The Poetry of
Yehuda Amichai

WITH TRANSLATIONS BY

GLENDA ABRAMSON

ROBERT ALTER

YEHUDA AMICHAI

CHANA BLOCH

ASSIA GUTMANN

BARBARA HARSHAV

BENJAMIN HARSHAV

TED HUGHES

CHANA KRONFELD

STEPHEN MITCHELL

RUTH NEVO

TUDOR PARFITT

HAROLD SCHIMMEL

LEON WIESELTIER

The Poetry of Yehuda Amichai

EDITED BY ROBERT ALTER

FARRAR, STRAUS AND GIROUX NEW YORK

FOR HANA

Farrar, Straus and Giroux
18 West 18th Street, New York 10011

Copyright © 2015 by Hana Amichai
Introduction and selection copyright © 2015 by Robert Alter
All rights reserved
Printed in the United States of America
Published in 2015 by Farrar, Straus and Giroux
First paperback edition, 2017

Owing to limitations of space, all acknowledgments for permission to
reprint previously published material can be found on page 551.

The Library of Congress has cataloged the hardcover edition as follows:
Amichai, Yehuda.
 [Poems. Selections. English]
 The poetry of Yehuda Amichai / edited by Robert Alter. — First edition.
 pages cm
 Includes index.
 ISBN 978-0-374-23525-3 (hardback) — ISBN 978-0-374-71515-1 (ebook)
 1. Amichai, Yehuda—Translations into English. I. Alter, Robert, editor.
II. Title.

PJ5054.A65 A2 2015
892.41'6—dc23

 2015010115

Paperback ISBN: 978-0-374-53658-9

Designed by Jonathan D. Lippincott

Our books may be purchased in bulk for promotional, educational,
or business use. Please contact your local bookseller or the Macmillan
Corporate and Premium Sales Department at 1-800-221-7945, extension 5442,
or by e-mail at MacmillanSpecialMarkets@macmillan.com.

www.fsgbooks.com
www.twitter.com/fsgbooks • www.facebook.com/fsgbooks

1 3 5 7 9 10 8 6 4 2

Contents

Introduction

The poetry of Yehuda Amichai (1924–2000), who with the passage of time seems more and more one of the great poets of the twentieth century, is deceptively accessible in translation. He was part of a group of young Israeli poets in the early 1950s who effected a vernacular revolution in Hebrew verse, rejecting the high literary language and the rhetorical thrust of the previous generation of Hebrew poets and finding ways to make poetry out of the plain words of everyday speech. His first volume of poetry, *Now and in Other Days* (1955), was widely recognized after it appeared as the turning point in the vernacular revolution. This effort to use the plain language and images of ordinary experience is clearly visible in a good deal of what Amichai wrote. It has a lot to do with the enormous popularity his work has enjoyed in Israel from the late 1950s to the present. It is also what makes at least some of his poems seem perfectly transparent in English, almost as if nothing were lost in translation. But his language is scarcely as vernacular, and not at all as simple, as it is often imagined to be.

Amichai arrived in Palestine from Germany with his parents at the age of twelve, in 1936. In addition to his German mother tongue, he knew enough Hebrew when he came to get along immediately, for from the age of three he had gone to a bilingual school in his native Wurzburg, following a curriculum that included religious instruction (his parents were Orthodox). He naturally retained some attachment to his mother tongue, though English modernist verse appears to have been a more decisive influence on him than German poetry, however much he admired Rilke and, later, Celan. German renderings of a few of his Hebrew poems have been found in the Amichai archive at Yale, but the extravagant claim of one recent critic that much of his poetry is essentially a recasting of German originals is quite groundless. Amichai was manifestly enamored of the Hebrew language—not only its sounds and its rich historical associations but even its grammatical structures—and his poetry plays vigorously and inventively with the formal properties and the cultural backgrounds of its Hebrew medium in ways that cannot easily cross the barrier of translation. One

extreme and therefore instructive example is an early poem, never translated (for good reason), called "The Sonnet of the Conjugations." It is one of the finest Ages of Man poems of the previous century, but it chooses to trace the movement from infancy to the last sad decrepitude by following the sequence of the seven conjugations of Hebrew verbs as they are taught in school, from *qal*, "simple," to *hitpaʿel*, "reflexive." Uncannily, the paradigms of Hebrew grammar are transformed into a haunting expression of the human condition, a tour de force that cannot be conveyed in English.

Amichai obviously relished the directness of the only recently revived spoken Hebrew that he quickly mastered in the pressure cooker circumstances of his adolescent immigration. Yet, unlike most Hebrew poets of his generation, he also never let go of the language of the Bible, the prayer book, and other traditional sources to which he was extensively exposed both in his German childhood and at a religious school in his teens in Jerusalem.

Amichai's relation to his Orthodox upbringing and to the new Israeli reality in which he flourished makes him in some ways atypical of the Hebrew poets of his generation. He never underwent a crisis of faith, he once told me; he merely became bored with the world of observance—the constant repetitions in the liturgy, the endless round of rituals and ceremonies. But even as, by the time he left high school, he became what one would have to call a secular Jew, he never entirely jettisoned the baggage of Jewish tradition. In his poems, he sometimes regarded it as comical, sometimes with fondness, and his last volume of verse exhibits some nostalgia about the pious milieu in which he grew up. He surely no longer believed in the God of Jewish tradition, yet God is not absent from his work, persisting as an idea to grapple with, a being to challenge or turn inside out, even occasionally as a kind of lingering ghostly presence.

The local reality that Amichai entered was more military than he would have liked. At the age of eighteen he enlisted in the British army and was stationed for a while in Egypt. In the Israeli War of Independence of 1948–49, he saw frontline action (as he would again in 1956) in the Negev, and though it would be wrong to say that he suffered from posttraumatic stress, the experience certainly haunted him for the rest of his life. In several of his poems he remembers in particular carrying the bleeding body of a friend who did not survive; and

in his poetry the mayhem of the battlefield is sometimes turned into an image of what modern life is all about. Once, in the 1970s, at a reading in Berkeley, a belligerent questioner wanted to know whether he had seen God on the battlefield. No, he answered quietly, he had seen only men dying, and it was the job of the poet to name these harsh realties plainly, not to envelop them in pseudotheological rhetoric in the way of the politicians and the generals.

One might say that war and love were the two poles of his life. If he was scarred by war ("I go out to all my wars," he wrote in an early poem), he also exhibited a kind of alacrity for falling in love. The first signal instance was in high school, when he was actually prepared to marry his teenage girlfriend—a step predictably vetoed by his parents and hers. He had other deeply felt romantic involvements afterward; and unlike most people, he continued to brood over them many years after they ended, sometimes writing poems about the pain of the breakup decades later. He married Tamar Horn in 1950 and had a son with her, Roni. In the mid-1960s he met Hana Sokolov, who would be the great love of his life, and with whom he had two children, David and Emanuella. He attended first a teachers' seminary and then the Hebrew University of Jerusalem, where he studied Bible and Hebrew literature. For two years he was a schoolteacher, and he subsequently earned his living at a teachers' seminary and then in a program for college students from abroad. By the 1970s he had a firmly established international reputation, with his work translated into many languages, and his books in Hebrew were the Israeli equivalent of bestsellers, so after a time he began to realize a degree of appreciable income from his writing. Though he became a celebrated public figure in Israel, he studiously avoided assuming any public role as "the poet," mocking those who did, and he always claimed that real poets should be simple foot soldiers, not preening generals.

One of the piquant aspects of his poetry is that a writer who was so immersed in the gritty actualities of constant warfare and in the sensual and emotional experience of love should have drawn so inventively from the language of Hebrew tradition to express these realities. Such traditional elements show up in surprising places. Some will be recognizable to the biblically literate English reader and others will not. In the former category, "We Did It," a poem about rapturous lovemaking and the world's indifference to it, invokes the six-winged

seraphim of Isaiah's vision in the temple as well as Ezekiel's divine chariot as images of the two lovers' exuberant gyrations. More recondite is the beginning of "Bitter and Brusque," a poem about the breakup of a love affair (one of Amichai's great subjects), which is a citation of a phrase from the prophet Habakkuk. I have identified this as a citation rather than as an allusion because the phrase has become a kind of idiomatic expression for disaster in literary Hebrew, often invoked in connection with untimely death. The Hebrew for those first words sounds like this: *mar venimhar*. Existing translations render this as "bitter and swift" or "bitter and quick," but the double alliteration and the internal rhyme (the phrase is repeated in the poem) are inseparable from the striking elegiac effect, and in any case *nimhar* is not the normal form for the word that means "swift." Translations are inevitably no more than earnest approximations, so in the new version I did for this volume, I opted for "brusque," which yields an alliteration of both *b* and *r*, while giving up on the internal rhyme in the Hebrew.

Amichai's poetry has understandably attracted many English translators, and through the various English versions his work has had a strong and sustained following both in America and in England, perhaps especially among poets. Indeed, there are very few foreign poets who have had the sort of presence in the English-speaking world that he has enjoyed. (His poetry has also had considerable popularity in Poland, Albania, Slovenia, and even China and Japan.) A good many of the existing English translations are quite accomplished, and it has been my pleasure to incorporate in this volume hundreds of poems by a variety of translators. One whole book of verse, *Time*, was translated by Amichai himself in collaboration with his good friend the British poet Ted Hughes, and generous selections of their work appear here, though for some poems it seemed to me that other versions were actually preferable. There remain many fine poems by Amichai that have never been translated. A good many of these I have done myself, and for some I have recruited translations by Chana Bloch and Chana Kronfeld and by Leon Wieseltier. The splendid collaborative translation by Bloch and Kronfeld of *Open Closed Open* appears here nearly in its entirety, with poems untranslated in the original American version of that book added and the order of the poems in the Hebrew volume restored. Though it was scarcely feasible to do a complete edition of Amichai's poetry in English (the book would have been more

than three times the size of this one), I thought it would be instructive to provide readers with one complete volume of verse as part of the present large selection, a choice further justified by the fact that Amichai's last book of poetry is in certain ways a kind of summary and synthesis of his general enterprise and a reflection on his life.

Though, as I have suggested, there is much to admire in the available English versions of Amichai, there are also translations of many poems in which something is awry. The problems vary from wrong diction, defective rhythms, failure to convey significant biblical echoes or other allusions, excessive liberties with the original, and even egregious errors in construing the Hebrew. It seemed altogether unwise for me to revise the work of other translators and thus to get involved in the messy complications of negotiating with them about the revisions, so in those instances where I found a translation wanting—in a few cases, it was a matter of a single strongly offending word—I have done my own versions.

Let me offer one small example. "Poems of Akhziv," a vivid cycle of erotic poems written in the 1970s, has been rendered in English by three different translators. One poem begins startlingly with the words (each of the three versions uses the same sexual term) "I have learned to relate to your cunt as to a face." But the Hebrew word Amichai uses, 'ervah, is by no means an obscenity—modern Hebrew has a monosyllabic word, borrowed from the Arabic, that would correspond to the English four-letter term, but Amichai invariably avoids it. 'Ervah is a biblical term, the "nakedness" that one is enjoined not to uncover in the various sexual prohibitions in Leviticus and elsewhere. It is, then, a perfectly decorous term that refers to the sexual part, female or male, with a certain association of taboo. To translate it as an obscenity is a serious violation of the poem. Since there was no way to get the biblical resonance in English ("nakedness" in the context of the poem would misleadingly imply the whole naked body), I represented the line in my own version as "I have learned to relate to your sex as to a face," at least preserving the tone of the original, which is at once erotically frank and decorous.

Another sort of challenge to the translator is presented by the poem "Farewell." The original is framed in virtuosic quatrains. Two of the three existing translations reproduce the quatrains, one a bit awkwardly and the other more resourcefully, but in order to create

the rhymes, both translators have had to exercise certain liberties with the exquisitely expressive imagery of the Hebrew, and none of the three does anything with the blatant breaking of normal Hebrew grammar at the beginning that is a correlative of the shattering of the lovers' union. It seemed to me prudent in this case to surrender rhyme in order to hew more closely to the powerful images and the evocative syntax, trying to let strong rhythms in the English stand in for the fuller musicality of the Hebrew. Elsewhere, I have included rhymed translations—several published ones and a number of admirable versions done for this volume by Bloch and Kronfeld—in order to give some sense of one kind of verse that Amichai was drawn to, especially early on. Yet it must be said that despite the often remarkable ingenuity of the translators, these for the most part do not entirely equal the striking deftness of the Hebrew and so, whatever their virtues, can be satisfying only to a certain point.

In this particular poem, "Farewell," there is also the matter of a powerful pun in the original, depending on Amichai's familiarity with the language of Jewish tradition, that is entirely lost—indeed, misconstrued—in the three English versions: "For all came through our word, a profane all." All three translators mistakenly represent the last phrase, *shehakol shel ḥol*, as "all is sand" (one of them has "a world of sand"). The Hebrew *ḥol* can mean either "sand" or "profane." *Shehakol* is the popular designation among observant Jews of a blessing recited over certain foods: "for all came through His word." In the high compression of this allusive pun, what the speaker is saying is that in love's exultation, it seemed as though everything came about through the lovers' word, an everything that was not divine nor theological but wonderfully human. Though my version does at least reproduce the plain sense of the Hebrew, the pregnant allusion is invisible and, alas, has to be brought to light for the English reader through the kind of annotation I have just provided. I have appended to this volume a set of concise notes in order to provide where strictly necessary this sort of background of allusion and cultural reference that could not be communicated in the English versions of the poems. (Biblical allusions with which most readers will be familiar, such as grinding swords into plowshares and the parting of the Red Sea, are not annotated.)

A good many subtleties and complexities, then, in Amichai's poetry will inevitably disappear in translation. What I have tried to

keep in mind in putting together these different versions and in doing my own is to avoid as much as possible English renderings that are more effortlessly smooth or more flatly colloquial than the original. A translated poem, of course, has to be readable in the target language, but while honoring this reasonable requirement, I have also sought in my editorial choices and in my translations to intimate the artful disjunctions and disruptions and the purposeful disorientations of the Hebrew. Amichai remains one of the most appealingly accessible of twentieth-century poets, but it is an accessibility often marked by unanticipated complications and challenges. Perhaps one cannot altogether convey this in a translation, but it seemed to me worth the effort to point in that direction.

In regard to the substance of Amichai's poems as well as their language there are more complexities and greater depth than meet the casual eye. He is obviously an intensely personal poet, with a large number of his poems explicitly anchored in autobiographical experience. This is surely part of his appeal to readers, first in Israel, then in America and England and across the globe. In fact, many of his early poems are a plea for the preciousness of private experience in a time of continuing warfare. Poems such as "God Takes Pity on Kindergarten Children," "The Smell of Gasoline in My Nose," and "I Waited for My Girl and Her Steps Were Not There" resonated powerfully for Israeli readers between one war in 1948–49 and another in 1956, and well beyond that period, because they expressed with such poignant directness the desperate cherishing of a private world and private loves when historical reality tore lovers apart and dragged young people who had once been sheltered children to the pitiless exposure of the battlefield.

But there are elements in much of Amichai's poetry that go beyond the merely autobiographical and beyond the local Israeli situation, even as both are vividly evoked. Thus, "The Smell of Gasoline" concludes with these two lines: "A jet makes peace in the sky for all, / For us, and all those who love in the fall." These lines explicitly echo the concluding words of the kaddish, which any Hebrew reader would immediately recognize: "He who makes peace in his heights, may He make peace for us and for all Israel." The poem about a young soldier's wrenching experience when his call to the front compels him to part from his girl (the smell of gasoline is from the jeep or truck

that is about to take him away) becomes a larger statement about the fragility of life in violent times. Instead of God in his heavens providentially protecting his people, modern lovers live under the provisional and intermittent protection of a fighter plane circling above. The poet's personal plight, without the slightest didactic insistence or affectation, is ultimately played out on the big stage of life in the upheavals of the twentieth century, between the arch of the heavens above and the earth below.

Some of Amichai's poems about the anguish of living in a world of relentless armed conflict are general statements about this condition rather than explicit expressions of the poet's personal experience. A few of the justly famous among these are "God Takes Pity on Kindergarten Children," "Rain Falls on the Faces of My Friends," "God Full of Mercy," and "To the Full Severity of Compassion." The last of these, characteristically, evokes two biblical allusions—God's promise to make Abraham's seed as countless as the sand on the shore and the writing on the wall of Belshazar's feast in the book of Daniel—in order to define a world where we are all lonely people, vulnerable and countable, and where the dire writing on the wall is everywhere, like graffiti.

Amichai more usually makes his way to the global through a concrete imagining of the personal. The moving love poem, "But We Must Praise," is a vivid case in point. The poem begins with a strong allusion to the opening words of one of the most familiar prayers of the traditional liturgy, "We must praise the Lord of all." Here, however, the object of the praise is "a familiar night. Gold borrowed from the abyss." The Hebrew original of that second phrase is one of Amichai's untranslatable puns, *zahav mosh'al mishe'ol*. The night of rapturous love is a treasure "borrowed from the abyss," presided over not by the God of tradition but by the "Lord of the loss of all," because sweet love is bitterly transient—perhaps necessarily transient—and our existence is shadowed by inevitable, painful loss. This poem definitely seems to bear the imprint of personal experience, but its articulation gives it a world-embracing reach. At the end, the lover is conscious of the stars overhead in this night of love, of his beloved's body as a token or model of the sky above "in the hollow / of this narrow world." The largeness of meaning conveyed by the poem is effected without the slightest strain in what looks like simple language, but the speaker's

sense of the preciousness and the fragility of his love plays out under the starry sky, above the abyss, becoming an intimation of the human condition itself.

From beginning to end, Amichai is an extravagantly playful poet. The playfulness is exhibited in such manifestly exuberant poems as "The Visit of the Queen of Sheba," but it also has an essential role in some of his saddest poems—about personal loss, about the death of his parents, about the Nazi genocide. A good deal of this playfulness is enacted through puns, acoustic effects, and allusions and thus will not be fully visible in translation, though several of the translators represented in this volume have been remarkably resourceful in conveying at least some of the lively inventiveness of the Hebrew. But the playfulness is also often evident in the vigor and originality of the figurative language, which can be conveyed in translation, and in the poet's bold reimagining of familiar stories and common everyday situations. Let me quote, as a foretaste of what readers have in store for them in this collection, one complete poem from Amichai's last book, *Open Closed Open*. It is a take on the Exodus story—that last ghastly night in Egypt when the Egyptian firstborn perished and the Israelites were protected by blood smeared on the lintels, when the liberated Hebrew slaves fled in haste, with no time for the rising of the dough for their bread—that resembles nothing written by any other writer on this story, from the ancient Midrash to Thomas Mann's *The Tables of the Law*.

> I don't imagine that on the night of the exodus from Egypt,
> between midnight and dawn, any couple could lie together
> in love. (We could have.) In haste,
> blood dripping from lintels and doorposts,
> silver and gold dishes clanging in the dark, between the
> firstborn's
> stifled death cry and the shrieking of mothers' wombs
> emptying like wineskins. And standing over them, legs wide
> apart,
> the Angel of Death, crotch gaping male and female
> like a bloody sun in the thick of frizzled black death.
> Sandaled feet slapping against the soft dough of matza
> and the flesh of belly and thigh, hard belts

cinched tight at the waist, buckles
scraping against skin, tangled in one another.
To roll like that, locked in eternal love,
with all the rabble from the house of slavery
into the Promised Desert.

There is an almost shocking explosiveness in the figurative language here, a power of mythic imagining, a mingling of the erotic and the theological, that might be surprising to those who think of Amichai primarily as a vernacular poet of everyday experience. He is this as well, of course, but there are also murky depths and soaring heights in his poetic world that are realized through his metaphors and through his often densely allusive Hebrew. As is usually the case with poets of the first order, there is more in his work than meets the casual eye. One hopes that American readers will be able to discern at least some of that richness in this volume.

Now and in Other Days

1955

חִכִּיתִי לְנַעֲרָתִי
וְלֹא הָיוּ צְעָדֶיהָ

חִכִּיתִי לְנַעֲרָתִי וְלֹא הָיוּ צְעָדֶיהָ.
אַךְ שָׁמַעְתִּי קוֹל יְרָיָה. - חַיָּלִים
מִתְאַמְּנִים לַמִּלְחָמָה.
חַיָּלִים תָּמִיד מִתְאַמְּנִים לְאַחַת הַמִּלְחָמוֹת.

אָז פָּתַחְתִּי צַוְּארוֹן חֻלְצָתִי
וּשְׁנֵי קְצוֹת הַדַּשִּׁים הִצְבִּיעוּ
לַכִּוּוּן הָאֶחָד וְלַכִּוּוּן הַשֵּׁנִי,
וְצַוָּארִי עָלָה בֵּינֵיהֶם - וְעָלָיו
אֲמִיר רֹאשִׁי הַשָּׁקֵט
וּבוֹ פֵּרוֹת עֵינַיִם.

וּלְמַטָּה, בְּכִיסֵי הַחֵם, נָתַן לִי צִלְצוּל הַמַּפְתְּחוֹת
קְצָת בִּטָּחוֹן
שֶׁל כָּל הַדְּבָרִים שֶׁאֶפְשָׁר עוֹד
לִסְגֹּר וְלִשְׁמֹר.

וְנַעֲרָתִי עֲדַיִן הוֹלֶכֶת בָּרְחוֹבוֹת
וְהִיא עֲנוּדַת תַּכְשִׁיטֵי הַקֵּץ
וַחֲרוּזֵי הַסַּכָּנָה הַנּוֹרָאָה
עַל צַוָּארָהּ.

(TRANSLATION ON PAGE 8)

When I Was a Child

When I was a child
grasses and masts stood at the seashore,
and as I lay there
I thought they were all the same
because all of them rose into the sky above me.

Only my mother's words went with me
like a sandwich wrapped in rustling waxpaper,
and I didn't know when my father would come back
because there was another forest beyond the clearing.

Everything stretched out a hand,
a bull gored the sun with its horns,
and in the nights the light of the streets caressed
my cheeks along with the walls,
and the moon, like a large pitcher, leaned over
and watered my thirsty sleep.

STEPHEN MITCHELL

My Mother Baked the Whole World for Me

My mother baked the whole world for me
In sweet cakes.
My beloved filled my window
With raisins of stars.
And my yearnings closed inside me
Like bubbles in a loaf of bread.
On the outside, I am smooth and quiet and brown.
The world loves me.
But my hair is sad as reeds in a drying swamp—
All the rare birds with beautiful plumage
Flee from me.

BENJAMIN AND BARBARA HARSHAV

The Two of Us Together and Each of Us Alone

"The two of them together and each of them alone."
—from a rental contract

Another summer, my girl, is over and gone,
And Dad didn't come to Luna Park to play.
Still, all the swings go on swinging away.
The two of us together and each of us alone.

The sea's horizon keeps losing its ships—
Holding onto anything now is hard indeed.
The fighters are waiting behind the hills.
Compassion is what we dearly need.
The two of us together and each of us alone.

The moon is sawing the clouds in half.
Come, let's step forth for a lovers' duel.
Just the two of us at love before the warring camps.
It still may be possible to change it all.
The two of us together and each of us alone.

My love turns me like a salt sea, it seems,
Into sweet drops of autumn's first rain.
I'm brought to you slowly as I fall. Take me in.
For us there's no angel who will come to redeem.
For we are together. Each of us alone.

CHANA BLOCH AND CHANA KRONFELD

God Takes Pity on Kindergarten Children

God takes pity on kindergarten children.
Less on schoolchildren.
On grown-ups, He won't take pity anymore.
He leaves them alone.
Sometimes they have to crawl on all fours
In the blazing sand,
To get to the first-aid station
Dripping blood.

Maybe He will take pity and cast His shadow
On those who truly love
As a tree on someone sleeping on the bench
On a boulevard.

Maybe we too will spend on them
The last coins of favor
Mother bequeathed us,
So their bliss will protect us
Now and in other days.

BENJAMIN AND BARBARA HARSHAV

Autobiography in the Year 1952

My father built a great worry around me like a dock
Once I left it before I was finished
And he remained with his great, empty worry.
And my mother—like a tree on the shore
Between her arms outstretched for me.

And in '31 my hands were merry and small
And in '41 they learned to use a rifle
And when I loved my first love
My thoughts were like a bunch of colored balloons
And the girl's white hand clutched them all
With a thin string—and then let them fly.

And in '51, the movement of my life
Was like the movement of many slaves rowing a ship,
And the face of my father like the lantern at the end of a parting
 train,
And my mother closed all the clouds in her brown closet.
And I climbed up my street,
And the twentieth century was the blood in my veins,
Blood that wanted to go out to many wars,
Through many openings.
It pounds on my head from inside
And moves in angry waves to my heart.

But now, in the spring of '52, I see
More birds have returned than left last winter.
And I return down the slope of the mountain
To my room where the woman's body is heavy
And full of time.

BENJAMIN AND BARBARA HARSHAV

I Waited for My Girl and
Her Steps Were Not There

I waited for my girl and her steps were not there.
But I heard a shot—soldiers
training for war.
Soldiers always train for some war.

Then I opened the collar of my shirt
and the two lapel edges pointed
in two directions.
And my neck rose between them—
on it the crest of my quiet head
bearing the fruit of eyes.

And below, in my warm pocket, the clinking keys
gave me the small sense of security
of those things that could still
be locked and kept.

But my girl yet walks through the streets
adorned in the jewels of the end-time
and the beads of the terrible danger
round her neck.

ROBERT ALTER

Two Poems About the First Battles

I

The first battles brought out
terrible flowers of love
with kisses nearly as lethal as mortar fire.
The lovely buses of our city
transport the boy-soldiers:
all of lines 12, 8, and 5 travel
to the front.

II

On the way to the front we slept in a kindergarten,
I placed a wooly teddy bear under my head,
tops and dolls and trumpets descended
onto my tired face—
not angels.
My feet, in their heavy boots,
knocked over a tower of brightly colored blocks
that were piled on each other,
each block smaller than the one beneath it.
And in my head was a chaos of memories large and small
and out of it they made dreams.

Beyond the window there were flames . . .
and so, too, in my eyes under my eyelids.

LEON WIESELTIER

Rain Falls on the Faces of My Friends

In memory of Dicky

Rain falls on the faces of my friends;
on the faces of my living friends
who cover their heads with a blanket—
and on the faces of my dead friends
who cover no more.

ROBERT ALTER

The Smell of Gasoline in My Nose

The smell of gasoline in my nose,
In my palm I hold your soul that rose,
Like an etrog in a bowl of soft cotton—
My dead father did it every autumn.

The olive tree stopped wondering—it knows
There are seasons and it's time to go.
Wipe your face, my girl, stand by me for a while,
As in a family picture, show your smile.

I packed my shirt and my gloom,
I won't forget you, girl in my room,
My last window before the desert and the gore,
That has no windows and has a war.

Once you laughed, now there's silence in your eyes,
The beloved country never cries,
The wind will rustle in the rumpled bed—
When will we sleep again head to head?

In the earth, raw materials leave their mark,
Not extracted like us from silence and dark,
A jet makes peace in the sky for all,
For us, and all those who love in the fall.

<div align="right">BENJAMIN AND BARBARA HARSHAV</div>

Six Poems for Tamar

1
The rain is speaking quietly,
you can sleep now.

Near my bed, the rustle of newspaper wings.
There are no other angels.

I'll wake up early and bribe the coming day
to be kind to us.

2
You had a laughter of grapes:
many round green laughs.

Your body is full of lizards.
All of them love the sun.

Flowers grew in the field, grass grew on my cheeks,
everything was possible.

3
You're always lying on
my eyes.

Every day of our life together
Ecclesiastes cancels a line of his book.

We are the saving evidence in the terrible trial.
We'll acquit them all!

4
Like the taste of blood in the mouth,
spring was upon us—suddenly.

The world is awake tonight.
It is lying on its back, with its eyes open.

The crescent moon fits the line of your cheek,
your breast fits the line of my cheek.

5
Your heart plays blood-catch
inside your veins.

Your eyes are still warm, like beds
time has slept in.

Your thighs are two sweet yesterdays,
I'm coming to you.

All hundred and fifty psalms
roar hallelujah.

6
My eyes want to flow into each other
like two neighboring lakes.

To tell each other
everything they've seen.

My blood has many relatives.
They never visit.

But when they die,
my blood will inherit.

STEPHEN MITCHELL

Yehuda Ha-Levi

The soft hairs on the back of his neck
are the roots of his eyes.

His curly hair is
the sequel to his dreams.

His forehead: a sail; his arms: oars
to carry the soul inside his body to Jerusalem.

But in the white fist of his brain
he holds the black seeds of his happy childhood.

When he reaches the belovèd, bone-dry land—
he will sow.

STEPHEN MITCHELL

Ibn Gabirol

Sometimes pus,
sometimes poetry—

always something is excreted,
always pain.

My father was a tree in a grove of fathers,
covered with green moss.

Oh widows of the flesh, orphans of the blood,
I've got to escape.

Eyes sharp as can-openers
pried open heavy secrets.

But through the wound in my chest
God peers into the universe.

I am the door
to his apartment.

STEPHEN MITCHELL

My Father

The memory of my father is wrapped in white paper
like slices of bread for the workday.

Like a magician pulling out rabbits and towers from his hat,
he pulled out from his little body—love.

The rivers of his hands
poured into his good deeds.

STEPHEN MITCHELL

From All the Spaces Between Times

From all the spaces between times,
from all the gaps in soldiers' ranks,
from cracks in the wall,
from doors we did not close tight,
from hands we did not hold,
from the distance between body and body
when we didn't come close to each other—
the great sprawling expanse adds up,
the plain, the desert,
where our souls will walk, hopeless, after death.

ROBERT ALTER

But Now See How Exaggerated

But now see how exaggerated parting is compared to meeting—
no longer twin sisters, no longer sisters,
no longer standing together,
just the petal of meeting, the butterfly of lingering,
against the sky of parting, and for the length of the journey without
 memory,
just the small warm air in the mouth of the beloved,
just the inside of the palm of a boy's hand
in the autumnal storms, between the high vaults of winter,
just the small brown eye
in this terrible, visible expanse.

See what the seasons do to the fields and the mountains,
what the wars do to the cities,
and what my words did not do to you,
and how my hands did not change the hue of your hair,
and the parting!

<div align="right">LEON WIESELTIER</div>

Now That the Water Presses Hard

Now that the water presses hard
On the walls of the dam,
Now that the returning white storks
In the middle of the firmament
Turn into flocks of jet planes,
We will feel again how strong are the ribs,
How bold the warm air in the lungs,
How urgent the daring to love in the open plain,
When great dangers arch overhead,
And how much love is needed
To fill all the empty vessels
And the watches that stopped telling time,
And how much breath,
A blizzard of breath,
To sing the little Song of Spring.

BENJAMIN AND BARBARA HARSHAV

Two Hopes Away

1958

מֵעֵין אַחֲרִית הַיָּמִים

הָאִישׁ תַּחַת תְּאֵנָתוֹ טִלְפֵּן לָאִישׁ תַּחַת גַּפְנוֹ:
"הַלַּיְלָה הֵם בְּהֶחְלֵט עֲלוּלִים לָבוֹא.
שַׁרְיֵן אֶת הֶעָלִים סְגֹר הֵיטֵב אֶת הָאִילָן,
קְרָא לַמֵּתִים הַבַּיְתָה, וֶהֱיֵה מוּכָן".

הַכֶּבֶשׂ הַלָּבָן אָמַר לַזְּאֵב:
"בְּנֵי אָדָם פּוֹעִים וְלִבִּי כּוֹאֵב:
הֵם יַגִּיעוּ שָׁם לִידֵי קְרָבוֹת כִּידוֹן.
בַּפְּגִישָׁה הַבָּאָה בֵּינֵינוּ, הָעִנְיָן יִדּוֹן".

כָּל הַגּוֹיִים (הַמְאֻחָדִים) יִנְהֲרוּ לִירוּשָׁלַיִם
לִרְאוֹת אִם יָצְאָה תּוֹרָה, וּבֵנְתַיִם

הֱיוֹת וְעָבְשׁוּ אָבִיב
יְלַקְטוּ פְּרָחִים מִסָּבִיב.

וְכִתְּתוּ חֶרֶב לְמַזְמֵרָה וּמַזְמֵרָה לְחֶרֶב
וְחוֹזֵר חֲלִילָה וְשׁוֹב בְּלִי הֶרֶף.

אוּלַי מִכְּתוּתִים וְהַשְׁחָזוֹת הַרְבֵּה,
בַּרְזֶל הָרִיב בָּעוֹלָם יִכְלֶה.

(TRANSLATION ON PAGE 27)

A Military Operation

A military operation changed the map.
Not your face. Not as the wind blows here.
For the world between the table and the chair
Remained all quiet, ours, and flat
Even post-Copernicus,
And the infinite sea begins just at the door,
And the faithful table laden as before,
Yesterday's talk and a scrap of hope between us.

Under the net of airline company routes
City planners set aside terrain
For lovers, bus stops, and destruction sites.
A new road paved. New distance comes to be.
But the border guards of possibility
Permitted us to enter their domain.

CHANA BLOCH AND CHANA KRONFELD

God's Hand in the World

1

God's hand is in the world
like my mother's hand in the guts of the slaughtered chicken
on Sabbath eve.
What does God see through the window
while his hands reach into the world?
What does my mother see?

2

My pain is already a grandfather:
it has begotten two generations
of pains that look like it.
My hopes have erected white housing projects
far away from the crowds inside me.
My girlfriend forgot her love on the sidewalk
like a bicycle. All night outside, in the dew.

Children mark the eras of my life
and the eras of Jerusalem
with moon chalk on the street.
God's hand in the world.

STEPHEN MITCHELL

A Corpse in the Field

His blood was flung hastily and carelessly
like the clothes
of someone much too tired.
How the night has grown!
The windows were right
like my parents, when I was a child.

Monastic winds
passed over the hills, serious, head bent.

Mayors, UN army officials
measured the distance from living
to dead,
with right angles and compasses and little rulers,
with cigar boxes, with hard emotions,
with sharpened hopes
and bloodhounds.

ROBERT ALTER

God Full of Mercy

God full of mercy.
Were God not full of mercy
there would be mercy in the world, and not just in Him.
I, who plucked flowers on the mountain
and looked in all the valleys,
I, who hauled from the hills dead bodies,
can say that the world is empty of mercy.

I who was Salt King by the sea,
who stood indecisive at my window,
who counted the steps of angels,
whose heart lifted the weights of pain
in the terrible competitions,
I, who use just a small part
of the words in the dictionary.

I, who must solve riddles despite myself,
know that were God not full of mercy,
there would be mercy in the world
and not just in Him.

ROBERT ALTER

Sort of an Apocalypse

The man under his fig tree telephoned the man under his vine:
"Tonight they definitely might come. Assign
positions, armor-plate the leaves, secure the tree,
tell the dead to report home immediately."

The white lamb leaned over, said to the wolf:
"Humans are bleating and my heart aches with grief.
I'm afraid they'll get to gunpoint, to bayonets in the dust.
At our next meeting this matter will be discussed."

All the nations (united) will flow to Jerusalem
to see if the Torah has gone out. And then,
inasmuch as it's spring, they'll come down
and pick flowers from all around.

And they'll beat swords into plowshares and plowshares
 into swords,
and so on and so on, and back and forth.

Perhaps from being beaten thinner and thinner,
the iron of hatred will vanish, forever.

STEPHEN MITCHELL

And That Is Your Glory

(Phrase from the liturgy of the Days of Awe)

I've yoked together my large silence and my small outcry
like an ox and an ass. I've been through low and through high.
I've been in Jerusalem, in Rome. And perhaps in Mecca anon.
But now God is hiding, and man cries Where have you gone.
And that is your glory.

Underneath the world, God lies stretched on his back,
always repairing, always things get out of whack.
I wanted to see him all, but I see no more
than the soles of his shoes and I'm sadder than I was before.
And that is his glory.

Even the trees went out once to choose a king.
A thousand times I've given my life one more fling.
At the end of the street somebody stands and picks;
this one and this one and this one and this one and this.
And that is your glory.

Perhaps like an ancient statue that has no arms
our life, without deeds and heroes, has greater charms.
Ungird my T-shirt, love; this was my final bout.
I fought all the knights, until the electricity gave out.
And that is my glory.

Rest your mind, it ran with me all the way,
it's exhausted now and needs to knock off for the day.
I see you standing by the wide-open fridge door, revealed
from head to toe in a light from another world.
And that is my glory
and that is his glory
and that is your glory.

STEPHEN MITCHELL

Of Three or Four in a Room

Of three or four in a room
there is always one who stands beside the window.
He must see the evil among thorns
and the fires on the hill.
And how people who went out of their houses whole
are given back in the evening like small change.

Of three or four in a room
there is always one who stands beside the window,
his dark hair above his thoughts.
Behind him, words.
And in front of him, voices wandering without a knapsack,
hearts without provisions, prophecies without water,
large stones that have been returned
and stay sealed, like letters that have no
address and no one to receive them.

STEPHEN MITCHELL

Not Like a Cypress

Not like a cypress,
not all at once, not all of me,
but like the grass, in thousands of cautious green exits,
to be hiding like many children
while one of them seeks.

And not like the single man,
like Saul, whom the multitude found
and made king.

But like the rain in many places
from many clouds, to be absorbed, to be drunk
by many mouths, to be breathed in
like the air all year long
and scattered like blossoming in springtime.

Not the sharp ring that wakes up
the doctor on call,
but with tapping, on many small windows
at side entrances, with many heartbeats.

And afterward the quiet exit, like smoke
without shofar-blasts, a statesman resigning,
children tired from play,
a stone as it almost stops rolling
down the steep hill, in the place
where the plain of great renunciation begins,
from which, like prayers that are answered,
dust rises in many myriads of grains.

STEPHEN MITCHELL

Through Two Points
Only One Straight Line Can Pass

(Theorem in geometry)

A planet once got married to a star,
and inside, voices talked of future war.
I only know what I was told in class:
through two points only one straight line can pass.

A stray dog chased us down an empty street.
I threw a stone; the dog would not retreat.
The king of Babel stooped to eating grass.
Through two points only one straight line can pass.

Your small sob is enough for many pains,
as locomotive power can pull long trains.
When will we step inside the looking glass?
Through two points only one straight line can pass.

At times it stands apart, at times it rhymes
with *you*, at times *we*'s singular, at times
plural, at times I don't know what. Alas,
through two points only one straight line can pass.

Our life of joy turns to a life of tears,
our life eternal to a life of years.
Our life of gold became a life of brass.
Through two points only one straight line can pass.

STEPHEN MITCHELL

Half the People in the World

Half the people in the world
love the other half,
half the people
hate the other half.
Must I because of this half and that half
go wandering and changing ceaselessly
like rain in its cycle,
must I sleep among rocks,
and grow ragged like the trunks of olive trees,
and hear the moon barking at me,
and camouflage my love with worries,
and sprout like frightened grass between the railroad tracks,
and live underground like a mole,
and remain with roots and not with branches,
and not feel my cheek against the cheek of angels,
and love in the first cave,
and marry my wife beneath a canopy
of beams that support the earth,
and act out my death, always
till the last breath and the last
words and without ever understanding,
and put flagpoles on top of my house
and a bomb shelter underneath. And go out on roads
made only for returning and go through
all the appalling stations—
cat, stick, fire, water, butcher,
between the kid and the angel of death?

Half the people love,
half the people hate.
And where is my place between such well-matched halves,
and through what crack will I see

the white housing projects of my dreams
and the barefoot runners on the sands
or, at least, the waving
of a girl's kerchief, beside the mound?

STEPHEN MITCHELL

I Want to Die in My Bed

All night Joshua's army had to climb
To make it to the killing fields on time.
Deep in the ground, the weft and woof of the dead.
I want to die in my bed.

Like gun slits on a tank, their eyes took a narrow view.
They are the many and I am always the few.
Let them question me. I'll have to say what I said.
But I want to die in my bed.

O sun, stand still at Gibeon! Your light
Sees fit to shine for war makers who murder all night.
I may not even see my wife struck dead,
But I want to die in my bed.

Samson's a hero, thanks to his long black hair.
I had to be taught to bend the bow, to dare,
They made me a hero-on-call, they sheared my head.
I want to die in my bed.

I've learned that one can manage anywhere,
Even the lion's maw, with room to spare.
So what if I die alone. That's not what I dread.
But I want to die in my bed.

CHANA BLOCH AND CHANA KRONFELD

34

To the Mother

1
Like an old windmill,
two hands always raised to shout to the sky
and two lowered to prepare sandwiches.

Her eyes are clean and gleaming
as on Passover eve.

At night she puts all the letters
and photos side by side,

to measure with them
the length of the finger of God.

2
I want to walk through
the deep ravines between her sobs.

I want to stand in the heat wave
of her silence.

I want to lean
on the rough tree trunks of her pain.

3
She puts me,
as Hagar put Ishmael,
under one of the bushes.

So she wouldn't see my death, in the war,
under one of the bushes,
in one of the wars.

ROBERT ALTER

The Ones Who Blew Up Houses

The ones who blew up houses
are now abandoned like an abandoned village
and still
the earth turns,
carpeted in countries.
The rain goes through its paces before an empty world.
Words are switched like changings of the guard:
some are always asleep at their posts.
The wind weeps coming and going
the whole way from the sea.
My thoughts have opened and darkened
like a sliced apple.
But my body is free and glad
like a destroyed house though which one can see
the sky.

LEON WIESELTIER

Poet

Like the mouth of a baby not yet weaned—his eyes
Were not yet weaned and still he wanted it all.
He senses, yes, the changes of summer and fall
Though something inside him always lags behind.

And in the place where all the other trees
Are growing roots, two legs are what he has.
When suddenly the poems within him rise,
He thinks he'll write for a while, until he sees

What in truth his line of work is for.
And his eyes, that opened belatedly,
Search beyond the window, but the pen

Writes on, as if from the stress of memory.
Now he has stationed his body like a dam
Behind whose walls everything is stored.

CHANA BLOCH AND CHANA KRONFELD

King Saul and I

1

They gave him a finger, but he took the whole hand.
They gave me the whole hand: I didn't even take the little finger.
While my heart
Was weightlifting its first feelings
He rehearsed the tearing of oxen.

My pulse-beats were like
Drips from a tap.
His pulse-beats
Pounded like hammers on a new building.

He was my big brother.
I got his used clothes.

2

His head, like a compass, will always bring him
To the sure north of his future.

His heart is set, like an alarm clock
For the hour of his reign.
When everyone's asleep, he will cry out
Until all the quarries are hoarse.
Nobody will stop him!

Only the asses bare their yellow teeth
At the end.

3

Dead prophets turned time-wheels
When he went out searching for asses
Which I, now, have found.

But I don't know how to handle them.
They kick me.

I was raised with the straw,
I fell with heavy seeds.
But he breathed the winds of his histories.
He was anointed with the royal oil
As with wrestler's grease.
He battled with olive trees
Forcing them to kneel.

Roots bulged on the earth's forehead
With the strain.
The prophets escaped from the arena;
Only God remained, counting:
Seven . . . eight . . . nine . . . ten . . .
The people, from his shoulders downwards, rejoiced.
Not a man stood up.
He had won.

4
I am tired,
My bed is my kingdom.

My sleep is just.
My dream is my verdict.

I hung my clothes on a chair
For tomorrow.

He hung his kingdom
In a frame of golden wrath
On the sky's wall.

My arms are short, like string too short
To tie a parcel.

His arms are like the chains in a harbor
For cargo to be carried across time.

He is a dead king.
I am a tired man.

<div align="right">ASSIA GUTMANN</div>

Ballad of the Long Hair and the Short Hair

His hair was shaved when he came to the camp.
Her hair remained long and without response.
"I can't hear you at all with this noise everywhere."
—Your long hair, girl. —And your short hair.

All summer long the flowers trained to bloom
Inside the patient earth; they gathered strength.
"I returned to you, girl, but wasn't the same as before."
—Your long hair, girl. —And your short hair.

The wind shattered the tree; the tree the wind.
They had plenty of choices but no time to rest.
"The rain is falling, come home from there."
—Your long hair, girl. —And your short hair.

The world for them, like indirect speech,
didn't quite touch them. Slowly they began to sing.
"I've set my watch. When will you get here?"
—Your long hair, girl. —And your short hair.

Then they grew silent. Like retreating steps.
The skies opened wide. The law books shut once more.
"What are you saying, girl?"
"What are you saying?"
—Your long hair, girl. —And your short hair.

CHANA BLOCH AND CHANA KRONFELD

The Visit of the Queen of Sheba

1. Preparations for the Journey
Not resting but
moving her lovely butt,
the Queen of Sheba,
having decided to leave, a-
rose from her lair
among dark spells, tossed her hair,
clapped her hands,
the servants fainted, and
already she drew in the sand
with her big toe:
King Solomon, as though
he were a rubber ball, an
apocalyptic, bearded herring, an
imperial walking stick, an
amalgam, half chicken
and half Solomon.

The minister of protocol
went too far, with all
those peacocks and ivory boxes.
Later on,
she began to yawn
deliciously, she stretched like a cat
so that
he would be able to sniff
her odif-
erous heart. They spared no expense,
they brought feathers, to tickle
his ears, to make his last defense
prickle.
She had been brought
a vague report

about circumcision,
she wanted to know everything, with absolute precision,
her curiosity
blossomed like leprosy,
the disheveled sisters of her corpuscles
screamed through their loudspeaker into all her muscles,
the sky undid
its buttons, she made herself up and slid
into a vast commotion,
felt her head
spin, all the brothels of her emotions
were lit up in red.
In the factory
of her blood, they worked frantically
till night came: a dark night, like an old table,
a night as eternal
as a jungle.

2. *The Ship Waits*
A ship in the harbor, night
among the shadows, a white

ship, with a cargo of yearnings,
some temperate, some burning,

a ship that desire launches,
a ship without a subconscious.

Already among the sails
sway the Queen's colored veils,

made of the silk of sparrows
who had died of their tiny sorrows

before they could flutter forth
to the cool lands of the North.

It's worthwhile, at any rate,
for the white ship to wait

cheek to cheek with the dock
and let itself gently rock

between ideas of sand
and ideas of ocean, and

endure its insomnia
till morning, etc.

3. Setting Sail
She called her thighs to return to each other,
knee-cheek to knee-cheek, and her soul
was already a zebra of moods, good and bad.
In the oven of her body, her heart
rotated on a spit. The morning screamed,
a tropical rain fell.

The forecasters, chained to the spot, forecasted,
the engineers of her sleep went out on weary camels,
all the little fish of her laughter fled
before the shark of her awakening rage. In her armpits
faint-hearted corals hid,
night lizards left their footprints on her belly.

She sat in bed, sharpening her charms and her riddles
like colored pencils. From the beards
of old blowhards, she had had an African apron made,
her secrets were embroidered on scarves.

But the lions still held the laws
like the two tablets over the holy ark
and over the whole world.

4. *The Journey on the Red Sea*

Fish blew through the sea and through
the long anticipation. Captains
plotted their course by the map
of her longing. Her nipples preceded her like scouts,
her hairs whispered to one another
like conspirators. In the dark corners between sea and ship
the counting started, quietly.
A solitary bird sang
in the permanent trill of her blood. Rules fell
from biology textbooks, clouds were torn like contracts,
at noon she dreamt about
making love naked in the snow, egg yolks dripping
down her leg, the thrill of yellow beeswax. All the air
rushed to be breathed inside her. The sailors cried out
in the foreign language of fish.

But underneath the world, underneath the sea,
there were cantillations as if on the Sabbath:
everything sang each other.

5. *Solomon Waits*

Never any rain,
never any rain,
always clouds without closure,
always raw-voiced love.

Shepherds of the wind returned
from the pasture.
In the world's court-
yards, blossoms of stone opened
consecrated to strange gods.
Trembling ladders dreamt about
humans dreaming about them.

But he
saw the world,
the slightly torn

lining of the world.
And was awake like many lit stables
in Megiddo.

Never any rain,
never any rain,
always raw-voiced love,
always quarries.

6. *The Queen Enters the Throne Room*
The dewy rose of her dark pudenda
was doubled in the mirrored floor. His agenda

seemed superfluous now, and all the provisions
he had made for her, the decrees and decisions

he had worked out while he was judging the last
of the litigants. Then he rolled up his past

like a map; and he sat there, reeling, giddy,
and saw in the mirror a body and a body,

from above and below, like the queen of spades.
In the bedroom of his heart he pulled down the shades,

he covered his blood with sackcloth, tried
to think of icebergs, of putrefied

camel flesh. And his face changed seasons
like a speeded-up landscape. He followed his visions

to the end of them, growing wiser and warm,
and he knew that her soul's form was like the form

of her supple body, which he soon would embrace—
as a violin's form is the form of its case.

7. *Who Could Stump Whom*

In the ping-pong of questions and answers
not a sound was heard
except:
ping . . . pong . . .
And the cough of the learned counselors
and the sharp tearing of paper.

He made black waves with his beard
so that her words would drown in it.
She made a jungle
of her hair, for him to be lost in.
Words were plunked down with a click
like chessmen.
Thoughts with high masts
sailed past one another.
Empty crossword puzzles filled up
as the sky fills with stars,
secret caches were opened,
buckles and vows were unfastened,
cruel religions
were tickled, and laughed
horribly.
In the final game,
her words played with his words, her tongue
with his tongue.
Precise maps
were spread, face up, on the table.
Everything was revealed. Hard.
And pitiless.

8. *The Empty Throne Room*

All the word games
lay scattered out of their boxes.
Boxes were left gaping
after the game.

Sawdust of questions,
shells of cracked parables,
woolly packing materials from
crates of facile riddles.

Heavy wrapping paper
of love and strategies.
Used solutions rustled
in the trash of thinking.

Long problems
were rolled up on spools,
miracles were locked in their cages.
Chess horses were led back to the stable.

Empty cartons that had
"Handle With Care!"
printed on them
sang hymns of thanksgiving.

Later, in ponderous parade, the King's soldiers arrived.
She fled, sad
as black snakes
in the dry grass.

A moon of atonement spun around the towers
as on Yom Kippur eve.
Caravans with no camels, no people,
no sound, departed and departed and departed.

STEPHEN MITCHELL

from The Right Angle

The right angle between the dead and his mourner—
From now on, let it be the place where I sit, my corner.
The woman sits with me, the girl in a burning cloud
Rose up to the heavens and into my open heart.

CHANA BLOCH AND CHANA KRONFELD

Poems, 1948–1962

1963

רְחוֹב

אוֹר מְכוֹנִיּוֹת חוֹלְפוֹת
סִדֵּר לִי אֶת מַחְשְׁבוֹתַי בְּשָׁחוֹר וְלָבָן.

אֲנִי, שֶׁחוֹצֶה אֶת הָרְחוֹב
רַק בִּמְקוֹמוֹת שֶׁבָּהֶם מֻתָּר,
לִי קָרְאוּ פִּתְאֹם
אֶל בֵּין וְרָדִים.

וּכְעָנָף כֵּהֶה שֶׁהוּא בָּהִיר
בְּמָקוֹם שֶׁבְּרוֹ,
גַּם אֲנִי בָּהִיר
בְּאַהֲבָתִי.

(TRANSLATION ON PAGE 63)

As for the World

As for the world,
I am always like one of Socrates' students:
walking beside him,
hearing his seasons and generations,
and all I can do is say:
Yes, certainly that is true.
You are right again.
It is exactly as you have said.

As for my life, I am always
Venice:
everything that is streets
is in other people.
In me—love, dark and flowing.

As for the scream, as for the silence,
I am always a shofar:
hoarding, all year long, its one blast
for the terrible Days of Awe.

As for the deeds,
I am always Cain:
a fugitive and a vagabond before the deed that I won't do,
or after the deed that
can't be undone.

As for the palm of your hand,
as for the signals of my heart
and the plans of my flesh,
as for the writing on the wall,
I am always an ignoramus: I can't
read or write
and my head is empty as a weed,

knowing only the secret whisper
and the motion in the wind
when a fate passes through me, to
some other place.

STEPHEN MITCHELL

In the Middle of This Century

In the middle of this century we turned to each other
With half faces and full eyes
like an ancient Egyptian picture
And for a short while.

I stroked your hair
In the opposite direction to your journey,
We called to each other,
Like calling out the names of towns
Where nobody stops
Along the route.

Lovely is the world rising early to evil,
Lovely is the world falling asleep to sin and pity,
In the mingling of ourselves, you and I,
Lovely is the world.

The earth drinks men and their loves
Like wine,
To forget.
It can't.
And like the contours of the Judean hills,
We shall never find peace.

In the middle of this century we turned to each other,
I saw your body, throwing shade, waiting for me,
The leather straps for a long journey
Already tightening across my chest.
I spoke in praise of your mortal hips,
You spoke in praise of my passing face,
I stroked your hair in the direction of your journey,
I touched your flesh, prophet of your end,

I touched your hand which has never slept,
I touched your mouth which may yet sing.

Dust from the desert covered the table
At which we did not eat
But with my finger I wrote on it
The letters of your name.

ASSIA GUTMANN

Farewell

Farewell, O face of you, already face of memory.
Parting ascends, a ghost, and flies and flies.
Face of beasts, face of water, face of going,
and grove of whispers, face of lap, face of child.

Not ours again the hour when we could touch,
not ours to say: yes now, yes now.
A name of winds was yours once, woman
of directions and intentions, mirror and fall.

For what we did not grasp we sang together.
Ages and darkness, face of alternation.
No longer mine, now undeciphered,
Blocked nipples, buckles, mouths, and screws.

And so farewell, forever sleepless,
for all came through our word, a profane all.
From now you weave
your own dreams, world and all.

Farewell, death's bundles and suitcases,
threads, feathers, dwelling's tangle, token of hair.
For that which will not be no hand can write,
and what was not the body's we forget.

ROBERT ALTER

My Parents' Migration

And my parents' migration has not yet calmed in me.
My blood goes on shaking at its walls,
As the bowl after it is set down.
And my parents' migration has not yet calmed in me.
Winds continually over stones.
Earth forgets the footsteps of those who walk.
An awful fate. Stumps of talk after midnight.
An achievement, a retreat. Night reminds
And day forgets.
My eyes, which have looked a long time into a vast desert,
Are a little calmed. One woman. The rules of a game
Nobody had ever completely explained. The laws of pain and weight.

Even now my heart
Makes only a bare living
With its daily love.
My parents in their migration.
On the crossroads where I am forever orphaned,
Too young to die, too old to play.
The weariness of the miner
The emptiness of the quarry
In one body.
Archaeology of the future,
Museums of what is still to happen.
And my parents' migration has not yet calmed in me,
And from bitter peoples I learned bitter languages
For my silence among the houses
Which are always
Like ships.

Already my veins, my tendons
Are a tangle of ropes I will never undo.

Finally, my own
Death
And an end to my parents' migration.

ASSIA GUTMANN

Jerusalem

On a roof in the Old City
laundry hanging in the late afternoon sunlight:
the white sheet of a woman who is my enemy,
the towel of a man who is my enemy,
to wipe off the sweat of his brow.

In the sky of the Old City
a kite.
At the other end of the string,
a child
I can't see
because of the wall.

We have put up many flags,
they have put up many flags.
To make us think that they're happy.
To make them think that we're happy.

STEPHEN MITCHELL

It's Been a While Since They Asked

It's been a while since they asked, Who lives in between these
 houses,
And who was he, the last of the last to speak,
And who forgot his coat between these houses,
And who was the one who stayed. Why didn't he flee?

Among the blossomers a dead tree stands, dead tree.
A long-standing error, a misunderstanding of yore,
The edge of the Land, where an era begins to be
For somebody else. A bit of stillness there.

And the current events of body and of hell,
The reeds of the end, their spells of sway and sough.
The wind passed on its way through that locale
And a serious dog saw the humans laugh.

CHANA BLOCH AND CHANA KRONFELD

And Till Abu Gosh

And till Abu Gosh we were silent
and till old age I will love you
at the foot of the hill of terrors,
in the den of the winds. And at Sha'ar Hagai
the angels of the three faiths came down to the road. Belief
in one God is still heavy. And with words of pain
I must describe the fig leaves
and what happened to me, not through my fault. Sand
flew into my eyes and turned to tears. And at Ramla
small planes were standing with the great nameless dead. The
 fragrance
of oranges groves touched my blood. My blood looked over
its shoulder to see what had touched. Winds, like actors,
began to put on new costumes to act before us
and to don masks of home and mountain and grove,
eye shadow of sunset and night.

From there the other roads began.
And my heart was covered with dreams, like
my shiny shoes that were covered with dust,
for dreams, too, are a long road
with an end I will not reach.

<div align="right">ROBERT ALTER</div>

Street

The light of passing cars
sorted my thoughts in black and white.

I, who cross the street
only in the places permitted,
was suddenly called among roses.

And like a dark branch that is white
where it is broken,
I too am bright in my love.

<div align="right">ROBERT ALTER</div>

A House Toward Evening

Constant moving of furniture
in the cramped apartment. A place for sitting
becomes a bed, a bed an altar,
an altar—to what was.

And white sheets flap in the windows:
a surrender to the night, before battle.

And like one who, still alive,
buys a gravesite for himself,
already now I love
all that's given me to love
in the hours of the night and the heart of the double cave.

ROBERT ALTER

Laundry

In a place where laundry is hung
no people die,
none are in the wars,
they'll stay at least
two or three days.
They won't be replaced
and they won't flutter.
They aren't like the dry grass.

LEON WIESELTIER

The Place Where We Are Right

From the place where we are right
flowers will never grow
in the spring.

The place where we are right
is hard and trampled
like a yard.

But doubts and loves
dig up the world
like a mole, a plow.
And a whisper will be heard in the place
where the ruined
house once stood.

STEPHEN MITCHELL

Mayor

It's sad to be
the mayor of Jerusalem—
it's terrible.
How can a man be mayor of such a city?
What can he do with it?
Build and build and build.

And at night the stones of the mountains crawl down
and surround the stone houses,
like wolves coming to howl at the dogs,
who have become the slaves of men.

STEPHEN MITCHELL

Resurrection

Afterward they will get up
all together, and with a sound of chairs scraping
they will face the narrow exit.

And their clothes are crumpled
and covered with dust and cigarette ashes
and their hand discovers in the inside pocket
a ticket stub from a very previous season.

And their faces are still crisscrossed
with God's will.
And their eyes are red from so much sleeplessness
under the ground.

And right away, questions:
What time is it?
Where did you put mine?
When? When?

And one of them can be seen in an ancient
scanning of the sky, to see if rain.
Or a woman,
with an age-old gesture, wipes her eyes
and lifts the heavy hair
at the back of her neck.

STEPHEN MITCHELL

The Hair Dried Last

The hair dried last,
when we were already far from the sea,
when words and salt, which had mingled upon us,
parted in a sigh,
and your body no longer showed
signs of terrible antiquity.
And in vain we forgot some things on the beach
so we could have a reason to return.
We did not return.

And these days I remember days
that were not called by your name, like the name of a ship.
And how we saw through two open doors
a man thinking and how we looked
at the clouds with the ancient look inherited from our fathers
who waited for rain.
And how at night, when the world turned cool,
your body kept its warmth a long time
like a sea.

ROBERT ALTER

Like Our Bodies' Imprint

Like our bodies' imprint
Not a sign will remain that we were in this place.
The world closes behind us,
The sand straightens itself.

Dates are already in view
In which you no longer exist,
Already a wind blows clouds
Which will not rain on us both.

And your name is already in the passenger lists of ships
And in the registers of hotels,
Whose names alone
Deaden the heart.

The three languages I know,
All the colors in which I see and dream:

None will help me.

ASSIA GUTMANN

If with a Bitter Mouth

If with a bitter mouth you say
sweet words, the world will not sweeten
nor will it turn bitter.

And it is written that we should not fear.
And it is written also that we should not change,
like words,
like past and future,
in the plural and in the loneliness.

And soon, in the nights to come,
we'll appear like traveling players,
one in the other's dreams
and in the dreams of strangers we did not know together.

ROBERT ALTER

During Our Love Houses Were Finished

During our love houses were finished
and someone who didn't know how
learned to play the flute, his exercises
rising and falling. One can hear
them now, when we no longer fill each other
as birds fill the treetop.
And you're already exchanging currency incessantly
from country to country and from will to will.

And though we acted crazy,
now it seems we didn't go much beyond
what's normal and we didn't disturb the world,
its people and their slumber.
But now, the end.
And soon of the two of us neither will remain
to forget the other.

ROBERT ALTER

It Was Summer, or Its End

It was summer, or its end, and I heard then
your steps as you went from east to west
for the last time. And in the world
kerchiefs and books and people were forgotten.

It was summer, or its end,
there were hours of afternoon
you were.
And for the first time you put on your shroud
and didn't know.
For there were flowers embroidered on it.

ROBERT ALTER

Once More

Once more be for me my kingdom of the here and now,
Beyond the door, from which there is no return.
Once more I'll hear, "It's a good thing you came."
And then to die, not pieced together again.

Once more inside my pocket
The feel of your house-door key.
And with the cold midnight wind, to whisper
Suddenly: "Pull up the covers." "No, you cover me."

And once more the curved basin of your pelvis.
Once more to die and rise the same.
To be with you waters within waters
And come to an end. They'll not divide us again.

And to lie in the dark and to hear
The voice above the voice that calls.
Once more at night to touch the brow
And then—to fall:

Not in the wars, not in them will I fall again,
But here and now, in the land without compare,
The land without me, the land without you,
The land of gray hills. Forever there.

CHANA BLOCH AND CHANA KRONFELD

To the Full Severity of Compassion

Count them.
Yes, you can count them. They
are not like the sand upon the seashore. They
are not like the stars of the heaven for multitude.
They're like lonely people.
On the corner and in the street.

Count them. See them
seeing the sky through ruined houses.
Find a way out of the stones and come back. What
will you come back to? But count them, for they
do their time in dreams
and they walk around outside and their hopes, unbandaged,
are gaping, and they will die of them.

Count them.
Too soon have they learned to read the terrible
handwriting on the wall. To read and to write upon
other walls. And the feast goes on in silence.

Count them. Be present for they
have already used up all the blood and there's still not enough,
as in a dangeous operation, when one is exhausted
and beaten down like ten thousand. For who's judge and what's
 judgment
unless it be to the full extent of night
and the full severity of compassion.

CHANA BLOCH AND CHANA KRONFELD

Jacob and the Angel

Toward morning she sighed and grabbed him
so, and defeated him.
And he grabbed her so, and defeated her.
The two of them knew that the hold
brings death.
They dispensed with the saying of names.

But in the first light of dawn
he saw her body,
which had stayed white
in the places the bathing suit
yesterday covered.

After, they called her suddenly from above
twice,
as one calls a little girl from her game
in the yard.
And he knew her name and he let her go.

ROBERT ALTER

And Let Us Not Get Excited

And let us not get excited, for a translator
must not get excited. Quietly, let us pass down
words from one to another, one tongue to other lips,

unawares, the way a father passes down
the features of his dead father's face to his son
though he doesn't resemble either of them:
he's just a go-between.

Let us remember the things we held onto
that slipped from our hands,
whatever belongeth to me, or belongeth not.
It is not for us to get excited.
The calls and their callers are drowned.
Or was it that my beloved
entrusted a few words to me before she went away
so I would grow them up for her sake.

And let us no longer say unto other sayers
what has been said unto us. To be silent is to concede. No,
it is not for us to get excited.

CHANA BLOCH AND CHANA KRONFELD

But We Must Praise

"We must praise the Lord of all."
—*Hebrew liturgy*

But we must praise
a familiar night. Gold borrowed from the abyss.
Cypresses rose forever. Far away,
long hair still flows, Lord of the loss of all.

What are you doing to me, faraway woman?
You hung me as on branches with weeping thoughts.
From far away your hand touches me as if testing
my bridges. They bear the weight and tremble. Yours is the
 kingdom.

Behind my words dark as a moon
come to me, make me tired.
But we must praise the loins of all: your lap.
Shout of the shoulder

that bore you to me on the night of reversal,
stars of forgetful man above us.
Your body's style, sky's manner here in the hollow
of this narrow world. But we must.

ROBERT ALTER

Now in the Uproar:
Poems, 1963–1968

1968

הַפַּר חוֹזֵר

הַפַּר חוֹזֵר מִיּוֹם עֲבוֹדָתוֹ בַּזִּירָה,
אַחֲרֵי שֶׁשָּׁתָה קָפֶה עִם לוֹחֲמָיו
וְהִשְׁאִיר לָהֶם פֶּתֶק שֶׁבּוֹ כְּתָבְתּוֹ
הַמְדֻיֶּקֶת וּמְקוֹם הַמִּטְפַּחַת הָאֲדֻמָּה.
הַחֶרֶב נִשְׁאֲרָה בְּעָרְפּוֹ קְשֵׁה-הָעֹרֶף.
וּמָתַי הוּא בַּבַּיִת. עַכְשָׁו
הוּא יוֹשֵׁב עַל מִטָּתוֹ בְּעֵינָיו
הַיְּהוּדִיּוֹת הַכְּבֵדוֹת. הוּא יוֹדֵעַ
שֶׁגַּם לַחֶרֶב כּוֹאֵב לָחֲדֹר לְתוֹךְ הַבָּשָׂר.
בְּגִלְגּוּל הַבָּא יִהְיֶה חֶרֶב: הַכְּאֵב יִשָּׁאֵר.
("הַדֶּלֶת פְּתוּחָה. אִם לֹא, הַמַּפְתֵּחַ מִתַּחַת
לַסַּף".).
הוּא יוֹדֵעַ עַל חֶסֶד עַרְבַּיִם וְעַל חֶסֶד
שֶׁל אֱמֶת. בַּתַּנַ"ךְ הוּא כָּתוּב עִם חַיּוֹת טְהוֹרוֹת.
הוּא כָּשֵׁר מְאֹד, מַעֲלֶה גֵרָה
וַאֲפִלּוּ לִבּוֹ מְחֻלָּק וְשָׁסוּעַ כַּפַּרְסָה.
מִתּוֹךְ חָזֵהוּ פּוֹרְצוֹת שְׂעָרוֹת
יְבֵשׁוֹת וַאֲפֹרוֹת כְּמִתּוֹךְ מִזְרָן בָּקוּעַ.

(TRANSLATION ON PAGE 96)

Jerusalem, 1967

To my friends Dennis, Arieh, and Harold

1

This year I traveled a long way
to view the silence of my city.
A baby calms down when you rock it, a city calms down
from the distance. I dwelled in longing. I played the hopscotch
of the four strict squares of Yehuda Ha-Levi:
My heart. Myself. East. West.

I heard bells ringing in the religions of time,
but the wailing that I heard inside me
has always been from my Yehudean desert.

Now that I've come back, I'm screaming again.
And at night, stars rise like the bubbles of the drowned,
and every morning I scream the scream of a newborn baby
at the tumult of houses and at all this huge light.

2

I've come back to this city where names
are given to distances as if to human beings
and the numbers are not of bus routes
but: 70 After, 1917, 500
B.C., Forty-eight. These are the lines
you really travel on.

And already the demons of the past are meeting
with the demons of the future and negotiating about me
above me, their give-and-take neither giving nor taking,
in the high arches of shell orbits above my head.

A man who comes back to Jerusalem is aware that the places
that used to hurt don't hurt anymore.

But a light warning remains in everything,
like the movement of a light veil: warning.

3

Illuminated is the Tower of David, illuminated is the Church of Maria,
illuminated the patriarchs sleeping in their burial cave, illuminated
are the faces from inside, illuminated the translucent
honey cakes, illuminated the clock and illuminated the time
passing through your thighs as you take off your dress.

Illuminated illuminated. Illuminated are the cheeks of my childhood,
illuminated the stones that wanted to be illuminated
along with those that wanted to sleep in the darkness of squares.

Illuminated are the spiders of the banister and the cobwebs of churches
and the acrobats of the stairs. But more than all these, and in them all,
illuminated is the terrible, true X-ray writing
in letters of bones, in white and lightning: *MENE
MENE TEKEL UPHARSIN.*

4

In vain you will look for the fences of barbed wire.
You know that such things
don't disappear. A different city perhaps
is now being cut in two; two lovers
separated; a different flesh is tormenting itself now
with these thorns, refusing to be stone.

In vain you will look. You lift up your eyes unto the hills,
perhaps there? Not these hills, accidents of geology,
but The Hills. You ask
questions without a rise in your voice, without a question mark,
only because you're supposed to ask them; and they
don't exist. But a great weariness wants you with all your might
and gets you. Like death.

Jerusalem, the only city in the world
where the right to vote is granted even to the dead.

5

On Yom Kippur in 1967, the Year of Forgetting, I put on
my dark holiday clothes and walked to the Old City of Jerusalem.
For a long time I stood in front of an Arab's hole-in-the-wall shop,
not far from the Damascus Gate, a shop with
buttons and zippers and spools of thread
in every color and snaps and buckles.
A rare light and many colors, like an open Ark.

I told him in my heart that my father too
had a shop like this, with thread and buttons.
I explained to him in my heart about all the decades
and the causes and the events, why I am now here
and my father's shop was burned there and he is buried here.

When I finished, it was time for the Closing of the Gates prayer.
He too lowered the shutters and locked the gate
and I returned, with all the worshipers, home.

6

It's not time that keeps me far away from my childhood,
it's this city and everything in it. Now
I've got to learn Arabic too, to reach all the way to Jericho
from both ends of time; and the length of walls has been added
and the height of towers and the domes of prayer houses
whose area is immeasurable. All these
really broaden my life and force me
always to emigrate once more from the smell
of river and forest.

My life is stretched out this way; it grows very thin
like cloth, transparent. You can see right through me.

7

In this summer of wide-open-eyed hatred
and blind love, I'm beginning to believe again
in all the little things that will fill
the holes left by the shells: soil, a bit of grass,

perhaps, after the rains, small insects of every kind.
I think of children growing up half in the ethics of their fathers
and half in the science of war.
The tears now penetrate into my eyes from the outside
and my ears invent, every day, the footsteps of
the messenger of good tidings.

8

The city plays hide-and-seek among her names:
Yerushalayim, Al-Quds, Salem, Jeru, Yeru, all the while
whispering her first, Jebusite name: Y'vus,
Y'vus, Y'vus, in the dark. She weeps
with longing: Ælia Capitolina, Ælia, Ælia.
She comes to any man who calls her
at night, alone. But we know
who comes to whom.

9

On an open door a sign hangs: Closed.
How do you explain it? Now
the chain is free at both ends: there is no
prisoner and no warden, no dog and no master.
The chain will gradually turn into wings.
How do you explain it?
Ah well, you'll explain it.

10

Jerusalem is short and crouched among its hills,
unlike New York, for example.
Two thousand years ago she crouched
in the marvelous starting-line position.
All the other cities ran ahead, did long
laps in the arena of time, they won or lost,
and died. Jerusalem remained in the starting crouch:
all the victories are clenched inside her,
hidden inside her. All the defeats.
Her strength grows and her breathing is calm
for a race even beyond the arena.

11

Loneliness is always in the middle,
protected and fortified. People were supposed
to feel secure in that, and they don't.
When they go out, after a long time,
caves are formed for the new solitaries.
What do you know about Jerusalem.
You don't need to understand languages;
they pass through everything as if through the ruins of houses.
People are a wall of moving stones.
But even in the Wailing Wall
I haven't seen stones as sad as these.
The letters of my pain are illuminated
like the name of the hotel across the street.
What awaits me and what doesn't await me.

12

Jerusalem stone is the only stone that can
feel pain. It has a network of nerves.
From time to time Jerusalem crowds into
mass protests like the tower of Babel.
But with huge clubs God-the-Police beats her
down: houses are razed, walls flattened,
and afterward the city disperses, muttering
prayers of complaint and sporadic screams from churches
and synagogues and loud-moaning mosques.
Each to his own place.

13

Always beside ruined houses and iron girders
twisted like the arms of the slain, you find
someone who is sweeping the paved path
or tending the little garden, sensitive
paths, square flower-beds.
Large desires for a horrible death are well cared for
as in the monastery of the White Brothers next to the Lions' Gate.
But farther on, in the courtyard, the earth gapes:
columns and arches supporting vain land

and negotiating with one another: crusaders and guardian
 angels,
a sultan and Rabbi Yehuda the Pious. Arched vaults with a
column, ransom for prisoners, and strange conditions in
 rolled-up
contracts, and sealing stones. Curved hooks holding
air.
Capitals and broken pieces of columns scattered like chessmen
in a game that was interrupted in anger,
and Herod, who already, two thousand years ago, wailed
like mortar shells. He knew.

14

If clouds are a ceiling, I would like to
sit in the room beneath them: a dead kingdom rises
up from me, up, like steam from hot food.
À door squeaks: an opening cloud.
In the distances of valleys someone rapped iron against stone
but the echo erects large, different things in the air.
Above the houses—houses with houses above them. This is
all of history.
This learning in schools without roof
and without walls and without chairs and without teachers.
This learning in the absolute outside,
a learning short as a single heartbeat. All of it.

15

I and Jerusalem are like a blind man and a cripple.
She sees for me
out to the Dead Sea, to the End of Days.
And I hoist her up on my shoulders
and walk blind in my darkness underneath.

16

On this bright autumn day
I establish Jerusalem once again.
The foundation scrolls
are flying in the air, birds, thoughts.

God is angry with me
because I always force him
to create the world once again
from chaos, light, second day, until
man, and back to the beginning.

17
In the morning the shadow of the Old City falls
on the New. In the afternoon—vice versa.
Nobody profits. The muezzin's prayer
is wasted on the new houses. The ringing
bells roll like balls and bounce back.
The shout of *Holy, Holy, Holy* from the synagogues will fade
like gray smoke.

At the end of summer I breathe this air
that is burnt and pained. My thoughts have
the stillness of many closed books:
many crowded books, with most of their pages
stuck together like eyelids in the morning.

18
I climb up the Tower of David
a little higher than the prayer that ascends the highest:
halfway to heaven. A few of
the ancients succeeded: Mohammed, Jesus,
and others. Though they didn't find rest in heaven;
they just entered a higher excitement. But
the applause for them hasn't stopped ever since,
down below.

19
Jerusalem is built on the vaulted foundations
of a held-back scream. If there were no reason
for the scream, the foundations would crumble, the city would
 collapse;
if the scream were screamed, Jerusalem would explode into the
 heavens.

20

Poets come in the evening into the Old City
and they emerge from it pockets stuffed with images
and metaphors and little well-constructed parables
and crepuscular similes from among columns and crypts,
from within darkening fruit
and delicate filigree of hammered hearts.

I lifted my hand to my forehead
to wipe off the sweat
and found I had accidentally raised up
the ghost of Else Lasker-Schüler.
Light and tiny as she was
in her life, all the more so in her death. Ah, but
her poems.

21

Jerusalem is a port city on the shore of eternity.
The Temple Mount is a huge ship, a magnificent
luxury liner. From the portholes of her Western Wall
cheerful saints look out, travelers, Hasidim on the pier
wave goodbye, shout hooray, hooray, bon voyage! She is
always arriving, always sailing away. And the fences and the piers
and the policemen and the flags and the high masts of churches
and mosques and the smokestacks of synagogues and the boats
of psalms of praise and the mountain waves. The shofar blows:
 another one
has just left. Yom Kippur sailors in white uniforms
climb among ladders and ropes of well-tested prayers.

And the commerce and the gates and the golden domes:
Jerusalem is the Venice of God.

22

Jerusalem is Sodom's sister city,
but the merciful salt didn't have mercy on her
and didn't cover her with a silent whiteness.
Jerusalem is an unconsenting Pompeii.

History books that were thrown into the fire,
their pages are strewn about, stiffening in red.

An eye whose color is too light, blind,
always shattered in a sieve of veins.
Many births gaping below,
a womb with numberless teeth,
a double-edged woman and the holy beasts.

The sun thought that Jerusalem was a sea
and set in her: a terrible mistake.
Sky fish were caught in a net of alleys,
tearing one another to pieces.

Jerusalem. An operation that was left open.
The surgeons went to fake a nap in faraway skies,
but her dead gradually
formed a circle, all around her,
like quiet petals.
My God.
My stamen.
Amen.

STEPHEN MITCHELL

My Child Has the Fragrance of Peace

My child has the fragrance of peace.
When I lean over him,
it's not just the scent of soap.

All the grown-ups were children once, fragrant with peace.
(And all through the land,
not a single gristmill still turns.)

O, country torn apart
like clothes that can never be mended.
Fathers hard and lonely even in the Cave of the Patriarchs.
Childless silence,

my child has the scent of peace.
His mother's womb promised him
what even God Himself cannot
promise us.

CHANA BLOCH AND CHANA KRONFELD

All the Generations Before Me

All the generations before me donated me
little by little so I'd rise up all at once in Jerusalem
like a house of prayer or a charitable institution.
That's a big obligation. My name is the name of my donors.
That's a big obligation.

I am getting close to the age when my father died.
My will is patched in many places.
Each day I have to change my life and my death
to fulfill all the prophecies
that prophesied me. So they won't be lies.
That's a big obligation.

I have passed my fortieth year. There are
places where I wouldn't be hired
for that very reason. If I'd been in Auschwitz,
they wouldn't have sent me to work,
they would have burned me on the spot.
That's a big obligation.

CHANA BLOCH AND CHANA KRONFELD

The Time Has Come to Collect Evidence

When did I cry for the last time?
The time has come to collect evidence
among those who saw me doing it. Some of them dead.
I wash my eyes with water
to see the world once again
through the moist and the hurt. I need
to collect evidence. These days
I felt sharp stabbing pains for the first time
in my heart:
I wasn't afraid. I was almost as proud as a boy
who discovers the first hair under his arms
and down there, between his legs.

CHANA BLOCH AND CHANA KRONFELD

With My Mother

My mother always calls me home
when I'm playing outside. And once she called me
and I returned only years later,
and not from playing.

When I sit before her now,
she is like mute stones.
All my language and all my poems
are like the oily outpouring of words
of a carpet salesman,
a pimp, and a slick travel agent.

ROBERT ALTER

Bitter and Brusque

The end came bitter and brusque,
but slow and sweet was the time between us,
slow and sweet were the nights
when my hands did not touch each other in despair
but, in love, your body, that kept them apart.
And when I entered you, it was the only way
for great happiness to be measured
with the precision of sharp pain. Bitter and brusque.

Slow and sweet were the nights,
bitter and gritty as sand the time now.
"Let's be sensible," and similar curses.

And the further we grow from love,
the more we're compelled to talk,
words and long composed sentences.

If we had stayed together,
we could have been silence.

ROBERT ALTER

My Father, My King

My father, my king, groundless love and groundless hatred
have made my face resemble the face of this ruined land.
The years have transformed me into a pain taster.
Like a wine taster I distinguish
between varieties of silence,
knowing what is dead, and who.

My father, my king, act so that my face will not be ripped apart
by laughter or by tears.
My father, my king, act so that I will not be tormented
by all that befalls me
between desire and sadness; and so that
all that I do against my will
will seem like my will. And my will like flowers.

<div align="right">LEON WIESELTIER</div>

The Bull Returns

The bull returns from his day of work in the ring
after a cup of coffee with his opponents,
having left them a note with his address and
the exact location of the red scarf.
The sword remains in his stiff-necked neck.
And when he's usually at home. Now
he sits on his bed, with his heavy
Jewish eyes. He knows
that the sword too is hurt when it pierces flesh.
In his next incarnation he'll be a sword: the hurt will remain.
("The door is open. If not, the key is under
the mat.")
He knows about the mercy of twilight and about the final
mercy. In the Bible, he's listed with the clean animals.
He's very kosher: chews his cud,
and even his heart is divided and cloven like a hoof.
From his chest, hairs burst forth
dry and gray, as though from a split mattress.

STEPHEN MITCHELL

Poem in the Orange Grove

I am godforsaken. "You are
godforsaken," said my father.
God forsook me. Afterward, he, too.

The fragrance of blossoming orange groves
lingered in me for a time. The hands were sticky
with juice and desire. You screamed loud,
committed two of your final thighs
to battle. Afterward, silence. You, who studied
history with your lovely head, know that only what's past
is quiet; even battles, even the fragrance
of orange groves. Fruit and flower were in a single tree
that double season, in spring.

And already then we spoke in the strange foreign accent
of those who will die or be parted.

ROBERT ALTER

God's Fate

God's fate now
is like the fate
of trees and stones, sun and moon,
when people stopped believing in them
and began to believe in Him.

But He has to stay with us:
at least like the trees, like the stones
and the sun and the moon and the stars.

<div align="right">ROBERT ALTER</div>

I Am Invited to Life

I am invited to life. But
I see that my hosts show signs of fatigue and impatience.
Trees sway, clouds fall ever more
silent. Mountains move
from place to place, the heavens gape.
And in the nights, winds move around
objects uneasily, smoke, people, lights.

I sign the guestbook
of God: I was, I lingered,
it was good, I enjoyed, I was guilty, I betrayed,
I was impressed by the reception
in this world.

ROBERT ALTER

I Am a Living Man

I am a living man,
son of a dead father,
father of a living son,
with many plans for blossoming and withering,
similar to the seasons of the year.

I hear the slightly hoarse voice
of this full life,
I smell the perfumed odors
that rise early to kill me.
And in these Passover days I recline,
perhaps to die,
I place my watch on the table before me,
a remembrance before you.
Easily will the brittle matzah break
between my fingers. Easily
will the door move at the midnight of miracles
and my desire's hair stand on end
again and in this time.

<div align="right">LEON WIESELTIER</div>

Capital Crime and Ashes

They are gilding the dome of the mosque.
You are leaving me. It's the same thing.
Ash from the cigarette
flies off in a western wind toward the Old City,
adding to the ashes there
from the Temples and the thorns of last year.

Capital crimes are not for the court
but when you love and burn and gild.

On the Ninth of Av every year my mother
riffles through the photos of her dead and not yet dead,
the ruins of my life.

Ashes and capital crimes. Titus didn't intend
to set fire to the Temple. He only wanted to peek,
to lift the edge of a thick sacred curtain
like a teenager: just to peek.
But the panicked priests began to sing
songs of death and hallelujah, and he panicked and set fire
like a madman: ashes, capital crimes.

ROBERT ALTER

Lullaby

Sleep, my child, sleep.
The song is not a song
and the cradle's not a cradle.
I am not by your side
but the distance lulls me there
and you here.

Sleep, my child, sleep.
In my heart there is nothing
even like the wildflowers
in the empty lot
after the rains.
But there are words in my mouth
for your sleep, there are words.

Sleep, my child, sleep.
The orange peels
will rise again
and make an orange
out of your dream, my child,
and Trumpeldor again will find
his amputated arm. Sleep.

Sleep, my child, sleep,
free of all your clothes.
In a mosque we remove our shoes,
in a synagogue we wear hats,
in a church, we take them off.
You are without all these,
you should sleep, my child, sleep.

ROBERT ALTER

I Am Their Last

Because it is time now. The courtyards are empty,
and half my life is shadowed by its final half.
Only peace and two cypresses. A single utterance.
Who else will speak and who will wander and who will rest?
Even in the awful houses there is a contraption
for a holiday flag, so that it may flutter and make us forget.

Leave me alone, God, I am tired now,
do not intervene again with Satan. You won
and he won. I have blessed God and also cursed.
I have suffered this and that. Grant me a respite
between "while he was yet speaking" and "there came another."

Gather me into the combinations of my full unspoken name,
disperse my voice like ashes that have forgotten what came before
and remember me from a time when I was what I was, You will be
 what You will be.

My heart's visage still shows on my face.
Remember me with Abraham, Isaac, and Jacob,
add me to the list of the dead of Machpelah
at the end of the dark stairs. I am their last.

<div style="text-align: right">LEON WIESELTIER</div>

A Pity, We Were Such a Good Invention

They amputated
Your thighs off my hips.
As far as I'm concerned
They are all surgeons. All of them.

They dismantled us
Each from the other.
As far as I'm concerned
They are all engineers. All of them.

A pity. We were such a good
And loving invention.
An aeroplane made from a man and wife.
Wings and everything.
We hovered a little above the earth.

We even flew a little.

ASSIA GUTMANN

Hike with a Woman

When after hours of walking
you suddenly discover
that the body of the woman striding beside you
was not meant
for travel and war,

that her thighs become heavy
and her buttocks sway like a tired flock,
you are filled with great joy
for the world
in which women are like that.

ROBERT ALTER

Praise of Summer

In these days God leaves the earth
to go to his summer home
in the dark mountains that are you
and abandons us to heat wave, sword, and jealousy.

We won't go on talking. We won't go on
existing at all. Eternity is
a perfected form of mutual loneliness.

A sweet sensation between the legs
tells us of the weakness of the stay
and of the sadness of words.

ROBERT ALTER

We Did It

We did it in front of the mirror
and in the light. We did it in darkness,
in the water and the high grass.

We did it in honor of man
and in honor of beast and in honor of God.
But they didn't want to know about us,
they had already seen that sort of thing.

We did it with flair and in colors,
with the mingling of reddish hair and brown
and with difficult exercises
gladdening the heart. We did it
like the wheel-shaped angels and the holy beasts
and the divine chariot of the prophets.
We did it with six wings
and six legs, but the heavens
were hard above us
like the summer earth beneath us.

ROBERT ALTER

Red Bride

Here are the hills of Moab,
Here the hills of Edom lie before me.
Here I stand now
At the gallows tree.

Thou art hereby sanctified,
Right away, right here,
I'll tie you up
With your own red hair.

I'll harrow your skin
With thorns like nails,
Add you to the reckoning
of the End of Days.

You will scream:
Your belly's an open gash.
Because this world
Is dust and ash.

Down we went to the walnut grove,
You and I,
On a hypnotized night:
You and I.

CHANA BLOCH AND CHANA KRONFELD

The Travels of the Last Benjamin of Tudela

You ate and were full, you came
twelve years old in the thirties of the world
trailing fringes of your undershawl
that stuck between your legs in the scorching country.
Your skin smooth and firm without protective hair.
Brown, round eyes, the size of ripe cherries. You will get used
to oranges. The whole innocent orange.
Watches were set to the round heart's beat, railway ties
to a child's stride.

The days bent over me quietly, like a doctor
and a mother, and began to whisper together,
while the grass bent, flattened by the bitter wind
on the hills I shall never climb again.
Moon and stars and the ancient deeds of adults
were put high on a shelf
out of my reach;
in vain I stretched up to the forbidden bookshelves.
But even then I was marked for death like an orange
for peeling, like chocolate for breaking, like a hand grenade
for explosion. The hand of fate held me tight.
My heaven was the soft palm—its outside
coarse skin, hard stars; its protruding veins,
airlines; its black hairs, the trajectory of shells
silent or shining, in darkness or with flares.
And before I was real and here to stay,
my heart shouldered sorrows not my own,
and strange ideas entered me, muffled, slow,
jolting like a train
into a listening, hollow station.

You ate and were full and blessed
alone and in company and alone.

In the marriage room, and outside after
the wedding, stood the bearded witnesses listening
for the voices of love, the sighs and the moans and the cries,
mine and yours in the marriage room. And at the door
wedding gifts mounted up like gifts for the dead
in the tombs of Egyptian kings.
The stone lions on the bridges in the city of my childhood
stood guard with the stone lions of the old house in Jerusalem.

You did not eat. Were not full. Spoke big words
from a small mouth. Your heart will never learn
to judge distances. The thing farthest from it
is the nearest tree, the pavement's edge, the lover's face.
The blind heart taps, like the blind,
its stick against obstacles and still taps
and gropes without progress. Taps and taps.
Loneliness is a tense in which actions can be
declined. Tap, will tap. Time is a flavor. For example
the flavor of 1929, when sadness said over you
the blessing of the first fruits. "Who hath preserved us to this day."
And you did not know you were her first fruit.

You went to a Montessori kindergarten.
You were taught to love, to do things alone, with your own hands.
You were educated to loneliness. You masturbated,
wet dream of the day and wet dream of the night. "I'll tell your father."
Hollow halls of New Year echoing.—Yom Kippur machines
in white, bright metal, caterpillar tracks
of prayers, conveyor belts of bowing and prostrating,
with a threatening hum. You have sinned. You have transgressed.
In a dark womb shaped like a synagogue dome,
round, ancient cave of prayer, the open ark
blinding, like an interrogation, a third degree.
Do you confess? Do you confess? I confess
before thee in the morning, when sunshine is outside. What
is your name? Do you surrender? You have trespassed. You have grown
fat. Are you alive?
Who are you? (Do you love me?) You have remembered. You have
forgotten.

Oh Montessori, Montessori, white-haired woman,
the first of the dead I loved. "Child, child!" Still
I turn in the street when I hear that called out
behind me.
Slowly and in great pain "I" turns into "he" after
resting a little in "you." You into them.
The operation is performed under a local. Open-eyed.
Only the place anesthetized with ice, or the drug of love.
They will call after you too, "Dreamer! Dreamer?"
You won't be able to, you can't. What is your name now?
I took no name in vain. Names are for children.
Adults vanish from their names. Only their surnames remain.
Afterwards, Father, Sir, Uncle, Mister. Hey Mister,
You there! (Do you love me? That's different,
that's more than a name.) Afterwards numbers and
perhaps: He. He went out. They will return, they—hey there,
 hey you.
The forest of names is withered, and the kindergarten
has shed the leaves of its trees, is black and will die.

On Fridays they stitched my handkerchief
to the corner of my pocket, to prevent me from carrying,
a sin on the Holy Sabbath. On festivals priests blessed me
from the white caves of their shawls, blessed me
with cramped epileptic fingers. I looked at them
and God didn't thunder. Since then his thunder
has rolled back and become a great silence.
I looked and my eyes were not blinded.
Since then my eyes have opened wider and wider
from year to year, beyond sleep,
to the rim of pain, beyond eyelids, beyond clouds, beyond years.
Death is not sleep but open eyes, the whole body
gaping with eyes, pressed in the narrow space of the world.

Angels like sacred scrolls in velvet robes
and white silk petticoats, with crowns and silver bells. Angels
flew about me and sniffed at my heart and cried to each other,
Ah, Ah, with adult smiles. "I will tell your father."
And even now, after thirty-three years my father's blessing

remains in my hair, though it grew wild in the desert,
sticky with blood and Negev dust, though I cropped
and chopped it to a war brush, and later
stylish French fashion stuck sadly to my forehead.
Still the blessing remains in the hair of my blessed head.

You came via Haifa. The harbor was new. The child was new.
You lay on your belly, not to kiss the Holy Land
but because of the riots of 1936.
British soldiers, wearing the cork helmets of a crumbling empire,
threw open to you your life's new kingdom. What's your name?
Threw open to you with their tattooed arms: dragons,
women's breasts, thighs, a dagger, the coiled serpent, a rose,
girls' buttocks. Since then this view has sunk deep within you
not to be seen from outside; painfully engraved and as deep
as your soul, itself an inscribed parchment, a mezuzah
lying aslant the length of your inner body.
You became a collector of pain in the tradition of this country.
My God, my God, why? Have you forsaken me?
My God, my God. Even then you had to call him twice.
The second time already a question, a first doubt: my God?

I haven't said the last word yet. I haven't
eaten yet, and I am already full. My cough is not
from smoking or illness. It is a compact
and economical form of inquiry.
Whatever has been is as if it never was.
And the rest I do not know. Perhaps
it is written in the difficult books on the shelf,
in the concordances of pain and the dictionaries of joy,
in the encyclopedias with stuck pages, like eyes
not wanting to let their dream go at dawn,
in the terrible correspondence
of Marx and Engels, you and I, he and God,
in the book of Job, in the hard words. Lines
that are deep cuts in my flesh. Long wounds
red from whips, wounds full of white salt, like meat
that my mother salted and koshered, so that there would be no blood

only pink salt soaked in blood, only the pain
of searing knowledge, the sacred, the pure.
The rest—unknown, alien in darkness.
We will wait, bow down on our knees like the brothers in Egypt in
 the dark,
hiding servile faces, till the world can no longer
resist and will weep and cry out: I am Joseph
your brother! I am the world!

The year the war broke out I passed your mother's belly
in which you crouched, as at night with me.
Our rhythm was the rhythm of the orchard pumps and the rhythm
 of shots.
It's started! Light and pain, iron and earth and stones.
Stones and flesh and iron in changing combinations
of matter. Render unto matter that which is matter's. Dust, dust,
from man thou cam'st and unto man thou shalt return.
It's started! My blood flows in many colors and puts on
red when it bursts out. My love's navel is an eye
to see the end. Beginning and end in her body.
Two creases in the right buttock, one in the left,
Glasses glitter against white skin of belly, eyebrow
arches to the eye's cry. Silk, soft and black on tense
skin of thick thighs. Shoulder distinct and prominent,
halved by a cloth strap, black, precise.
Shoulder to shoulder, flesh to flesh, dust to dust.

A story and a child, love and again, world and ear,
time in a curled smile, loving and opening:
the house to the night, the earth to the dead and the rain
after the gift of sun. Spring sprouted green words
in us, and the summer gambled on our arriving first,
and love burst out of us, all at once,
all over, like sweat, in the fear,
in the race of our lives, the game.
And children grew and ripened, for the water level
rises all the time with the terrible flood, and all their growth
is because of the rising flood, so as not to drown.

And still, his finger-tips dusted with moon,
like a schoolmaster's with chalk,
God strokes our head, his wrists already
song and angels! And what elbows! And what a face—
of a woman already turned to other matters. A profile
in a window.

The veins in my legs begin to protrude, because
my legs think a lot, their pace is thoughts. Into the desolate space
of my feelings wild beasts return, that left
when I tilled and drained, and made my life
a settled civilization. Long rows of books,
restful rooms and corridors. My body
built for good resonance like a concert hall,
cries and shouts don't get through. The walls
absorbent and impenetrable. Waves of memory
rebound. And up above, in the ceiling,
childish possessions, soft words, women's dresses,
my father's prayer shawl,
half bodies, big furry toys, clouds,
lumps of good night, heavy hair:
to heighten the resonance.

Dust, dust, my body, the frame of half my life. Still
bold scaffolding of hope, shaky ladders
against the unfinished outside. Even the head
is no more than the lowest
of the extra floors that were planned. My eyes,
one alert and interested, the other
distant and indifferent, as if receiving all from within,
and my hands drawing sheets
over the faces of the dead and the living. It is done.
Shaving, my face is a clown's, foamy white,
the only froth that isn't anger's. My face
is something between mad bull
and migratory bird that has lost its way
and lags behind the flock, but sees

slow, good things before its death in the sea.
Even then, and ever since, I met
the stagehands of my life, the shifters of walls,
and furniture and people, putting up and taking down,
new illusions of new houses,
new scenes, vistas
in perspective, not real. Resemblance
not truly close. Everyone, all,
all my lovers and haters are directors and stagehands,
electricians for rigging up a strange light which
dims and brings near, changes and alters,
hanging up and hanging about.

All his life my father tried to make a man of me,
so that I'd have a hard face like Kosygin and Brezhnev,
like generals and admirals and stockbrokers and administrators:
imaginary fathers I made to replace
my father.
I have to screw into my face the expression of a hero
like a bulb screwed into its hard threaded socket
screwed in and lit up.
All my life my father tried to make
a man of me, but I always slip back
into the softness of thighs and the longing to bless:
"Who hast made me according to his will." And his will is woman.
My father feared a useless blessing.
To bless the Creator of fruit trees and not to eat the apple.
To bless without loving. To love without fullness.
I ate and was not full and did not bless.
My life spreads out and separates:
in my childhood there were still tales of kings and ghosts
and blacksmiths, now glass houses and shining spaceships,
radiant silences without hope.
My hands are stretched out to a past not mine
and to a future not mine: it is hard to love,
hard to embrace, with hands like that.
Like a butcher sharpening knife on knife

I sharpen heart on heart. The hearts
get sharper and thinner and disappear. But my soul
still grinds, and my voice gets lost in the sound of metal.

On Yom Kippur, in tennis shoes, you ran.
And with Holy Holy Holy, you jumped up high
higher than anyone, nearly up to the angels on the ceiling.
And in the circlings of Simchat Torah
you circled seven times and seven
and arrived breathless.
Like pumping iron you thrust up
the Scrolls of the Law, in the Raising Up
with both trembling arms
so that all could see what was written, and the strength of your arms.

Bowing down, bending the knee, you fell to the ground,
like a starting leap into the whole of your life.
On Yom Kippur you started a fistfight
with yourself: "We have trespassed, we have dealt treacherously,"
bare fists, no gloves, nervous
featherweight against sad heavyweight
giving up. Prayers dribbled from the corners of the mouth
a thin red stream. With a prayer shawl
they wiped off your sweat between rounds.

The prayers of your childhood
return now, falling from above
like bullets that missed their mark and return
long afterwards, to earth,
arousing no attention, harmless.
When you lie with your beloved
they return. "I love you" "You
are mine." I confess before you. "Thou shallst love . . ."
the Lord your God. "With all my might."
Be angry and sin not, and be still. Selah. Pillar. Silence.
Hear O Israel in bed. In bed
without Hear O Israel. In a double bed
the double cave of the bed. Hear, oh hear.

Now listen again.
Without hearing. Without you.

Not one finger of God but ten
choke me. "I won't let you let me leave you." That too
is a meaning of death.
You forget the way you were.
Don't blame the Pharaoh's Butler who forgot
the dream of Joseph! Hands still sticky with candle wax
forget Chanukah. My face's wrinkled masks
have forgotten Purim. The body mortifying itself
on Yom Kippur forgot the High Priest (as beautiful
as you, this night), forgot the song of praise:
the appearance of the High Priest is like the sun,
like an onyx, a topaz. The appearance. Also your body
is Urim and Thummim. The nipples, the eyes,
the nostrils, dimple, navel, mouth, your mouth—
all these blaze for me like the Priest's breastplate,
all these spoke to me and prophesied what I should do.
I run away. Before your body
prophesies the future, I run away.

Sometimes I want to go back
to all that I had, the way you go back
in a museum, at random, not in order of periods,
in the opposite direction, not following the arrow,
to seek the woman you loved.
Where is she? The Egyptian Room,
The Far East, The Moderns, Cave
Paintings, all mixed up, worried guards
call after you: it's against the periods! No entry!
The exit to the left. You won't learn that way,
you know you won't. You search, you forget.
As you hear a parading military band
and you remain where you are in the street
hear them disappear. Slowly, slowly, the voices
vanish. First the cymbals, then the big horns fade out
then the oboes sink into the distance

then the sharp flutes and the small drums
but the bass drums remain a long while
the melody's skeleton, heartbeat, until
they too. And be still. Selah.
Amen. Selah.

On the New Year you give the blower of the ram's horn
orders: long blast, short blast, tremolo.
Wrath. Fierce wrath, long blasts, fire at every target before you, fire!
Cease fire. It's over. Be seated. Today the world's day.
Today all creatures on earth will be judged.
Synagogues are fortresses facing Jerusalem,
their windows slits facing the Holy East.

The ram's horn forgot my lips
the words forgot my mouth
the sweat steamed from my skin
the blood congealed and flaked off
the hand forgot my hand
the blessing evaporated from the hair of my head.
The radio is still warm,
the bed cooled first.
The seam between day and night
gapes, you might slip through it
out of your life, and disappear without anyone seeing.
Sometimes you need several days
to get over a single night.
History is a castrate
that wants mine too,
wanting to castrate,
to cut off with pages sharper than any knife
to stuff my mouth forever
with what was cut off—
like the mutilated corpses I saw on the battlefield—
so that my song becomes a barren chirp,
so that I will learn many languages
not one my own,

so that I will be scattered and disseminated
so that I will not be a Tower of Babel rising toward heaven.

Not to understand is my happiness
to be like stupid ignorant angels
soothing with their castrati songs.
The time has come to be busy
with mechanical toys, machines and their parts,
self-propelled, automatic, sprung,
doing it themselves, in their sleep,
wheels for turning, switches for turning on,
everything that moves and jumps and hops
and emits sweet sound, male and female slaves,
male and female tools, whores and concubines,
castrates and the castrates of castrates.
My life is spiced with heavy lies
and the longer I live the greater grows
my art of forgery and the truer it seems.
Artificial flowers seem more and more
natural, and the growing ones seem handmade.

Who in the end can distinguish
the true from the forged banknote?
Even the watermarks
stamped in me can be forged: my heart.
The unconscious has become immune to light
like bacteria to the latest antibiotic.
A new underground arises
below the below.

Forty-two light years and forty-
two night years. Drunkard and glutton
stuffing and feasting like the last Roman Caesars
in the secondhand history books, mad graffiti
and the writing on the wall in toilets,
heroic annals and conquest and decline,
vain life and vain death.

Revolt and rebellion and the suppression of rebellion
while banqueting. In a transparent nightdress
like a banner, you rose in revolt against me, hair
flying like a flag above, and bristling below.
Ram's horn blast, long blast. Crash of a broken bottle
and war cry. Suppression of revolt with the garter belt
of a woman. Suffocation with transparent stockings.
Stoning with the sharp heels of party shoes.
Arena combat between a broken bottleneck
and a net of flimsy petticoats. Shoes
against treacherous gauze, tongue against fork,
half a fish against half a woman. Straps and buttons,
brassieres decorated with buds, tangled with buckles
and army equipment. Fanfare and suppression of fanfare.
Football shouts from the nearby stadium.
And I was lying on you heavy and quiet
like a weight, so that the wind and time couldn't
blow you away like bits of paper and hours.

"Where do you feel your soul?"
Stretched between mouth-hole and asshole
a white thread, not transparent mist,
squeezed into a corner between two bones
in pain.
When satiated, vanishing like a cat.
I belong to the last generation
to separate body and soul.
"What will you do tomorrow?"
I can't wean myself from myself.
I'm weaned from smoking and drinking
and my father's God.
I'm weaned from everything liable to hasten my end.

Smell of a new bicycle I was given
when a child still in my nostrils,
blood not yet dried
and I already seek serenity, a different god,
a god of order, like the order of Passover. Four questions

and their ready-made answers, reward
and punishment, ten plagues, four mothers,
hard-boiled egg, knucklebone, bitter herbs,
all in order, a kid for two farthings,
familiar soup, the certainty of matzoh balls,
nine months of childbearing, forty
blows at sea. And the heart ajar a little
like the door for Elijah the Prophet.
"And it shall come to pass, in the dead of night." Now
the children are put to bed. In their sleep
they still hear the sound of munching jaws:
the world devours a great feast.

The sound of swallowing is the sound of history,
belch and hiccup and crunching of bones,
these are the sounds of history,
bowel movements—its movement. Digestion.
In digesting, all begin to be alike:
brother and sister, man and dog, saint and sinner,
flower and cloud, shepherd and sheep, all, governor
and governed, all descend into sameness.
My experimental life descends too.
All descends into the terrible sameness. All is fruit
of the intestinal tract.

Turn over now. Look, the crease down the back that
deepens through the buttocks. Who
can say where they begin and where
the thighs end: see the bold supports
of the loins, columns of legs
and Hellenistic curls of hair
above the genitals. The Gothic arch that rises
towards the heart and the reddish Byzantine flame
between the legs. A distinct
Crusader influence in the hard jaws,
protuberant chin. If she stoops she'll be perfect Arabesque.
She can touch the floor with both hands
without bending her knees. She touches the earth

I didn't kiss when I was brought to it, a child.
Visit the country again,
visit my tears and the east wind,
the true Western Wall, made of great stones
of wind. The sobbing of wind and the bits
of paper blown by the wind are the wishes
I stuck between the stones. Visit the country.
On a fine day, if the visibility is good, one can see
the miracle of my child
holding me in his arms, four years old.
And I forty-four.
And here is the zoo of greater love,
acres of love. Hairy animals breathing
in the cages of porous underpants, brown
feathers and fur, red fish with green eyes,
solitary hearts behind the bars of ribs
jumping like monkeys, furry fish and snakes
like round fat thighs.
A blazing body a flame
covered with a damp raincoat. That quiets.

This land speaks only if struck.
If hail rain and shells strike her,
like Balaam's ass who spoke
only after her master struck her. I speak,
I speak: I've been hit. Ram's horn blast, long blast.
Be seated. Today is the day of the world.

I want to make a bet with Job
on how God and Satan will behave:
who will be the first to curse man.
Like sunset red in Job's mouth
he was beaten and his last word
sinks, red, into his last face.
I left him like that, in the crowded station
in the noise and loudspeaker's voices.
"To hell with it, Job. Cursed be the day
you were created in my image. You are

your mother's shame, Job."
God cursed, God blessed. Job won.
And I must kill myself with the toy
pistol of my small son.

My child blossoms sadly.
He blossoms in spring without me,
he ripens in the sadness of my not being there.
I saw a cat playing with her kittens,
I shall not teach my son war,
I shall not teach him at all. I shall not be.
He puts sand in a small bucket.
He makes a sand cake.
I put sand in my body.
The cake crumbles. My body.

I ate and was full.
Birthdays caught me standing up
in haste. A moment's quiet on a floating log.
Forty-third birthday. Wedding day
with yourself, with no prospect of divorce.
Separate beds for dream and day,
for your desire and your love.
I live beyond my mother's law and in countries
not my father's faith. Stonemasons,
not prophets, built the walls of my house. And on
the gate I found my birth-date carved.
(What became of the house, and what became of me!)
Afternoons I take a quiet stroll
among my extra-territorial wounds:
a lighted window behind which perhaps
you are undressing now,
a street where we were, a black door,
a garden beside it, a gate
through which, a dress like yours,
on a body not like yours, a mouth singing like yours,
a word that is nearly. These are all alien wounds
in a large garden of wounds.

I wear colorful clothes,
I am a colorful male bird.
Too late I discovered that this is the order of nature.
The male dresses up. Red shirt, green coat.
Don't look at me that way, my son!
Don't laugh. You don't see me. I'm a part
of the wall. The collar of my shirt blackens. Under my eyes
there's a black shadow. The remains of coffee
are black and black the sadness under my nails.
Don't look at me like that, my son. With my hands,
smelling of tobacco and strange perfume, I knead
your future dreams. I prepare your subconscious.
The first memory of my child is the day
I left his house, my house. His memories
are as hard as gems in a clock which hasn't stopped
since. When the woman asks him,—that first
night of love, when they lie awake on their backs,
he will say to her: "When my father left the first time."

Blessed is the memory of my childhood. I had my ration
of rebellion, I did my duty as a prodigal son,
I paid my debt to the generation gap
and wildness of adolescence. Therefore I haven't
much time for ease and satiety. Such is
man, and blessed the memory of my childhood.
Sleeplessness made me a night watchman
without instruction on what to guard.
"Happy birthday to you, happy birthday to you."
Understanding and age, wisdom and white hair, knowledge
and death came over me all at once. Memory of childhood. Blessed.

I came home a big-game hunter of feelings.
Antlers, wings, heads on the walls,
stuffed feelings everywhere on the walls.
I sit and look at them peacefully. Do not
watch me at it, my son. Even my laughter
shows that I no longer know how to laugh,
and the mirror has known a long time

that I am its reflection.
Don't watch me, my son, your eyes are darker than mine,
perhaps you are already sadder than I am.
My heavy body shakes its hearts like the hand
of a gambler before he throws the dice
on the table. That is the movement
of my body, that is its game, and my fate.

Bialik, bald knight among olive trees,
wrote no poems in the land of Israel, for he kissed
the earth and chased away flies and mosquitoes
with his writing hand,
and wiped sweat
from his versifying brain and in the khamsin
placed on his forehead a handkerchief from the Diaspora.

The lion heart of Richard peers forth and
sticks out its long tongue between his ribs.
He came too with the traveling circus
to the Holy Land. He was the Lion Heart
and I am a kicking ass heart.
All in the *salto mortale*, colored clowns
smeared with white blood, feathers and armor,
swallowing swords and sharpened crosses,
acrobats with cap and bells. Saladin,
din of salad, empty clatter, swallowing
fire and spewing baptismal water.
Female dancers with male genitals.
The King David Hotel flies through the air,
its guests ask for milk, get a bottle of dynamite.
To destroy, to destroy. Blood and fire at the sweetmeat stalls,
you can get fresh frothing blood
from the juice squeezer of glory,
war casualties, twisted and rigid like bagels
threaded on a string.

Yehuda Halevi is bound in his books, caught
in the webs of the longing he exuded. He was kept

as a pledge, a dead poet, in Alexandria.
I don't remember his death, as I do not remember my own.
But I remember Alexandria: Number 66, Sisters Street.
General Shmuel Hanagid on his horse
burnt black like burnt olive trunks
riding round the round Abyssinian Church,
he imagined the Temple thus.
Napoleon, with his hand on his heart, equates the rhythm of
his heartbeats
with the rhythm of his cannon.
A woman's small triangular panties on a line
on a roof in Jerusalem—signal to an old sailor,
tired, from Tudela, a latter-day Benjamin.

I lived for two months in quiet Abu Tor.
I lived two weeks in the Valley of Gehenna
in a house destroyed after I left and in another house,
to which was added a floor, and in a house
whose sagging walls needed support. No one ever
supported me like that. A house has the advantage over a man.
Be seated in mourning now, get used to a low seat
from which all the living look like towers.
Eulogies for the dead scatter in the wind-cursed city.
Old Jerusalem murmurs in an evil golden silence a spell
of longing. The air of the valleys is whipped by olive branches
to new wars, olives black and
hard as a whip. There is no hope between
my eyes, no hope between my legs in the double
domes of my lusts. My Bar Mitzvah chapter
was double too: delivery—leprosy, telling
of skin diseases, vivid with sore colors,
deathly red and sulphurous Sodom yellow of pus.
Muttered calculations of apocalypse, numerology of torture,
barren acrostics of ruin, a game of chess:
twenty-four squares of lust
twenty-four squares of disgust
and Jerusalem a seething pot
of thick gruel, all her buildings raised bubbles,

eye-balls pressed from their sockets;
domes, towers, flat or sloping roofs—
all blisters before bursting. And God
takes the prophet nearest at the moment
and, as with a cook's spoon, stirs and stirs.

I am sitting here now with my father's eyes,
and with my mother's graying hair on my head,
in a house that belonged to an Arab
who bought it from an Englishman
who took it from a German
who hewed it from the stones
of Jerusalem, my city:
I look upon God's world of others
who received it from others.
I am composed of many things
I have been collected many times
I am constructed of spare parts
of decomposing materials
of disintegrating words. And already
in the middle of my life, I begin,
gradually, to return them,
for I wish to be a decent and orderly person
when I'm asked at the border, "Have you anything to declare?"
so that there won't be too much pressure at the end
so that I won't arrive sweating and breathless and confused
so that I won't have anything left to declare.
The red stars are my heart, the Milky Way
its blood, my blood. The hot khamsin
breathes in huge lungs, my life
pulses close to a huge heart, always within.

I live in the German Colony,
the Valley of Ghosts. Outside they call to each other,
a mother to her children, children to
each other, a man to God: come home!
Come, come! "and merciful."
Come home, God, be gathered to your people in Jerusalem

so that we can be gathered to you, in a mutual death
and with mutual prayers, with aired sheets and smooth pillows,
a putting out of reading lights and eternal lights,
the closing of books and the closing of eyes, and turning
crouched, to the wall.
Here in the valley, in the house upon whose gate
my birth-date is carved, with a verse in German:
"Open with God and close with God—That is the way
of life," a stone lion crouches, guards
the words and the date—four numerals.
On the gatepost a mezuzah, the flute
of my childhood's God, and two columns
in memory of the temple that never was.
The curtain stirs like the curtain in the hotel in Rome
that first morning, stirs, and is pushed aside
revealing the nakedness of the city
roofs and sky, and I was moved
to come to her. Please, now, please my love. Your hair
is parted in the middle, your back straight as you walk,
your strong face carries a heavy weight. Heavier
than the jar on the heads of the Arab women at the well,
and your eyes wide open, full to the brim. Outside
cars wail. Machines get the voices of human beings
when the going is rough, when in pain, when there's no fuel,
in the great heat and cold of morning, in old age and loneliness,
and they wail and cry.

Joseph Flavius, son of Matityahu, son of the dead like me,
the son of Matityahu gave up his citadels in Galilee
and threw his sword on the table in front of me
a ray of light from outside. He saw
my name carved on the gate as on a tombstone,
thought my house too was a grave. Son of
the dead, of ashes, son of the lit lamp outside in the evening.
The people outside the window are the legions
of Titus: they are storming Jerusalem
this Sabbath night, the cafés and the cinemas,

the lights and the cakes and the women's thighs:
the surrender of love, the pleading of love.
The rustle of trees
in the garden announces a change in my life
but not in my dreams. My inner garments
are unchanged, and the tattoo of my childhood
sinks deeper inward.
Go, happy commander, sad historian,
sleep between the pages of your book, like dried flowers,
pressed. Sleep there. Go.
My child still unborn is also a war orphan
of three wars in which I was not killed,
but he is a war orphan of all of them.
Go, pale commander of Galilee. I too
am always coming and going, as if into new apartments
through the barbed wire entanglements of memory.
You must be a shadow of water
to pass all those without breaking.
You're gathered again afterwards: a peace treaty
with yourself, a contract, conditions, like a real war.
A woman said to me once:
"Everyone goes to his own funeral." I didn't understand then.
I don't understand now, but
I go. Death is a senior clerk who arranges
our lives according to subject entries
in files and archives. This valley
is the rending of mourning in God's garment,
and nothing remains for poet or historian
except to hand over their citadels
and be mourners, for hire or gratis.
Yodfat opens wide her gates: a great light
breaks out, light of surrender, that had to be enough
for the darkness of thousands of years.
Blast, long blast, sad tremolo,
the blower's lips have cracked in the long heat,
his tongue cleaves to the roof of his mouth,
his right hand has lost its cunning. I remember

only the movement of a woman
pulling her dress off over her head.
What lifting of arms, what blind surrender,
what pleading, what passion, what surrender!
"I am no traitor." And between the columns my brother Josephus
disappears. "I must write history."
The columns are thick, their capitals leprous
with Greek decoration, whorled flutes and buds.
The house is sick. The English call a man "home-sick"
who longs for his house. The house
is man-sick. I am home-sick. Go, Josephus
my brother, flying flags also are curtains
in windows that no longer have a house.

I am a God-fearing Jew, my beard grows inward.
Instead of flesh and blood I am filled with the hair of my beard
like a mattress. Pain remains between phylacteries,
no remedy. My heart fasts nearly every week
whether I drop a scroll to the ground or not. Whether
the Temple is destroyed or rebuilt.
I don't drink wine, but whatever wine
does not do to me is a black pit, without
intoxication, a dark empty vat where the pressers tread
wounding their feet on the hard stone. My body is a dry dock
for what is called my soul. My body
will be dismantled and my soul
will go out to sea, its form the form of the body
in which it was, its form the form of the sea,
the form of the sea the form of my body.

My belovèd is Jobesque. It happened in summer, and the elastic straps
of her clothing snapped with the twang of a taut string. The wailings of
labor pains and rattle of death-agony already in a first night of love.
Rip, riiiiiip of light clothing,
Because it was summer, the end of a heavy summer of
thin, light clothing. A shofar like the hiccup
of a sick man. And in the beginning of the month of Elul
the blower blew the ram's horn and his face was sheepish

like a ram's face and his eye was bulging and glassy and rolled
in its socket like the eye of a closed tank. And his mouth was caught in
 the shofar, with no way to escape.
Jobesque: we met in the flight of the hemlock. With legs spread apart
wider than the spreading of wings, beyond the borders of your body.
In love always, despair lies with you now
and your movements and the writhing of your limbs and your
 screams with him
are the same as with me.
Sometimes I feel my soul rolling
as if it were inside an empty barrel. In the dull sound
of a barrel pushed from place to place. Sometimes
I see Jerusalem between two people
who stand in front of a window, with a space
between them. The fact that they aren't close and loving
allows me to see my life, between them.
"If only it were possible to grasp the moment
when two people first become strangers to each other."*

This could have been a song of praise
to the sweet imaginary God of my childhood.
It was Friday, and black angels
filled the Valley of the Cross, their wings
black houses and abandoned quarries.
Sabbath candles rose and fell like ships
at the entrance to the harbor. Come Sabbath bride, come bride,
wear the clothes of your mourning and your glory
the night you thought I would not come to you
and I came. The room was drenched with the smell
of black cherry preserve. Papers
scattered on the floor rustling below,
bitter wings scythed from above.
Love comes with parting, like a record—
music with applause at the end, love
with a cry, love with the stammered despair
of the proud departure into exile from each other.

*Translation of the twenty-four preceding lines by Stephen Mitchell.

Come bride, hold something of clay in your hand
at the hour of sunset, for flesh dissolves
and iron doesn't keep. Hold clay in your hand
for future archaeologists to find and remember.
They do not know that poppies after rain
are also an archaeological find, rich evidence.

The time has come to close like the Bible,
the canonical books of my life.
Chapters and books will be finally excluded,
will remain apocryphal, their days will
not be counted, they will be flourishes and marginalia
and addenda and glosses,
but not essential, and not sacred.
I imagine matches damp with tears
or blood, that cannot light again. I imagine
a ram's horn blast in the storming of an empty emplacement.
Bagpipes of Jewish ram's horn, Jeremiah of Anatot
storms an empty place at the head of a weeping mob.
But last Yom Kippur, at the end of the closing prayer
when everyone waited for the ram's horn
in dead silence, after the cries "Open to us the gate,"
a voice was heard, like the thin wail of an infant's
first cry. My life, the beginning of my life.

I chose you, I was King Ahasuerus
sitting on his throne, and choosing.
Through the fine clothes
I saw you, time passing
over your body, and the crest of curling hair
over your crotch. You wore black stockings,
but I knew you were the opposite. You wore
black dresses, like mourning, but I saw red
in your body, like a mouth. I saw
a red tongue of velvet protruding from a badly closed box,
pinched by the lid.
I was a bull for Purim and a bull for Kippurim

dressed in a living shroud.
Tremolo, long blast, love, long love.
Sit down. Today is pregnant with the future. Who
raped the future to make the day pregnant?
Today is pregnant, today you, today war.

Tanks from America, fighter planes from France, Russian
jet-doves, armored chariots from England, Sisera's regiments
who dried the swamp with their corpses, a flying Masada,
Beitar slowly sinking, Yodfat on wheels, the Antonia,
 ground-to-ground
ground, ground-to-air air, ground-to-sky sky. Masada won't fall
 again, won't again,
won't fall again, Masada, won't. Multiple automatic
prayer beads and also in single shots. Muezzins armed with
three-stage missiles, paper-rips and battle cries
of holy war in all seven kinds,
shtreimls like mines in the road and in the air, deep philosophical
depth charges, a heart lit up with a green light inside
the engine of a red-hot bomber, Elijah's ejection seat leaping up
at a time of danger, hurling circumcision knives, thundering
dynamite fuses from heart to heart, a Byzantine tank
with a decorated window in which an icon appears
lit up in purity and softness, mezuzahs filled with
explosives, don't kiss them or they'll blow up, dervishes
with powdered rococo curls, the Joint Chiefs of Staff
consisting of Job, his friends, Satan, and God, around a sand-table.
A pricking with bannered pins in the live flesh
of hills and valleys made of naked
humans lying in front of them,
underwater synagogues, periscope rabbis,
cantors out of the depths, jeeps armed with women's hair
and with wild girls' fingernails, ripping their
clothes in rage and mourning. Supersonic angels
with wings of women's fat thighs,
letters of a Torah scroll in ammunition straps, machine guns,
flowers in the pattern of a fortified bunker,

fingers of dynamite, prosthetic legs of dynamite,
eight empty bullet shells for a Hanukkah menorah,
explosives of eternal flame, the cross of a crossfire,
a submachine gun carried in phylactery straps,
camouflage nets of thin lacy material
from girlfriends' panties, used women's dresses
and ripped diapers to clean the cannon mouth,
offensive hand-grenades in the shape of bells,
defensive hand-grenades in the shape of a spice box
for the close of the Sabbath, sea mines
like the prickly apples used as smelling-salts on Yom Kippur
in case of fainting, half my childhood in
a whole armored truck, a grandmother clock
for starting a time-egg filled with
clipped fingernails of bad boys
with a smell of cinnamon, Dürer's
praying hands sticking up
like a vertical land mine, arms with an attachment
for a bayonet, a good-night fortified with sandbags,
the twelve little minor prophets
in a night ambush with warm breath,
cannon barrels climbing like ivy, shooting
cuckoo shells every fifteen minutes: cuckoo,
boom-boom. Barbed-wire testicles,
eye-mines bulging and hurting,
aerial bombs with the heads of
beautiful women like the ones that used to be carved
on ships' prows, the mouth of a cannon
open like flower petals,
M.I.R.V., S.W.A.T., I.C.B.M., I.B.M.,
P.O.W., R.I.P., A.W.O.L.,
S.N.A.F.U., I.N.R.I., J.D.L., L.B.J.,
E.S.P., I.R.S., D.N.A., G.O.D.
Sit down. Today is the day of judgment. Today there was war.*

*Translation of the preceding sixty-three lines by Stephen Mitchell.

The terrible angel brought his arm back
like a spring to his side, to rest or to strike
a new blow. Keep that arm occupied,
distract the attention of its muscles! Weigh it down
with heavy jewelry, gold and silver, bracelets,
diamonds, so that it will fall heavily, and
not strike again. Masada will not fall again.
Will not fall.

In the rising mists from below, in the bluish holy light
in his great hollow dome, I saw
the Lord of the world in all his sadness,
a radar God, lonely, circling round and round
with his huge wings, with sad movements
of primordial doubt.
Yes yes and no no, with the sadness of a God who knows
that there is no reply and no decision: only turning.
What he sees makes him sad. And what
he doesn't see makes him sad. What he records
is the code of sadness for humans to decipher.
I like the bluish light and the white of his eyes
which are blind, white screens
in which men read what will happen to them.
Again Masada. Again Masada. Not again.

One evening I tried to remember
the name of the one who fell beside me
on the pale sands of Ashdod. A foreigner.
Perhaps one of the sailors, lost, who thought
the Jewish people a sea, and those deathly sands
waves. His tattoo did not reveal his name,
only a flower, and a dragon, and fat women.
I could have called him Flower or Fat Women.
In the first light of dawn and retreat he died.
"Died in his arms." In Goethe's poem.
All evening, beside windows and tables
I was lost in the effort to remember,

like the effort of prophecy. I knew
that if I didn't remember his name I would
forget my name, it would dry up.
"Grass springs again." Also Goethe's. The grass
will not spring again, it remained crushed
alive and whispering to itself. It will not spring.
But will never die, and will not fear sudden death
beneath the heavy hobnailed soles.

The year the world got better
my heart fell sick. Am I to conclude
from this that my life is falling apart
without the sweet stifling cackles of danger?
I am forty-three. And my father died at sixty-three.
After the summer comes summer and summer and summer
like a broken record. Dying is when the last season
doesn't ever change again. The body
is the wax of the soul's candle
that drips and gathers and heaps up.
Paradise is when the dead remember
only the good things, the way even after the war
I remembered only the good days.

Last spring my child began
to fear death for the first time
too soon.
Flowers sprout from the earth,
fear flowers in his heart,
delicious fragrance to one
who enjoys fragrance like that.
And in summer I tried to take part in politics—
the questions of the time—
an attempt which also has the fragrance of flowers
and of their fading,
the attempt of a man to stage-manage his house, to move
the furniture to a new position, to take part.
As in the cinema
one moves his head and asks

those in front of him to move theirs too
so he'll have a clear view, at least.
I tried to go out into my times, and to know
but I didn't get further
than the woman's body beside me.
And there's no escape. Don't go to the ant, sluggard!
It will depress you to see that blind
industry, hurrying beneath the boot
raised to stamp.
There's no escape. Like a modern chess set
made of unusual pieces: the King
looks like the Queen, pawns like knights,
and the knights as smooth as the castles. But the game
sticks to the rules. Sometimes
you long for the old pieces, a king with a crown,
a castle round and fortified, the horse a horse.

The players sat inside, the talkers on the verandah:
half of my love, my left hand, a quarter of a friend,
a man half dead. The sound of the killed pieces
tossed into the wooden box is like
distant thunder, heralding evil.

I am a man who is nearing his end.
What seems to be the spirit of youth in me
is not the spirit of youth, it's the spirit of madness.
Only death can put a stop to this madness.
And what seems deep roots that I've struck
is only a tangle on the surface:
a disease of knots, a spasm of hands, a muddle
of ropes and crazy chains.

I am a solitary man, not a democracy.
The executive, the loving and the legislative power
in one body.
The hating power and the hurting power
the blind power and the dumb power.
I wasn't elected. I am a demonstration, I raise

my face like a poster. Everything is written there. Everything.
Please, there's no need to use tear gas.
I'm weeping already. There's no need to disperse me.
I'm dispersed.
The dead are also a demonstration.
When I visit my father's grave, I see
the tombstones raised by hands of dust below:
they're a mass demonstration.

Everyone hears a step at night,
not only prisoners, everyone hears.
Everything is steps at night,
receding or approaching,
but never arriving close enough
to be touched. That is man's
mistake about God and God's mistake about man.

Oh world, that everyone fills
to the brim. And bitterness will come and close
your mouth like stubborn, unyielding spring
so that it will fly wide open, wide open, in death.
What are we, what is our life. A child
hurt at play or beaten, chokes back his tears
and runs to his mother, a long way, through courtyards
and alleys, only there will he cry.
We too, all our lives, choke back our tears and run
a long way, our tears closed in, stifled in our throats.
Death is nothing but a good cry
that lasts forever. Blast. Long blast, *Tekiah gedolah*,
long cry, long silence. Be seated. Today.

The reader of the Scroll follows the silver hand
along the hard lines, like the lever of a big
holy machine. That large finger, bent and hard,
points as it passes to unchanging things.
Here you will read. Here you will die. Here.
And this is the eleventh commandment: Thou shalt not will.

I think of oblivion as of a ripening fruit
which will not be eaten when ripe
because it will not be, and will not be recalled:
its ripeness is its forgetting. When I lie
on my back, my bones fill with the sweetness
of my small son's breath.
He breathes the same air as I,
sees the same things,
but my breath is bitter and his is sweet
as rest to tired bones.
Blessed is the memory of my childhood. His childhood.

I did not kiss the earth
when they brought me, a child, to this country.
But now that I have grown upon it
it kisses me
it holds me
it clings to me in love
with its grass and thorns, sand and stone
with its wars and with this spring
until its last kiss.

RUTH NEVO

Takis Sinopolus, Greek Poet

Takis Sinopolus has eyes the color of the sea.
He is a doctor outside and a poet inside. But
Where is the sea?
As he climbed up to the fourth floor, he breathed heavily
And swallowed two pills from a flat, secret box.

He too is saved every day from death.
When he looks at Rome from his balcony,
When he hears the beat of his heart,
He is a poet outside and a doctor inside.

But I know that even if he is not the sea,
He is at least Odysseus
Tied by his friends to the mast, at his own wish.
When their ears are plugged with wax, he hears.

Takis Sinopolus, your friends abandoned you long ago!
For a long time, you haven't reached your true homeland!
For a long time, you have remained tied to the mast. Listening.

Thus you stand before me with salty eyes on the fourth floor
And your hand, that should have touched
Your heart in sudden pain doesn't touch,
For you are tied to the mast.

BENJAMIN AND BARBARA HARSHAV

Via Appia Antica

What are they saying in the graves
below the road from Rome?
They are saying this: one of us is passing by
who was given a few more days to live.
His resounding steps are one of the clocks
that measure our time, our heart above.
(*glaci frutti*)
He arrives from St. Sebastian's Gate,
the wind translates the language of the dead into his own tongue.
His shadow collapses onto the gravestones as he walks.
His shadow steals through the lattices of forbidden gardens.
He has squandered his last opportunity to become a cypress.
He is ordained to return just as he came, he is ordained to lie when
 he speaks,
so as to be even now silence like us. He is fated for what will not be.

These are the days of kindness toward the dead;
these dead who do not want it.
As in the moments after the end of the last broadcast,
when a gentle whistle persists briefly in the air.
After it, stillness.

LEON WIESELTIER

My Non-Credo

In the winter when my beloved saw snow for the first time
in her life, I told her what it is that I do not believe.
Inside they argued whether God is alive or dead.
She was dressed in a brown animal fur; she was an animal
of God; and outside, the snow.
I wake in the morning and kiss her for her sins
and sip, with kissing sounds, the warm drink.
But there is a great disquiet within me.
In the newspaper I saw a picture of people dancing.
This is a world where people dance. And my soul
miraculously still stands, like the Tower of Pisa: my body
surrounds it like a throng of tourists.
The sunlight falls across the table that is pawned to the devil,
the ground is not smooth, and even so

I still show kindness to the god of my childhood.
In my life's weariness I have turned into
a speech impediment: it is hard
for Him to praise His world in me.

<div align="right">LEON WIESELTIER</div>

Three Times I Came to Rome

Three times I came to Rome,
More and more entangled
In my problems. This time
We actually rolled into her
Like wrestlers entangled in each other,
I and my problems: beasts of prey,
Net and trident, sharp sword,
Early Christians, notched sword,
Stumbling in catacombs,
Emerging from the whistling Arch of Titus.
I didn't see any of those, I and my problems.
I could have stayed in Jerusalem.

Three times I came to Rome. This time
More honor, more pain,
More words in Italian—
Not just: Where is the train? How much?

And the gates are open to death all around.
Even the Porta San Sebastiano
I love.

BENJAMIN AND BARBARA HARSHAV

If I Forget Thee, Jerusalem

If I forget thee, Jerusalem,
Then let my right be forgotten,
Let my right be forgotten, and my left remember.
Let my left remember, and your right close
And your mouth open near the gate.

I shall remember Jerusalem
And forget the forest—my love will remember,
Will open her gate, will close my window,
Will forget my right,
Will forget my left,

If the west wind does not come
I'll never forgive the walls
Nor the sea, nor myself.
Should my right forget
My left shall forgive,
I shall forget all water,
I shall forget my mother.

If I forget thee, Jerusalem,
Let my blood be forgotten.
I shall touch your forehead,
Forget my own,
My voice changes
For the second and last time
To the most terrible of voices—
Or silence.

ASSIA GUTMANN

First Rain

First rain reminds me
of the rising dust of summer.
The rain does not remember last year's rain.
A year is a trained wild beast that has no memories.

Soon you will fasten your lovely embroidered
reins to hold up sheer stockings.
You are the mare and the one holding the reins in a single body.

The white startle of soft flesh
in the place where the stocking stops on the thigh,
a startle of sudden vision
of ancient saints.

ROBERT ALTER

Now in the Uproar

Now in the uproar before the stillness
I can tell you the things
that in the stillness before the uproar I did not say,
for they would have heard us and found our hiding-place.

That we were only neighbors in the blowing wind,
brought together in the ancient heat-blast from Aram of the Two
 Rivers,
and the Latter Prophets of the kingdom of my veins
prophesied into the sky of your flesh.

And the weather was good to us and to the heart
and the sun's muscles flexed within us in gold
in the Olympics of the emotions, before thousands of fans,
that we should know, that we should stay, that again there be clouds.

See, we met in the sheltered place, in the angle
where history began to rise, quiet
and safe from impetuous acts.
And the voice began to tell a tale at evening, by the children's bed.

And now it's too soon for archaeology
and too late to fix what was done.
Summer will come and the hard sound of the sandal
will sink in soft sand forever.

ROBERT ALTER

Spy

Many years ago
I was sent
to spy out the land
beyond the age of thirty.

I stayed there
and did not return to those who sent me,
so I would not have to tell them
about that land
and not have to lie.

ROBERT ALTER

They Fooled Us

They fooled us.
They told us: We'll die, we'll be wiped out
in one of the wars.
As long as I can remember, they told us:
Our blood will be spilled.
We ate and we drank and on the morrow
we didn't die.
We wasted whatever we saved,
flowers, for example, grass . . .

This spring I wonder sometimes:
What did you mean when you told me, "I will give you
one night only." Did you think
all the days of our lives meant nights, one night,
or did you say it out of the great terror?

They fooled us. To my students I passed on whatever
my teachers taught me; passed it on in great haste,
so I could be a bit freer and for myself in the end.
They fooled us:
unspilled blood
cries out louder than blood
that's spilled.

CHANA BLOCH AND CHANA KRONFELD

To Break Up Now

To break up now
the words between us
into sharp fragments:
"I won't ever be able to live without you,"
and to thrust them one by one
into the other's heart:
I won't ever be able.
To live,
won't ever,
without you.
To live.
Won't.

ROBERT ALTER

Poems of Akhziv

1

Broken near the sea,
My head a broken tin.
Seawater fills it
And seeps out.

Broken near the sea.
Elegy, song of my nest.
Foam on lips of the reefs.
Rabies has the sea,
Seabies it has.
More rabid than a dog
More sea than any sea.

Broken near the sea
Song of my nest, elegy.

BENJAMIN AND BARBARA HARSHAV

2

The wheels of ancient millstones were parted
And put on display, the lower stone, and the upper stone,
In two ends of the village.
Out of deep longing
They continue to grind between them
The time of lovers.
Naked people in the sand talk about
Political problems. Ridiculous!
In the distance, small heaps of clothes.
Birds shriek from an island. Pink buttocks
And muscles like sleeping fish. Ridiculous
Even to ask "what time is it"
When you're naked. A strip of white skin on your left wrist.
Better a dialogue:
"Dia," she said. "Logue," he said,
Dia, dia, dia, logue, logue.

Our friend hid a typewriter
In a broom bush. Camouflaged by branches,
Tick, tock, dia, dia, dia, logue.

BENJAMIN AND BARBARA HARSHAV

3

All night you lay awake on your back.
There was another wind
And there was a wind like you.
The light of the moon
Threw on the wall
One more lattice.
"The key's under the stone near the gate."
In the morning the outline of your body appeared
Marked by cigarette butts
On the floor.

HAROLD SCHIMMEL

4
Your green eyes were
Blue for my brown eyes
After this night.

Wrinkles appeared on the sheet;
Not of old age.

<div align="right">BENJAMIN AND BARBARA HARSHAV</div>

5

In midsummer, over the water
Near Akhziv, it suddenly came to me
"Rock of Ages let our song," a melody of snow
And Hanukah.

In my childhood I was in the places where the Maccabees
Fought in snow and in the forests. But even then
The voices were prepared to leap
Into time now. Suddenly,

Over the water, on my back, it came to me:
Rock of Ages. Sheltering tower. Praise.

BENJAMIN AND BARBARA HARSHAV

6

Around the dead word "we loved,"
Covered with seaweed in the sand.
Many onlookers crowded.

Till night we heard the testimonies
Of waves coming one by one.
Of how it happened.

BENJAMIN AND BARBARA HARSHAV

7

He who amasses waves amasses eyes,
He who amasses torments amasses salt,
He who amasses sleep amasses worms,
He who amasses sadness sings at night, amasses
Shells, amasses sand, sand, everything.

That means—to go on living.
What is our life: a few centimeters
Of madness and soft flesh
Between the hard skeleton inside
And the hard air outside.

BENJAMIN AND BARBARA HARSHAV

8
My friend saw horses bathing
In the sea at Acre. He saw, and I feel
Them galloping. What did we seek
In the sand on the third day and the fourth day,
What did we seek?
With a light puff I blew out your right ear.
With a light puff I blew out your left ear.
With light puffs in your two ears
I lit your lust. A great
Invasion into us
Began. Our throbbing, entangled
Bodies witnessed the immensity of the struggle. In vain.

BENJAMIN AND BARBARA HARSHAV

9

Tie up your weeping with a chain
and be inside me.

In the half-ruined house
the light lives alone.
From the darkness they make delicate silver vessels
for a last meal.

My mouth's a fish mouth
and a fish mouth your nipple
stuck together in the night.

After, there was a moonlit night
whiter than Yom Kippur.
Your weeping broke the chain.
It fled far off.

ROBERT ALTER

10

In the sand we were a two-headed Cerberus
Baring our teeth. At noon
Your one leg was in the east, the other in the west,
And I in the middle leaning on my forelegs,
Looking suspiciously to the sides, roaring terribly
So they wouldn't rob me of my prey.

Who are you?
A little Jewish boy from the Diaspora,
A yarmulke on his head. From there. From that time.

At night we are together with no
Heavy memory, no sticky feelings. Just
Ingathering of muscles and their dispersion.

Far away from here, in another continent of time.
Yon can clearly see the dead rabbis of my childhood,
Holding high above their heads
The tombstones. Their souls bound in the bond of my life.
My God, my God,
Why did You not forsake me!?

BENJAMIN AND BARBARA HARSHAV

11

With a daring Columbus gaze
I look through towels hung
At a window. The sun is setting
Into a red dress.
Four boats passed from evening
To evening behind a kerchief.
Salt in the little salt shaker on the table
And outside, all the salt in the world.

Seven creased underpants
Around your bed, for the seven
Days we were here. Like
Seven withering roses
In seven colors.

BENJAMIN AND BARBARA HARSHAV

12
One-piece bathing suit:
Many voices of the crowd.
Somersault of games.
Applause of my hands on your body,
Stormy applause.

Dry measure and wet
Measure in hard longing
Destroy each other.

Crossroads of veins.
Blue pretends to be pink.
In your ankle I shall live.
My member rises with great solemnity
As if to attention.

I shall leave you at the sea
Until your red hair turns green,
Until my black briefcase is covered with green moss
Like a ship sunk long ago.
I shall draw screams from inside you,
Reparations for all the silence I bled.
Vengeance.
God.

BENJAMIN AND BARBARA HARSHAV

13
Two-piece bathing suit.
Two small pieces
Bathing suit
Bathing
Suit.
Sea.

BENJAMIN AND BARBARA HARSHAV

14
Akhziv, flowing juices,
Flowing gold,
Naked butt,
But, but.

Soon the abandoned village
Will be abandoned again
By us. But you,
Brown hair, white skin,
Green eyes; but here,
In Akhziv, all the red
Breaks out of you,
Reveals: you are one
Of the thirty-six hidden red saints.
Moss between your thighs,
Red,
Like Esau.

BENJAMIN AND BARBARA HARSHAV

15

The Ladders of Tyre, the ladders of lust.
The ladders to the roof of Eli's house. Girls
Descend and ascend, carrying mattresses and lines,
Long hair and underwear to be dried. Shouts
Of laundry. The dampness of laughter won't dry
Girls ascend and descend the ladder.

You can see her soul;
Black and made of thin net.
You can see her pink underwear,
With delicate lace. You can see her,
See her, see her.

BENJAMIN AND BARBARA HARSHAV

16
Wind, what a waste of wind
You are. To shift sand to sand,
Me to you, smell to smell.
Wind, what a waste!

Clouds, what a waste of clouds.
Not to rain, just to change
The colors of the Western Galilee a bit
For us.
My life, what a waste of life
It is. Only for these days. Here.

<div align="right">BENJAMIN AND BARBARA HARSHAV</div>

17
I have learned
to relate to your sex
as to a face.

I speak its ancient tongue.
It is wrinkled and made of older stuff
than all the remembered generations written in books.

It relates to us
as to distant offspring,
playing.

ROBERT ALTER

18

The last night at the window,
Outside and inside. Seven o'clock,
Nine, ten. The eleventh hour:
Moonlight
Turned our bodies into scalpels,
Hard and glittering in evil.
Another hour, one o'clock, two, three,

Five: in the first light of dawn
Your body appears trapped in the net
Of its veins, like a sheet
That fell down at night and was caught
In the branches of a dead tree
In front of the window.

<div align="right">BENJAMIN AND BARBARA HARSHAV</div>

19

In the abandoned house
Live Tamarisk Dwarf, Mint
And Sage. We shall visit them
After noon, sit with them,
Rustle with them and exude a fragrant odor.

On your loins a ruddy line,
Memory of an elastic band,
As a line in the sand disappears with a wave,
And we shall know:
Our days here are ripe.

<div align="right">BENJAMIN AND BARBARA HARSHAV</div>

20

How is it to be woman?
How is it to feel
Emptiness between your legs and curiosity
In a skirt, in the summer, in the wind,
And boldness in your buttocks.

A man has to live with the strange bag
Between his legs. "Where would you want
It to be?" asked the tailor, measuring my pants
And didn't smile.

How is it a whole voice that won't break?
How is it to get dressed and undressed
Gliding and sliding and caressing,
Like wearing olive oil,
To anoint your body with soft cloth,
Something silky, murmuring nothings of pink or blue?

A man dresses with coarse movements of
Buckling and hard tearing,
Angles, bones, and punching the air.
And the wind is entangled in his whiskers.

How is it to feel woman?
Your body dreams you.
How is it to love me?
The vestiges of a woman in my male body
And the male signs in your body
Herald the hell
Waiting for us
And our mutual death.

<div align="right">BENJAMIN AND BARBARA HARSHAV</div>

21

If the longings begin
Among these houses near this sea,
We shall be far away.

The mourning women in my heart
Began too early, while I'm still here,
To lament and tear my blood and the sand of the sea
And its weeds; and to bang their fist on the rock,
On the sand, on your breasts.

The sea retreated from my face.
My face is like the floor of the sea: dry
With crevices and rocks and harsh winds.
Thus I am mature
And the memories of the soft green sea still on my face.

<div align="right">BENJAMIN AND BARBARA HARSHAV</div>

22

After these days, I don't know much
About you. The palm tree stayed bent to the east
Even without a west wind. A white boat
Passes along the shore, tough
And clear as God's finger. The will
I'm writing in Akhziv, in the sand,
Is different from the will I wrote in Jerusalem.
The voices of children buried in the layers
Of the mound reach us in this century
At this hour of noon. They did not
Stop playing.

Never shall the white, weather-beaten board
Be again in the ship, never will a rock be made
From the crushed gravel. This tears
My soul, as it was torn by the Prophets; in a rip
Of sharp pain a man becomes a prophet.
This is the landscape for forgetting and prophecy.
From now on, we shall seek other windows with other
Images. We shall wander from window to window, from vault to vault.

The anchor of the abandoned ship will soon
Decorate houses and yards. Our heart will be just an amulet
Hanging inside dreams and blood.

BENJAMIN AND BARBARA HARSHAV

Not for the Sake of Remembering

1971

שָׁלוֹם בַּר

לֹא זֶה שֶׁל שְׁבִיתַת נֶשֶׁק,
אֲפִילוּ לֹא שֶׁל חֲזוֹן זְאֵב עִם גְּדִי,
אֶלָּא,
כְּמוֹ בַּלֵּב אַחַר הַהִתְרַגְּשׁוּת:
לְדַבֵּר רַק עַל עֲיֵפוּת גְּדוֹלָה.
אֲנִי יוֹדֵעַ שֶׁאֲנִי יוֹדֵעַ לְהָמִית,
לָכֵן אֲנִי מְבַגֵּר.
וּבְנִי מְשַׂחֵק בְּרוֹבֶה צַעֲצוּעִים שֶׁיּוֹדֵעַ
לִפְתֹּחַ וְלַעֲצֹם עֵינַיִם וּלְהַגִּיד, אִמָּא.
שָׁלוֹם
בְּלִי רַעַשׁ כְּתוּת חֲרָבוֹת לְאִתִּים, בְּלִי מִלִּים, בְּלִי
קוֹל חוֹתָמוֹת כְּבֵדוֹת; שֶׁיִּהְיֶה קַל
מֵעַל, בְּקֶצֶף לָבָן וְעָצֵל.
מְנוּחָה לַפְּצָעִים;
אֲפִלּוּ לֹא אֲרוּכָה.
(וְזַעֲקַת יְתוֹמִים נִמְסֶרֶת מִדּוֹר
לְדוֹר, כְּמוֹ בְּמֵרוֹץ שְׁלִיחִים: מַקֵּל לֹא נוֹפֵל.)

שֶׁיִּהְיֶה
כְּמוֹ פִּרְחֵי בַּר,
פִּתְאֹם בְּכֹרַח הַשָּׂדֶה:
שָׁלוֹם בַּר.

(TRANSLATION ON PAGE 184)

Instead of Words

My love has a very long white gown
of sleep, of sleeplessness, of weddings.
In the evening she sits at a small table,
puts a comb down on it, two tiny bottles
and a brush, instead of words.
Out of the depths of her hair she fishes many pins
and puts them in her mouth, instead of words.

I dishevel her, she combs.
I dishevel again. What's left?
She falls asleep instead of words,
and her sleep already knows me,
wags her woolly dreams.
Her belly easily absorbs
all the wrathful prophecies of
the End of Days.

I wake her: we
are the instruments of a hard love.

CHANA BLOCH

Jews in the Land of Israel

We forget where we came from. Our Jewish
names from the Exile give us away,
bring back the memory of flower and fruit, medieval cities,
metals, knights who turned to stone, roses,
spices whose scent drifted away, precious stones, lots of red,
handicrafts long gone from the world
(the hands are gone too).

Circumcision does it to us,
as in the Bible story of Shechem and the sons of Jacob,
so that we go on hurting all our lives.

What are we doing, coming back here with this pain?
Our longings were drained together with the swamps,
the desert blooms for us, and our children are beautiful.
Even the wrecks of ships that sank on the way
reached this shore,
even winds did. Not all the sails.

What are we doing
in this dark land with its
yellow shadows that pierce the eyes?
(Every now and then someone says, even after forty
or fifty years: "The sun is killing me.")

What are we doing with these souls of mist, with these names,
with our eyes of forests, with our beautiful children,
with our quick blood?

Spilled blood is not the roots of trees
but it's the closest thing to roots
we have.

CHANA BLOCH

Jerusalem's Suicide Attempts

The tears here do not soften
The eyes. They only hone
And polish the hard face, like a rock.

Jerusalem's suicide attempts.
She tried again on the Ninth of Av,
She tried with red and fire
And with slow decay of white dust
In the wind. She'll never succeed,
But she'll try again and again.

BENJAMIN AND BARBARA HARSHAV

A Tourist in Jerusalem

A girl ripe
like Jericho oranges
with leaves attached
so people will believe
they are fresh.

A girl that way with her dreams
from her distant land,
so people will believe her.

And my love is carved
as from olivewood.
As for tourists.

Night with an Armenian suffix:
Nightean.
Bright as the white of the eye at night
Ay, wax, wax.

ROBERT ALTER

A Poem on the Renovation of My House

With eyes that have seen Kuwait's gold
and the black cream of oil,
Taleb works on rebuilding my house
in exchange for a few thousand liras
which he turns into dinars, and then
into the gold in his pupils.

He raises my fallen roof.
Like an elegant tennis player he spreads
plaster over the walls of my room,
changing my life's story.

He has springs beneath his feet. He passes through
the Old City after work.
A sweet river meanders and bends
in deep and blue flirtation,
as only ribbons do in full-bodied hair.
Taleb sees a foreign woman covered in golden down
all over her body. A foreign hairy beast making shadows
dance in the alleys. He sees
a policeman mounted on a white horse
and on his chest parachuted angel's wings.

Blessed is the summer, burnt is the grass on the slopes:
a fire, too, is a language.

<div align="right">ROBERT ALTER</div>

Love in the Afternoon Before Sabbath

A braided challah, you and I
in Sabbath love.

In the room I blacken your skin
with fresh newspaper fingers.

You hear a melody in your ear
that still contains the murmur of my lust
as in an ashtray.

The sunlight is too much for you.
Put dark glasses
over your eyes.

The world will see you
darker than I.

ROBERT ALTER

Three Commentaries

I

"And no longer shall your name be called Abram"
I am Abram who once was Abraham
and returned the *h* to his God,
the way a man proudly returns
a medal to the government.

II

"The guardian of Israel will not slumber or sleep."
I wish to say a few things about
the insomnia of God.
Even the white dead
do not make him drowsy.

III

"Do not cast us aside in the season of our old age" but
cast us aside in the season of our youth.
Cast us, carry us,
with love always.

LEON WIESELTIER

Abandoned House

The window is filled with stones,
doors are carried away like corpses,
doors from inside the house.

The entrance is blocked with beams and barbed wire.
The chain dangles free of dog and wall.

And what was a past will be
another's future
like a room in a hotel.

ROBERT ALTER

Wildpeace

Not the peace of a cease-fire,
not even the vision of the wolf and the lamb,
but rather
as in the heart when the excitement is over
and you can talk only about a great weariness.
I know that I know how to kill,
that makes me an adult.
And my son plays with a toy gun that knows
how to open and close its eyes and say Mama.
A peace
without the big noise of beating swords into ploughshares,
without words, without
the thud of the heavy rubber stamp: let it be
light, floating, like lazy white foam.
A little rest for the wounds—
who speaks of healing?
(And the howl of the orphans is passed from one generation
to the next, as in a relay race:
the baton never falls.)

Let it come
like wildflowers,
suddenly, because the field
must have it: wildpeace.

<div align="right">CHANA BLOCH</div>

Leah Goldberg Died

Leah Goldberg died on a day of drizzle
as only in the poems she wrote
and put off her funeral
to the next day, which was sunny,
as only she.

Her sad eyes are the only ones
that could compete with my father's eyes
in the ancient Jewish game
of heavy eyes sliding into
hollows beneath.
(Now they are both there.)
Leah Goldberg died two days
after the literary supplements
were already printed.
Thus she compels us
to write about her in sad composure
and with chaste words, as only she.
(In the Negev battles her little book
From My Old Home was always in my kit bag.
Its pages were torn and stuck together
with Band-Aid strips, but I knew
all the hidden words by heart
and also what was revealed.)
She learned many languages
through the driving sadness of man:
speech, writing, and quiet weeping.
(Three girls lived in a certain apartment in Jerusalem
after her,
one of whom I loved very much.)
We brought her the sweetness
of our lives, so that she might put it

into her poems, like jam inside a doughnut.
But the suffering
she provided on her own:
she had no need of others'.
(When my boy was two years old,
he called her "Goldberg."
Not Auntie. Not Leah.)

The professor in her was
perhaps ready to live many years more.
But the poet did not want
to grow old, and won out.

Leah has died. Of this stillness
she already owned here many shares.
She goes out there rich,
a queen going out to the exile of death.
And young men and women will still read
her poems in secluded rooms in her land
that life has conquered.

On this mountain, which they call "resting place,"
I think now of the words
"in sorrow to the grave" that are in the Torah:
sorrow should be something
lovely and very precious, like
silver and golden vessels placed with
dead kings in their tombs. So with you.

Go now. Gather all the voices
to you. Take them with you.
They are yours, finally.
Return there. The dead are precise like you.
They cannot say as we do: I want to say.
I think that it's. Perhaps I'll come.
The dead say: No. Not I. I'm not.

Go to your resting place, weary Leah.
As for us, what's left but standing
with head raised and awaiting
evil and good tidings
mingled with the scent of pines.

ROBERT ALTER

We Lay Exposed and Equal

We lay
exposed and equal, like two halves of an orange,
until the evening turned dark
from your voice.

Water may be cried over,
not stones: that's why I'm returning to Jerusalem.
"I'll miss you!"
Who taught you to say
such vulgar words?

LEON WIESELTIER

Not for the Sake of Remembering

Not for the sake of remembering
do you live, but to complete the work
that you (despite it all, you) must complete,
and not for the sake of staying do you love,
and not for the sake of loving do you hurt.

You're speedy and you hurry to exhaustion,
short-tempered as on those days when
you fly from country to country,
exchanging good hours for showers of blessings
for some unknown trade, in a passing lover's currency,
on Corientes Street, they flow by, they flow by.

Vamos, let's go. In other languages
it hurts less: let's go
together, is the illusion at first,
and then, from each other.

LEON WIESELTIER

End of the Archaeological Season in Eyn Gedi

The archaeologists went home,
Collected their sticks black and white.
Everything measured.
They left their threads
As secreted webs.

The Roman excavation
Lay gaping on her back,
Abandoned like a woman raped
In the field,
It's all in the open
Though she didn't scream.

<div align="right">BENJAMIN AND BARBARA HARSHAV</div>

Poems in Jericho

1

The leprosy of the scent of Jericho roses
and Sodom apples swollen like diseased testicles,
lazy explosions of fruit, rose concentrate,
dried childhood in sheep droppings,
sweet crushed cat,
anointment oil on hair.
And the water, the water: what
can be learned from the water?
A girl on the top of the *tel*. She is
the stratum of the end of the second millennium
of the era, the era, the era.

2

By the dead orange grove, near my kingdom:
And I have no tree and I have no crown and I have no death.
Where are my lands?
An alien life-story rests
at my feet
like an enchanted lion.
You promised
you promised.

3

If now, in the middle of my life, I think
about death, I do so confident
that in the middle of death I will suddenly think
about life, with the same calming sorrow
and the distanced look of those
who see their prophecies fulfilled.

ROBERT ALTER

Poems of the Hot Wind

1

A train pursued by oleanders
Flees between the thighs of hot hills,

Olive trees gape open in panic,
Shake off lizards and chameleons.

The sun gives birth to a sun,
And a sun, and a sun.
Curtain of dust removed, revealing
Stung air kicking in all directions.

Toothless earth, whispering
Crazy thorns, like Van Gogh.

2

The water mask of the mountains
Burst at night. Hot winds
Come, the true monks,
Essenes from Dead Sea caves,
Come upon us, white, to crack
Lips, dry hearts,
Remind, warn.

4

In girls rumpled at noon
You can see the lining of their thoughts.

Behind their eyes,
Hard, white teeth.

With whispering wails
They fall upon me.

With delicate and knowing fingers
They open the orange of my memories
Into pale segments.

With drilling dreams
They reach black oil inside me.

BENJAMIN AND BARBARA HARSHAV

6
And all the sleepers were swallowed
in the serpent's maw of death.

Moonlight and the smell of the field
wrestle and groan.

Little dead Ruth
gets up from her bed
covered with glass shards,
half of her is her dream, half is my dream,
passing through enemy lines.
Her heart cooks within her on a low Sabbath flame.
Passing beneath high arches
of allegory and heaven's stars.

The landscape is calmed like a baby
through sobbing.
I recited the prayer of forgetting.

ROBERT ALTER

In the Morning I Stand by Your Bed

In the morning I stand by your bed.
My shadow falls over your face
and deepens your sleep
and makes for you extra night.

Like a smoker's fingers, our soul
has been darkened, addicted to love.

I love you
with all my might and with all my life.

ROBERT ALTER

Try Again

And my scream is made of strange edges
like a complicated key.
It will be hard to open the world with it,
hard and hurting sleep.
Try again, come again.
Leaves on the tree rustle suddenly.
They know a bit before us
about the coming of the wind. Try again,
there's a rear door, through the garden.
Perhaps a miracle of quiet convincing speech
that will bring forth water from a rock. Not
striking, just speaking.

ROBERT ALTER

The Way It Was

The way it was.
When the water we drank at night, afterwards,
was all the wine in the world.

And doors, I never remember
if they open in or out,
and if those buttons in the entrance to your building
are for switching on the light, for ringing the bell
or ringing in silence.

That's the way we wanted it. Was that
the way we wanted it?
In our three rooms,
at the open window,
you promised me there wouldn't be a war.

I gave you a watch instead of
a wedding ring: good round time,
the ripest fruit
of sleeplessness and forever.

CHANA BLOCH

Akhziv

1

Clouds came from the south, the Nile
Overflows its banks. Then there is hope.
War here pretends to be peace,
This shore still believes everything,
Floating papers and all that is written on them,
Seaweed, kelp, gestures of distant,
Foreign nations the waves inherited.
The rock in the water is covered with mold,
Warm as a body under wet wool,
A man carries a tune passing through his shoulder strap.
Long-legged girls like vestiges
Of beautiful houses with tall vaults.
A wind from the sea cools my hot testicles,
I touch the skin of the sand,
I touch the muscles of the sea,
The shadow breaks in a ruin and doesn't tear,
A snake was cut by a glass sliver
And hangs from the wall like the pretty belt
Of a woman undressing.
On a threshold stone, whose house is destroyed,
A watermelon was slaughtered, cracked,
And a light face rises
From the heavy tear slowly descending.

2

Many dead nations left
Their vestiges here like forgotten clothes at the sea.
This is a convenient place to put my childhood,
To spread the tools of my memories.
In this cracked room, propped up in the middle
By a square pillar, between suspended fishing rods

That dried out long ago, a hurricane lamp forgotten by the
 hurricane,
Hooks to hold the air, a mast, a net
That hauled in fishermen and fish
Along with my forty-six years.

A man learns to talk in his childhood
So he can talk to himself
When he remains more and more alone,
Talking with others is an ephemeral stage.
Some things grow heavy
Some light, some are anchor and some are sails,
Only after time passes
Do you know which are which.
You don't want any more perspective, you want
Flat calm, not a table
You can put things on, not a house to enter,
But lines, like a child draws, not depth
Promising eternity, not a boulevard with trees
That grow smaller, not a ship vanishing on the horizon.

3
Return begins here. Return
Doesn't have to be to the house
Where you lived, it can be
To a different, distant place.
What do you promise yourself
Standing at the movement of the waves, that reminds you
Of breasts rising breathing excitedly
Of a girl suddenly falling in love, what
Do you promise? Another letter? Calm?
Our names squandered us,
Our roads can go without us.
Perhaps a wandering memory, whose rememberer was lost,
Will find these hours and descend on them,
Your heart counts its moments like a bank teller:
More rustling of paper than ringing of gold,
Than flesh and blood, than the murmur of sea waves.

Strange and superfluous always to take
Everything with you, like a beggar afraid
To deposit his meager belongings in a safe place,
Your hair, your legs, all your memories,
To put your ear to places where there is no sound,
Your liver, your guts,
And everything in them, when you need
Only a mouth, only a caressing hand,
One thought, a single sex organ.
And the more loves you collect,
The more obligations, dependence, arguments,
Claims on your body and soul,
All of you. And it turns out
That what you thought was strong will
Is just the hardness of Jerusalem stones,
When you leave it, you're different.

4

Again and again, you take up your position at the imaginary
Starting line, like chess pieces for a new game,
You're tired. You give yourself
As a secondhand gift, wrapped in pretty paper,
Accepted with no surprise, no cries of joy.

Sailboats and horses remain as toys,
Palmach war songs are played at weddings
Among aunts and insolent beggars.
The sea is calm and big. Your gaze,
Like a beacon directed at the distance,
Strikes the girl sitting near you
And turns her face into illuminated distances,
Without hope of closeness.

5

And thus my belated soul,
Perhaps the last one, begins now to grow on me
From outside, like ivy climbing a house
About to be abandoned, to adorn the ruin.

And there is still hope. Still
The clouds come in the middle of summer
And a young woman brought along her heart
like a big red ball to play with,
The sea still uses her tanned skin
For its rolling tears, its foamy laugh.

What can you put against all those?
My slow walk, not even love;
My walk is the fifth season that doesn't change.
My face wraps itself in the wind, not to break.
Above me, echoes of supernocturnal voices
And gray hair is gray hair.

BENJAMIN AND BARBARA HARSHAV

Behind All This
a Great Happiness Is Hiding

1976

הֶרוֹדְיוֹן

אֲנִי נוֹסֵעַ דֶּרֶךְ הַמִּדְבָּר
אֶל מָקוֹם עַתִּיק וּמְפֻרְסָם לָשֶׁבֶת בּוֹ
בְּשֶׁמֶשׁ הַחֹרֶף לְיַד שִׁיָּרֵי מִגְדָּלִים
שֶׁשָּׁמְרוּ עַל תַּעֲנוּגוֹת מֶלֶךְ.

וּכְסַכִּין מְקַלֶּפֶת פְּרִי עָגֹל, אֲנִי חָשׁ
אֶת תְּנוּעַת הַזְּמַן סָבִיב-סָבִיב.

חַיִּים וּמֵתִים נִפְגָּשִׁים בְּתוֹךְ חֲלוֹמִי
כִּנְצִיגִים שֶׁל שְׁנֵי עַמִּים אוֹיְבִים
בִּמְדִינָה שְׁלִישִׁית.
וּפָנַי פְּנֵי מְנַצֵּחַ שֶׁהִצְטַטְבְּעוּ בְּצִבְעֵי מְנַצֵּחַ.

אֲנִי שָׁקֵט: מָה שֶׁעוֹזֵב אוֹתָנוּ
אֵינֶנּוּ מִצְטָרֵף מִיָּד לָאֲבָנִים וְלַמִּדְבָּר.
יֵשׁ דְּבָרִים בָּאֶמְצַע וְתַחֲנוֹת,
כְּגוֹן מֶרְחָק, הֵד וָחֹשֶׁךְ
יָד וְגַנִּים.

(TRANSLATION ON PAGE 226)

from Songs of Zion the Beautiful

1

Our baby was weaned during the first days
of the war. And I rushed out to stare
at the terrifying desert.
At night I came home again to watch him
sleeping. He is starting to forget
his mother's nipples, and he'll go on forgetting
until the next war.

And that's how, while he was still an infant,
his hopes closed and his complaints
opened—
never to close again.

2

The war broke out in the fall, at the empty border
between grapes and citrus fruit.

The sky blue as the veins
in the thighs of a tormented woman.
The desert, a mirror for those who look into it.

Somber males carry the memory of their families, hunchback
in their gear, in knapsack, kit bags,
soul-pouches, heavy eye-bladders.

The blood froze in its veins. So
it can't spill now, it can only
shatter to bits.

3

The October sun warms our faces.
A soldier is filling bags with the soft sand
he used to play in.

The October sun warms our dead.
Grief is a heavy wooden board,
tears are nails.

4
I have nothing to say about the war, nothing
to add. I'm ashamed.

All the knowledge I've absorbed in my life I now
give up, like a desert
that has given up water.
I'm forgetting names that I never thought
I'd forget.

And because of the war
I repeat, for the sake of a last, simple sweetness:

The sun goes around the earth, yes.
The earth is flat as a lost drifting plank, yes.
There's a God in Heaven. Yes.

5
I've closed myself up, now I'm like
a dull heavy swamp. I sleep war,
hibernating.

They've made me commander of the dead
on the Mount of Olives.

I always lose, even
in victory.

8
What did the man who burned to death
ask of us?
What the water would have us do:
not to make noise, not to make a mess,
to be very quiet at its side,
to let it flow.

11

The city where I was born was destroyed by gunfire.
The ship that brought me here was later sunk, in the war.
The barn in Hamadiya where I made love was burnt down,
the kiosk in Ein Gedi was blown up by the enemy,
the bridge in Ismailiya that I crossed
back and forth on the eve of all my loves
was torn to tatters.

My life is being blotted out behind me according to a precise map.
How much longer can those memories hold out?
They killed the little girl from my childhood and my father
 is dead.

So don't ever choose me for a lover or a son,
a tenant, a crosser of bridges, a citizen.

12

On the last words of Trumpeldor,
It is good to die for our country, they built
the new homeland, like hornets in crazy nests.
And even if those were not the words,
or he never said them, or if he did and they drifted away,
they are still there, vaulted like a cave. The cement
has become harder than stone. This is my homeland
where I can dream without stumbling,
do bad deeds without being damned,
neglect my wife without feeling lonely,
cry without shame, lie and betray
without going to hell for it.

This is the land we covered with field and forest
but we had no time to cover our faces
so they are naked in the grimace of sorrow and the ugliness
 of joy.

This is the land whose dead lie in the ground
instead of coal and iron and gold:
they are fuel for the coming of messiahs.

14

Because of the will of the night, I left the land
of the setting sun.
I came too late for the cedars, there weren't any more.
I also came too late for A. D. Gordon, and most of the swamps
were already drained when I was a child.

But my held-back weeping
hardened the foundations. And my feet, moving
in desperate joy, did what ploughs do,
and pavers of roads.
And when I became a man, the voice
of Rachel-weeping-for-her-children broke too.

My thoughts come back to me toward evening
like those who harvested in the days of Degania, in dust and joy.
On top of the hay wagon.

Now I live in a city of hills where it gets dark
before it does at the seashore.
And I live in a house that gets dark before it does outside.
But in my heart, where I really live,
it's always dark.
Perhaps one day there will finally be light
as in the Far North.

15

Even my loves are measured by wars.
I say, "That happened after
the Second World War." "We met
a day before the Six-Day War." I would never say
"before the peace of '45–'48" or "in the middle of
the peace of '56–'67."

Yet the knowledge of peace
makes its way from one place to another
like children's games,
which are so much alike everywhere you go.

17

An Armenian funeral on Mount Zion: the coffin
is carried, wobbling, like a bit of straw
in a procession of black ants.

The widow's black purse gleams
in the setting sun. That you are
Our Father, that he is Our King, that we have
no Savior in our time.

18

The graves in Jerusalem are the openings
of deep tunnels
on the day of the groundbreaking ceremonies.
After that they stop digging.

The gravestones are magnificent
cornerstones of buildings
that will never get built.

21

Jerusalem's a place where everyone remembers
he's forgotten something
but doesn't remember what it is.

And for the sake of remembering
I wear my father's face over mine.

This is the city where my dream containers fill up
like a diver's oxygen tanks.

Its holiness
sometimes turns into love.

And the questions that are asked in these hills
are the same as they've always been: "Have you
seen my sheep?" "Have you seen
my shepherd?"

And the door of my house stands open
like a tomb
where someone was resurrected.

22
This is the end of the landscape. Among blocks
of concrete and rusting iron
there's a fig tree with heavy fruit
but even kids don't come around to pick it.
This is the end of the landscape.
Inside the carcass of a mattress rotting in the field
the springs stay put, like souls.

The house I lived in gets farther and farther away
but a light was left burning in the window
so that people would only see and not hear.
This is the end.

And how to start loving again is like the problem
of architects in an old city: how to build
where houses once stood, so it will look like
those days, yet also like now.

23
Nineteen years this city was divided—
the lifetime of a young man who might have fallen in the war.
I long for the serenity and for the old longing.
Crazy people would cross through the fence that divided it,
enemies breached it,
lovers went up to it, testing,
like circus acrobats who try out the net
before they dare to jump.

The patches of no-man's-land were like bays.
Longing floated overhead in the sky
like ships whose anchors stuck deep in us, and sweetly
ached.

24

The photos of divided Jerusalem
you burn, and the very beautiful
love letters of a quiet beloved.

The undivided noisy matron has returned
with her gold and bronze and precious stones
to her fat legitimate life.
But I don't love her.
I sometimes remember the quiet one.

27

The toys of an only God
who is rich and spoiled:
dolls, angels, marbles, a bell and glass,
golden wheels, bundles of flutes.

But the toys of the poor children
of a poor God: prayer rattles, dry
palm branches, matzohs. And at the very most,
a Havdoleh box for cheap spices
with a little flag on top that goes round and round.

29

People travel a long distance to be able to say: This reminds me
of some other place.
It's like that time, it's similar. But
I knew a man who traveled all the way to New York
to commit suicide. He claimed that the buildings in Jerusalem
were too low and besides, everyone knew him here.

I remember him fondly because once
he called me out of the classroom in the middle of a lesson:
"A beautiful woman is waiting for you outside, in the garden."
And he quieted the noisy children.

Whenever I think about the woman and the garden,
I remember him up on that high roof:
the loneliness of his death, the death of his loneliness.

31
Four synagogues are entrenched together
against bombardment from God.
In the first, Holy Arks with candies hidden away,
and sweet preserves of God's Word from a blessed season,
all in beautiful jars, for children
to stand on tiptoe and lick with a golden finger.
Also ovens with cholent and oatmeal running over.

In the second, four strong pillars for an everlasting
wedding canopy. The result
of love.
The third, an old Turkish bathhouse with small, high windows
and Torah scrolls, naked
or taking off their robes. *Answer, answer us*
in clouds of vapor and white steam,
Answer, answer till the senses swoon.

The fourth:
part of God's bequest.

Yes. These are thy tents, O Jacob, *de profundis.*
"From here we begin the descent. Please remain seated
till the signal lights up." As on a flight
that will never land.

32
In the lot through which lovers took a shortcut
the Rumanian circus is parked.

Clouds mill around the setting sun like refugees
in a strange city of refuge.

A man of the twentieth century
casts a dark purple Byzantine shadow.

A woman shades her eyes with a raised hand, ringing
a bunch of lifted grapes.

Pain found me in the street
and whistled to his companions: Here's another one.

New houses flooded my father's grave
like tank columns. It stayed proud and didn't surrender.

A man who has no portion in the world to come
sleeps with a woman who does.

Their lust is reinforced by the self-restraint
in the monasteries all around.

This house has love carved on its gate
and loneliness for supports.

"From the roof you can see" or "Next year"—
between these two a whole life goes on.

In this city, the water level
is always beneath the level of the dead.

34
Let the memorial hill remember instead of me,
that's what it's here for. Let the park in-memory-of remember,
let the street that's-named-for remember,
let the famous building remember,
let the synagogue that's named after God remember,
let the rolling Torah scroll remember, let the prayer
for the memory of the dead remember. Let the flags remember,
those multicolored shrouds of history: the bodies they wrapped
have long since turned to dust. Let the dust remember.
Let the dung remember at the gate. Let the afterbirth remember.
Let the beasts of the field and the birds of the heavens
eat and remember.
Let all of them remember so that I can rest.

35

In the summer whole peoples visit one another
to spy out each other's nakedness.

Hebrew and Arabic, that are like guttural
stones, like sand on the palate,
grow soft as oil for the tourists' sake.

Jihad and Jehovah's wars
burst like ripe figs.

Jerusalem's water pipes protrude
like the veins and sinews of a tired old man.

Its houses are like the teeth of a lower jaw,
grinding in vain
because the skies above it are empty.

Perhaps Jerusalem is a dead city
with people
swarming like maggots.

Sometimes they celebrate.

36

Every evening God takes his glittery merchandise
out of the shop window:
chariot works, tablets of law, fancy beads,
crosses and gleaming bells,
and puts them back into dark boxes
inside, and closes the shutter: "Another day,
and still not one prophet has come to buy."

37

All these stones, all this sorrow, all this
light, rubble of night hours and noon-dust,
all the twisted pipework of sanctity,
Wailing Wall, towers, rusty halos,

all the prophecies that—like old men—couldn't hold it in,
all the sweaty angels' wings,
all the stinking candles, all the prosthetic tourism,
dung of deliverance, bliss-and-balls,
dregs of nothingness, bomb and time.
All this dust, all these bones
in the process of resurrection and of the wind,
all this love, all these
stones, all this sorrow—

Go heap them into the valleys all around
so Jerusalem will be level
for my sweet airplane
that will come and carry me up.

38
And nevertheless, I have to
love Jerusalem and recall
him who died for her on the Gethsemane Bridge,
whose death was a watershed
between memory and memory, hope and hope,
who was the land and the fruit of the land,
in whom festival fronds and trumpets and angel wings
became one bundle, who was
the salvations and the consolations and the deaths
for the sake of heaven and the sake of earth,
who rose up and stood, who stood and fell,
his body an extra gate in the city wall
and his voice a roar like the roar in the resurrection.
Who for the sword, to the sword, who
for the night, to the night and who for the uproar to the stillness.
Powered by a small sleeping child's breath
he ascends now, spreads out in supernal joy,
all Jerusalem a commentary on his death.

CHANA BLOCH

(POEMS 24 AND 38, ROBERT ALTER)

I've Grown Very Hairy

I've grown very hairy all over my body.
I'm afraid they're going to start hunting me for my fur.

My shirt of many colors isn't a sign of love:
it's like an aerial photograph of a railroad station.

At night my body is wide open and awake under the blanket
like the blindfolded eyes of someone who's about to be shot.

I live as a fugitive and a vagabond, I'll die
hungry for more—

and I wanted to be quiet, like an ancient mound
whose cities were all destroyed,

and peaceful,
like a full cemetery.

<div align="right">CHANA BLOCH</div>

A Poem on God's Ways

God's ways in the old orange grove in the Sharon.
He lets me walk on them, among black trees.
Only I know green. I'm a man of below.

The nearby grass sways and the distant grass rests in splendor.
In the eyes of one lying in it through the hours of noon
now is more than forever.

At night I hear the voice of the owl by the roof.
I am a man of below. Every love
takes me far from my life and my death as well.

ROBERT ALTER

Love Song

This is how it started: suddenly it felt
loose and light and happy inside,
like when you feel your shoelaces loosening a bit
and you bend down.

Then came other days.

And now I'm like a Trojan horse
filled with terrible loves.
Every night they break out and run wild
and at dawn they come back
into my dark belly.

CHANA BLOCH

I Am Tired

I am tired like a very ancient language
invaded by foreign words.
I cannot defend.

I'll buy myself a dog
and teach him to long.

A door creaks:
it's not the one I love.

But in evenings of grace the street is full
of substitute fathers and substitute mothers.

<div style="text-align: right;">ROBERT ALTER</div>

Empty Remembering

Remembering empty of memory comes to me in these hours,
and sorrow, like carrying bundles and baskets in a baby carriage,
a suitcase, and a pot with a flower.

"Here it was, with the iron cup
fastened by a chain," you want to say, the well
in the little square with the shed over it.
The eye, maybe nipples, maybe squinting mouth
and the heart a box that wants to live without matches.
And the last words of many dead
flatter my face in the light of the waning day.

Alas, stations without journeys or vehicles,
waiting rooms with no reception behind them,
stones out of ancient visions,
blackening wine stains on the pages
of an old Passover Haggadah, a blue enamel kettle
dented, with ornaments of nevermore,
plains to the end of the eye,
and dust rising up, as only people
rise up against their fate.

And under it all, as under
many covers, a child sleeps.

ROBERT ALTER

When a Man Is Left

When a man is left
by his love, a round hollow spreads out
inside him like a cave
for wondrous stalactites. Slowly,
like the empty place kept within history
for meaning, for purpose and for tears.

ROBERT ALTER

A Great War Is Being Fought

A great war is being fought over my mouth
that it not harden and over my jaws
that they not become like the doors of an empty safe
and my life not be called pre-death.

Like a newspaper pinned to the fence by a wind
my soul is stuck to me.
If the wind subsides,
my soul will fall from me.

<div align="right">

LEON WIESELTIER

</div>

Seven Laments for the War-Dead

1
Mr. Beringer, whose son
fell at the Canal that strangers dug
so ships could cross the desert,
crosses my path at Jaffa Gate.

He has grown very thin, has lost
the weight of his son.
That's why he floats so lightly in the alleys
and gets caught in my heart like little twigs
that drift away.

2
As a child he would mash his potatoes
to a golden mush.
And then you die.

A living child must be cleaned
when he comes home from playing.
But for a dead man
earth and sand are clear water, in which
his body goes on being bathed and purified
forever.

3
The Tomb of the Unknown Soldier
across there. On the enemy's side. A good landmark
for gunners of the future.

Or the war monument in London
at Hyde Park Corner, decorated
like a magnificent cake: yet another soldier
lifting head and rifle,

another cannon, another eagle, another
stone angel.

And the whipped cream of a huge marble flag
poured over it all
with an expert hand.

But the candied, much-too-red cherries
were already gobbled up
by the glutton of hearts. Amen.

4
I came upon an old zoology textbook,
Brehm, Volume II, *Birds*:
in sweet phrases, an account of the life of the starling,
swallow, and thrush. Full of mistakes in an antiquated
Gothic typeface, but full of love, too. "Our feathered
friends." "Migrate from us to the warmer climes."
Nest, speckled egg, soft plumage, nightingale,
stork. "The harbingers of spring." The robin,
red-breasted.

Year of publication: 1913, Germany,
on the eve of the war that was to be
the eve of all my wars.

My good friend who died in my arms, in
his blood,
on the sands of Ashdod. 1948, June.

Oh my friend,
red-breasted.

5
Dicky was hit.
Like the water tower at Yad Mordechai.
Hit. A hole in the belly. Everything
came flooding out.

But he has remained standing like that
in the landscape of my memory
like the water tower at Yad Mordechai.

He fell not far from there,
a little to the north, near Huleikat.

6
Is all of this
sorrow? I don't know.
I stood in the cemetery dressed in
the camouflage clothes of a living man: brown pants
and a shirt yellow as the sun.

Cemeteries are cheap; they don't ask for much.
Even the wastebaskets are small, made for holding
tissue paper
that wrapped flowers from the store.
Cemeteries are a polite and disciplined thing.
"I shall never forget you," in French
on a little ceramic plaque.
I don't know who it is that won't ever forget:
he's more anonymous than the one who died.

Is all of this sorrow? I guess so.
"May ye find consolation in the building
of the homeland." But how long
can you go on building the homeland
and not fall behind in the terrible
three-sided race
between consolation and building and death?

Yes, all of this is sorrow. But leave
a little love burning always
like the small bulb in the room of a sleeping baby
that gives him a bit of security and quiet love
though he doesn't know what the light is
or where it comes from.

7

Memorial Day for the war-dead: go tack on
the grief of all your losses—
including a woman who left you—
to the grief of losing them; go mix
one sorrow with another, like history,
that in its economical way
heaps pain and feast and sacrifice
onto a single day for easy reference.

Oh sweet world, soaked like bread
in sweet milk for the terrible
toothless God. "Behind all this,
some great happiness is hiding." No use
crying inside and screaming outside.
Behind all this, some great happiness may
be hiding.

Memorial day. Bitter salt, dressed up as
a little girl with flowers.
Ropes are strung out the whole length of the route
for a joint parade: the living and the dead together.
Children move with the footsteps of someone else's grief
as if picking their way through broken glass.

The flautist's mouth will stay pursed for many days.
A dead soldier swims among the small heads
with the swimming motions of the dead,
with the ancient error the dead have
about the place of the living water.

A flag loses contact with reality and flies away.
A store window decked out with beautiful dresses for women
in blue and white. And everything
in three languages: Hebrew, Arabic, and Death.

A great royal beast has been dying all night long
under the jasmine,

with a fixed stare at the world.
A man whose son died in the war
walks up the street
like a woman with a dead fetus in her womb.
"Behind all this, some great happiness is hiding."

CHANA BLOCH

Herodion

I travel across the desert
to a famous ancient place to sit there
in the winter sun near the remains of towers
that guarded the king's pleasures.

Like a knife peeling a round fruit, I sense
the motion of time round and round.

The living and the dead meet in my dreams
as the emissaries of two enemy nations
in a third country.
My face is the face of the conquered painted in the colors of the
 conqueror.

I am quiet: what leaves us
does not immediately join the rocks and the desert.
There are middle things, stations,
such as distance, echo, and darkness,
hand and gardens.

LEON WIESELTIER

Akhziv 1973

I've forgotten what is as multitudinous as the sand on the shore
 of the sea.
I don't know what passes like a passing cloud,
what is like the blowing wind.

And I take myself a light chair
and carry it on my back to go and sit on the sand
and the waves bring what never will stay.

The tranquillity that descends from above meets
over my head the wrath ascending from me,
and it makes a whirl
above me, like lovely curls.

The woman's skin is tanned and cured
for pleasures, like the leather
of smooth and lovely wallets.

A few cries of "Horse and its rider He hurled into the sea."
So my divided soul remembers
the splitting of the Red Sea.

ROBERT ALTER

The Synagogue in Florence

Spring's softness in the courtyard,
tree blooming, four girls playing
between lessons in the Holy Tongue
in front of the marble memorial wall:
Levi, Sonnino, Cassuto and others
in straight lines as in a newspaper
or in a Torah scroll.

And the tree stands in memory of nothing,
just the memory of this spring,
arrivederci, our Father,
buona notte, our King.

Tears in the eyes
like dry crumbs in the pocket,
of a cake that once was.

Buona notte, Sonnino,
arrivederci, six million,
the girls and the tree and the crumbs.

ROBERT ALTER

The Synagogue in the Venetian Ghetto

A synagogue that knows of many waters
which will not extinguish this love.

I cover my head with my elbow
that comes out from the shoulder, not far from the heart.
No need for a skullcap. Thank you. This is
a museum, this is the empty grave
of those who rose from it to resurrection
or to a new death;
no need for the lovely glass jewelry from
Murano Island. This colored swelling
is the terrible cancer
of glass and remembering.
Enough for me the window and the gloomy light.

After, to be very quiet
like a buoy at the water entrance,
to shine with gold and love
and unreturning youth.

A head of longing slowly floats and bobs
on the many muddy waters.

ROBERT ALTER

A Prophecy Returns

A photo in a violet frame
for her granddaughter fifty years hence:
"My grandma was very beautiful
at my age, more beautiful than I am, and proud."

A sweet prophecy from then
returns on its circular way from the future
to me: that's how I fell in love with you.

I see you from the side:
a trembling of lashes and eyebrows, like
the trembling of a wing, in the angle
between brow and cheek, the eye nests like a bird.

Your whole body is a sweet clamorous nesting:
from head to toe
many warm nests.

<div align="right">ROBERT ALTER</div>

To a Convert

A son of Abraham is studying to be a Jew.
He wants to be a Jew in no time at all.
Do you know what you're doing?
What's the hurry? After all, a man isn't
a fig tree: everything all at once, leaves and fruit
at the same time. (Even if the fig tree is
a Jewish tree.)

Aren't you afraid of the pain of circumcision?
Don't you worry that they'll cut and cut
till there's nothing left of you
but sweet Jew pain?

I know: you want to be a baby again,
to be carried around on an embroidered cushion, to be handed
from woman to woman, mothers and godmothers
with their heavy breasts and their wombs. You want the scent
of perfume in your nostrils, and wine
for your little smacking lips.

Now you're in the hospital. You're resting, recovering.
Women are waiting under the window for your foreskin.
Whoever catches it—you'll be hers, hers, hers.

CHANA BLOCH

Time

1978

קֹטֶר הַפְּצָצָה הָיָה שְׁלֹשִׁים סֶנְטִימֶטְרִים
וְקֹטֶר תְּחוּם פְּגִיעָתָהּ כְּשִׁבְעָה מֶטְרִים
וּבוֹ אַרְבָּעָה הֲרוּגִים וְאַחַד עָשָׂר פְּצוּעִים.
וּמִסָּבִיב לָאֵלֶּה, בְּמַעְגָּל גָּדוֹל יוֹתֵר
שֶׁל כְּאֵב וּזְמַן, פְּזוּרִים שְׁנֵי בָּתֵּי-חוֹלִים
וּבֵית קְבָרוֹת אֶחָד. אֲבָל הָאִשָּׁה
הַצְּעִירָה, שֶׁנִּקְבְּרָה בַּמָּקוֹם שֶׁמִּמֶּנּוּ
בָּאָה, בְּמֶרְחָק לְמַעְלָה מִמֵּאָה קִילוֹמֶטְרִים,
מַגְדִּילָה אֶת הַמַּעְגָּל מְאֹד מְאֹד,
וְהָאִישׁ הַבּוֹדֵד הַבּוֹכֶה עַל מוֹתָהּ
בְּיַרְכְּתֵי אַחַת מִמְּדִינוֹת הַיָּם הָרְחוֹבוֹת,
מַכְלִיל בַּמַּעְגָּל אֶת כָּל הָעוֹלָם.
וְלֹא אֲדַבֵּר כְּלָל עַל זַעֲקַת יְתוֹמִים
הַמַּגִּיעָה עַד לְכִסֵּא הָאֱלֹהִים
וּמִשָּׁם וָהָלְאָה וְעוֹשָׂה
אֶת הַמַּעְגָּל לְאֵין סוֹף וְאֵין אֱלֹהִים.

(TRANSLATION ON PAGE 245)

1

Songs of continuity, land mines and graves:
that's what turns up when you're making a house or a road.
Then come the black crow people from Meah She'arim
with their bitter screeching: "A body! A dead body!"
Then the young soldiers with their hands
of the night before,
dismantling iron to decipher death.

So come on, let's not build a house, let's not pave a road!
Let's make a house that's folded inside the heart,
a road wound up on a spool in the soul, deep inside,
and we won't die, ever.

People here live inside prophecies that have come true
as inside a heavy cloud that didn't disperse
after an explosion.
And so in their lonely blindness they touch one another
between the legs, between day and night,
because they have no other time and they
have no other place, and the prophets
died a long time ago.

CHANA BLOCH

3

On this evening I think again
about many days
that have sacrificed themselves
for just one night of love.
I think about this waste and this waste's fruit,
about abundance and about fire
and how without pain—time.

I've seen roads leading from one man
to another woman,
I've seen a life blurred
like a letter in the rain.
I've seen a dining table on which
things were left,
and wine on which was written, "The Brothers,"
and how without pain—time.

YEHUDA AMICHAI, WITH TED HUGHES

5

The bodies of two lovers hurt
after rolling all day long in the grass.

Their lying-awake-together at night
brings salvation to the world,
but not to them.

A bonfire burning in the open field
repeats blind with pain
the sun's work during the day.

Childhood is far away.
War is near. Amen.

YEHUDA AMICHAI, WITH TED HUGHES

9

What's this? This is an old
toolshed.
No, this is a great past love.

Anxiety and Joy were here together
in this darkness
and Hope.
Perhaps I've been here once before.
I didn't go near to find out.

These are voices calling out of a dream.
No, this is a great love.
No, this is an old toolshed.

YEHUDA AMICHAI, WITH TED HUGHES

10

No eye has ever seen,
nor any ear heard,
no bird has ever told it:
This child, sleeping, like a compass needle
trembling slightly at night.
But his head doesn't
move, secure in the holy ark
of his father's worry.

No eye has ever seen,
no dream ever dreamt
no mouth ever spoken this child.

In ancient times they used to say:
"Loved, like the apple of his eye." What, what,
like the apple of his eye? This child.
What is the apple of an eye? A ball made
from tears and paint.

Oh, all my words, sad
and happy nails of my life.

YEHUDA AMICHAI, WITH TED HUGHES

Shifra and Batya promised
With their loins eternal youth.

The years of their birth are so fresh.
They fill their thighs with a sweet tension
And my brain with a sound, like a bright chord.

They said: men are strange and crazy:
A sword that comes to kill, they adorn
With ornaments and diamonds

And the penis that brings joy
They don't.

<div style="text-align: right">BENJAMIN AND BARBARA HARSHAV</div>

15

I walked past a house where I lived once:
a man and a woman are still together in the whispers there.
Many years have passed with the quiet hum
of the staircase bulb going on
and off and on again.

The keyholes are like little wounds
where all the blood seeped out. And inside,
people pale as death.

I want to stand once again as I did
holding my first love all night long in the doorway.
When we left at dawn, the house
began to fall apart and since then the city and since then
the whole world.

I want to be filled with longing again
till dark burn marks show on my skin.

I want to be written again
in the Book of Life, to be written every single day
till the writing hand hurts.

CHANA BLOCH

To my love, combing her hair
without a mirror, facing me,

a psalm: you've shampooed your hair, an entire
forest of pine trees is filled with yearning on your head.

Calmness inside and calmness outside
have hammered your face between them to a tranquil copper.

The pillow on your bed is your spare brain,
tucked under your neck for remembering and dreaming.

The earth is trembling beneath us, love.
Let's lie fastened together, a double safety-lock.

<div align="right">CHANA BLOCH</div>

"One sees all kinds of things" said the Swedish
officer observing at the armistice line.
"All kinds of things" and said nothing more.

"One sees a lot of things" said the old
shoeshine man by the Jaffa Gate
when a Swedish girl in a very short dress
stood above him, without looking at him
with her proud eyes.

The prophet who looked into the opening heaven saw,
and so did God, "all kinds of things" down there beyond the smoke,
and the surgeon saw when he cut open a cancerous belly
and closed it again.

"One sees all kinds of things," said
our ancestor Jacob on his bed after the blessing
which took his last strength. "All kinds
of things," and he turned
toward the wall and he died.

YEHUDA AMICHAI, WITH TED HUGHES

19

How did a flag come into being?
Let's assume that in the beginning
there was something whole, which was
then torn into two pieces, both big enough
for two battling armies.

Or like the ragged striped fabric
of a beach chair in an abandoned
little garden of my childhood,
flapping in the wind. This
too could be a flag making you arise
to follow it or to weep at its side,
to betray it or to forget.

I don't know. In my wars
no flag bearer marched in front
of the gray soldiers in clouds of dust and smoke.
I've seen things starting as spring,
ending up with hasty retreat
in pale dunes.
I'm now far away from all that, like one
who in the middle of a bridge
forgets both its ends
and remains standing there
bent over the railing
to look down into the streaming water:
This too is a flag.

YEHUDA AMICHAI, WITH TED HUGHES

20

The diameter of the bomb was thirty centimeters
and the diameter of its effective range about seven meters,
with four dead and eleven wounded.
And around these, in a larger circle
of pain and time, two hospitals are scattered
and one graveyard. But the young woman
who was buried in the city she came from,
at a distance of more than a hundred kilometers,
enlarges the circle considerably,
and the solitary man mourning her death
at the distant shores of a country far across the sea
includes the entire world in the circle.
And I won't even mention the howl of orphans
that reaches up to the throne of God and
beyond, making
a circle with no end and no God.

<div style="text-align: right">CHANA BLOCH</div>

24

When I banged my head on the door, I screamed,
"My head, my head," and I screamed, "Door, door,"
and I didn't scream "Mama" and I didn't scream "God."
And I didn't prophesy a world at the End of Days
where there will be no more heads and doors.

When you stroked my head, I whispered,
"My head, my head" and I whispered, "Your hand, your hand,"
and I didn't whisper "Mama" or "God."
And I didn't have miraculous visions
of hands stroking heads in the heavens
as they split wide open.

Whatever I scream or say or whisper is only
to console myself: My head, my head.
Door, door. Your hand, your hand.

<div align="right">CHANA BLOCH</div>

26

This garden with your confession in it:
"Destroyed by love," you said,
and other things I have forgotten. I recall
the treetops that already had gone dark above
and the words below, that were still in the light.

And there is a window, which he who opens
will not be the one to close.

And there is a number on the house that is incised
and burnt into my heart like the brand on a horse.

"Destroyed by love" and the last voices
have already turned into
food for the birds and the little animals of night.

ROBERT ALTER

The old ice factory in Petah Tikvah:
a wooden tower, boards blackened by rot.
In my childhood a weeping lived there.
I remember the tears
dripping from board to board
to still the summer's rage
and make ice below
which slid out of a deep opening.

And immediately, behind the dark cypresses,
they started to talk! "You live
only once."

I didn't understand then
and now that I understand, it's too late.

The cypresses are just as they were
and the water goes on
dripping somewhere else.

YEHUDA AMICHAI, WITH TED HUGHES

31

I was weaned from the curse of Adam.
The flaming sword is far away
And flickers in the sun like a propeller.
I already love the taste of salty sweat
On my bread with dust and with death.

But the soul that was given me, is still like a tongue
Remembering sweet tastes between the teeth.

And I am already the second Adam, banished
From the Garden of the Great Curse where
I made do after the Garden of Eden.

And under my feet, a small cave grew
In the precise shape of my body.
I am a man of refuge: the third Adam.

<div align="right">BENJAMIN AND BARBARA HARSHAV</div>

The door opened by mistake;
"You shouldn't be here now."

A thin whistle in the dark;
This was a young fig tree.

A slight despair lifted its head for a moment
like a watchdog and didn't even bark.

Rapists as in deep slumber in the forest
dreaming about real love.

"You shouldn't be here."
But here I am now.

Together we sailed to the sources of your madness:
a thundering waterfall. But in the morning
tranquil water.

YEHUDA AMICHAI, WITH TED HUGHES

41

The evening lies along the horizon and donates blood.
Flights of birds move up the sky like black mist.

Love is a reservoir of tenderness and care
like the hoarding of food for times of siege.

A little boy sits upright in his bed.
His kingdom an eternal kingdom.

People put a fence around their house,
so that their hope will not be in vain.

In a white and closed room
a woman decides to grow her hair long again.

The earth is turned up for the seed.
A secret military installation blossoms in the dark.

YEHUDA AMICHAI, WITH TED HUGHES

43

A song, a psalm, on Independence Day.
All of it so far off, but still remembered
like the echo of footsteps whose bodies
turned to dust of the desert long ago.
The sound of trumpets that I hear—
not for me anymore.
Even the warm breath inside the trumpets—
not for me anymore.
And the remembered dust has turned
into forgetting fields.

Builders and destroyers gather
in my house in the evening
to sit all night through on the balcony
watching the fireworks
which are the many-colored sighs of the Jewish people.

Come, let's not talk about the famous six million,
let's talk about just one of them—me:
I am a man like a dead mound.
But in each of my layers
something still moves.

YEHUDA AMICHAI, WITH TED HUGHES

46

You carry the weight of heavy buttocks,
but your eyes are clear.
Around your waist a wide belt that won't protect you.

You're made of the kind of materials that slow down
the process of joy
and its pain.

I've already taught my penis
to say your name
like a trained parakeet.

And you're not even impressed. As if
you didn't hear.
What else should I have done for you?

All I have left now is your name,
completely independent,
like an animal:

it eats out of my hand
and lies down at night
curled up in my dark brain.

CHANA BLOCH

48

There came upon me a terrible longing
like people in an old photograph
who want to be back among the others
who are looking at them
in the good light of a lamp.

Here in this house I think
how love has turned into friendship
in the chemistry of our life.
I think about friendship which calms us for death
and how our lives are like single threads
without any hope of being rewoven
into another cloth.

Out of the desert
come muffled sounds,
dust prophesies dust, an airplane
fastens above our heads
the zipper of a huge bag of fate.

And the memory of a girl I once loved
moves along the valley tonight, like buses—
many lighted windows passing, many her faces.

YEHUDA AMICHAI, WITH TED HUGHES

49

I am a man "planted beside streams of water,"
but I'm not "blessed be the man."
The desert is calm all around me, but there's no peace in me.
Two sons I have, one still small,
and whenever I see a child crying
I want to make another one
as if I hadn't got it right
and wanted to start afresh.
And my father is dead, and God is only one, like me.
And the Hill of Evil Counsel sails into the night
all covered with antennae up to heaven.

I'm a man planted beside streams of water,
but I can only weep it,
and sweat it, and urinate it
and spill it from my wounds—
all this water.

YEHUDA AMICHAI, WITH TED HUGHES

52

Jerusalem the cradle city that rocks me.
When I wake up things happen to me in the middle of the day
As to a man descending the stairs of his lover's house
For the last time and his eyes are still shut.
But my days force me to open my eyes and to remember
The faces of passersby: maybe he will love me,
Maybe he planted a bomb wrapped like a package
Gift-wrapped for a lover. I see
The flaws in the stone buildings, the hole
Through which electricity flows, the slit for water,
The nakedness of the telephone connection and the sighing mouths.

I am a man of Jerusalem. Swimming pools and their voices
Are not part of my spiritual life. Dust is my consciousness,
Stone my subconscious,
And all my memories are closed yards on summer afternoons.

BENJAMIN AND BARBARA HARSHAV

62

Departure from a place where you had no love
includes the pain of all that did not happen
together with the longing for what will happen after you leave.

On my last evening I saw on the floor
of the balcony across the street
a small and exact square of light
bearing witness to great emotions
which have no limits.

And when I went early in the gray morning
to the railway station
many people were passing me
carrying lists of wonderful strange names
which I'll never come to know,
postmen, tax collectors, municipal clerks
and others. Perhaps angels.

YEHUDA AMICHAI, WITH TED HUGHES

63

When a man has been away from his homeland a long time,
his language becomes more and more precise
less and less impure,
like precise clouds of summer
on their blue background
which will never rain.

Thus, all those who were once lovers
still speak the language of love, sterile
and clear, never changing, and never
getting any response.

But I, who have stayed here, dirty my mouth
and my lips and my tongue.
In my words there is garbage of soul
and refuse of lust and dust and sweat.
Even the water I drink in this dry land,
between screams and memories of love,
is urine recycled back to me
through complicated circuits.

YEHUDA AMICHAI, WITH TED HUGHES

67

We walked together, you and I,
like Abraham and his son Isaac.
But although we were a man and a woman,
and although we did not go to the sacrifice,
the knowledge of things still to happen
and the ignorance of what will befall
were close together, like lovers.

After that jaws of suitcases gaped open
and it turned out that what
we thought would be a few days of separation
became forever.

But since then there have remained between us
signs and special marks
like those exchanged by people who don't know each
other
when they plan
to meet in places where they have never been.

YEHUDA AMICHAI, WITH TED HUGHES

You are so small and slight in the rain. A small target
for the raindrops, for the dust in summer,
and for bomb fragments too. Your belly is slack,
not like the tight flat skin of a drum: the flabbiness
of the third generation. Your grandfather, the pioneer,
drained the swamps. Now the swamps have their revenge.
You're filled with a madness that pulls people down,
that seethes in a fury of colors.

What are you going to do now? You'll collect loves
like stamps. You've got doubles and no one
will trade with you. And you've got damaged ones.
Your mother's curse broods at your side like a strange bird.
You resemble that curse.

Your room is empty. And each night your bed
is made up again. That's true damnation
for a bed: to have no one sleeping in it,
not a wrinkle, not a stain, like the cursed
summer sky.

CHANA BLOCH

69

My son, in whose face there is already a sign
of eagle—
like a daring prefix to your life,
let me kiss you once more while you still love it,
softly, like this.
Before you become a hairy Esau of open fields
be for a little while
soft-skinned Jacob for my blind hands.

Your brain is well packed in your skull,
efficiently folded for life. Had it stayed
spread out you might have been happier,
a large sheet of happiness without memory.

I'm on my way from believing in God
and you're on your way toward it: This too
is a meeting point of a father and a son.

It's evening now. The earthball is cooling,
clouds that have never lain with a woman
pass overhead in the sky, the desert
starts breathing into our ears,
and all the generations
squeeze a bar mitzvah for you.

YEHUDA AMICHAI, WITH TED HUGHES

71

"He left two sons," that's
what they say about someone
who died. Sometimes he is still alive.

The echo of a great love is like
the echo of a huge dog's barking
in an empty Jerusalem house
marked for demolition.

YEHUDA AMICHAI, WITH TED HUGHES

72

My former student is in the traffic police.
She stands at a crossroads in the middle of the city:
She opens a little cupboard, like a makeup cabinet
And changes the colors of the traffic light according to her mood.
Her pupils, an assortment of green, red, and yellow,
And her hair is very short, like an insolent boy's.
With her black, high shoes, she leans
On the cabinet. Her skirt is short and tight
And I don't even dare imagine
The awesome splendor at the end of all that golden brown.

I don't understand anymore. I'm lost.
When I pass in the street, legions of young men
And women are hurled at me, every year
In increasing waves, endless reserves.
And my student the policewoman couldn't stop them.
She even joins them!

BENJAMIN AND BARBARA HARSHAV

74

So I find myself always on the run
from blows and from pain,
from sweaty hands and from hard hits.
Most of my life in Jerusalem, a bad place
to evade all these. All my wars took
place in deserts among hard stones and sharp wounding
gravel.
I never had the luck to have a war
in a cool green forest
or in a wavy battle at sea.

And so I am on the run, evasive like
a pathetic dancer amid hurled stones
and falling shells, between strong
hands and outstretched arms,
a very clumsy and heavily loaded
man I am on the run,
my whole body loaded down from head to toe,
on my shoulder a rifle, around my belly
an ammunition belt, on my head
heavy guilt, my feet in shoe-cages,
on my back the heavy yoke of family care,

and even my knees, moving up and down,
activate a terrible time-motor.

Only my penis is still free and happy,
no good for sword fights and no good
for any work, or even for hanging things on,
or for digging trenches.
Praise be to God that it is so. Even onto
God I've loaded praise.

And so, much too heavy. I'm
on the run till the last pain
causes me no more pain.

YEHUDA AMICHAI, WITH TED HUGHES

75

A bird at dawn is singing
with too strong a voice
prophesying a day of dry hot winds.

At noon the shutters are pulled down
against the burning sun.
Then my soul makes love to me
from behind, all along my back
and I'm unable to return
to work because of all this pleasure.

Toward evening, the so-called Present Situation
lifts itself up from the people and
hangs up there, in one piece, like a high canopy,
and the quantity
of all the water in the world is turned
into the quality
of one tear in the eye.

YEHUDA AMICHAI, WITH TED HUGHES

77

My God, the soul you gave me
Is smoke
From the eternal fire of love memories.
We are born and start burning right away,
Until the smoke vanishes like smoke.

BENJAMIN AND BARBARA HARSHAV

78

Here on the ancient beach of Tantura I sit
in the sand with my sons and my sons' sons not yet born.
But they are assembled with me in my crouched squatting.
The happiness of the water equals the happiness of heaven.
And the waves' foam penetrates my mind and becomes clear there.

And my past's future is here and now in my rest.
I see children playing in the sand:
The happy ones always destroy and
the sad ones build again.
But the voices of both are stronger
than the sound of the breaking waves.

There on that hillock beside the railway tracks
an old concrete pillbox still stands.
Thorns cover it. Its iron died long ago,
but its shooting slits have become
real eyes, sometimes seeing
and sometimes weeping thin sand.

There I stood in the summer of 1942
facing the sea, guarding against the enemy
to protect the continuation of my life
to reach until this moment.
New enemies come now from the east,
but the same wind still nestles
in sleepless reddened eyes.

<p align="right">YEHUDA AMICHAI, WITH TED HUGHES</p>

Now the lifeguards have all gone home. The bay
is closed and what's left of the sunlight
is reflected in a piece of broken glass,
as an entire life in the shattered eye of the dying.

A board licked clean is saved from the fate
of becoming furniture.
Half an apple and half a footprint in the sand
are trying to be some whole new thing together,
and a box turning black
resembles a man who's asleep or dead.
Even God stopped here and didn't come closer
to the truth. The mistake that occurs once only
and the single right action
both bring a man peace of mind.
The balance pans have been overturned: now good and evil
are pouring out slowly into a tranquil world.

In the last night, near the rock pool, a few young people
are still warming themselves with the feelings
I once had in this place.
A green stone in the water
seems to be dancing in the ripples with a dead fish,
and a girl's face emerges from diving,
her wet eyelashes
like the rays of a sun resurrected for the night.

CHANA BLOCH

So I went down to the ancient harbor: human actions
bring the sea closer to the shore, but other actions
push it back. How should the sea know
what it is they want,
which pier holds tight like love
and which pier lets go.

In the shallow water lies a Roman column.
But this isn't its final resting place. Even if
they carry it off and put it in a museum
with a little plaque telling what it is, even that won't be
its final resting place: it will go on falling
through floors and strata and other ages.

But now a wind in the tamarisks
fans a last red glow on the faces of those who sit here
like the embers of a dying campfire. After this, night
and whiteness.
The salt eats everything and I eat salt
till it eats me too.
And whatever was given to me is taken away
and given again, and what was thirsty has drunk its fill
and what drank its fill has long since rested in death.

<div style="text-align: right">CHANA BLOCH</div>

A Great Tranquillity:
Questions and Answers
1980

אֶקוֹלוֹגְיָה שֶׁל יְרוּשָׁלַיִם

הָאֲוִיר מֵעַל לִירוּשָׁלַיִם רָווּי תְּפִלּוֹת וַחֲלוֹמוֹת
כְּמוֹ הָאֲוִיר מֵעַל לְעָרֵי תַּעֲשִׂיָּה כְּבֵדָה.
קָשֶׁה לִנְשֹׁם.

וּמִזְּמַן לִזְמַן מַגִּיעַ מִשְׁלוֹחַ חָדָשׁ שֶׁל הִיסְטוֹרְיָה
וְהַבָּתִּים וְהַמִּגְדָּלִים הֵם חָמְרֵי אֲרִיזָתָהּ,
שֶׁאַחַר כָּךְ מֻשְׁלָכִים וְנֶעֱרָמִים בָּעֲרֵמוֹת.

וְלִפְעָמִים בָּאִים נֵרוֹת בִּמְקוֹם בְּנֵי אָדָם,
אָז שֶׁקֶט.
וְלִפְעָמִים בָּאִים בְּנֵי אָדָם בִּמְקוֹם נֵרוֹת,
אָז רַעַשׁ.

וּבְתוֹךְ גַּנִּים סְגוּרִים, בֵּין שִׂיחֵי יַסְמִין
מְלֵאֵי בֹּשֶׂם, קוֹנְסוּלְיוֹת זָרוֹת,
כְּמוֹ כַּלּוֹת רָעוֹת שֶׁנֻּדְּחוּ,
אוֹרְבוֹת לְשַׁעְתָּן.

(TRANSLATION ON PAGE 298)

The Doors Are Closed

The doors are closed that were meant to be
open forever. And those that I can open
guard emptied places
like ancient looted graves.
I think of the love of people
who forgot to take down the holiday decorations:
what do they have left?
Farewell to you, too. The hour when
we got up early in order to part
remains fixed within me, like an alarm clock
that no longer needs to wake one, and just
gives off a dry rattle.

ROBERT ALTER

An Arab Shepherd Is Searching
for His Goat on Mount Zion

An Arab shepherd is searching for his goat on Mount Zion
and on the opposite mountain I am searching
for my little boy.
An Arab shepherd and a Jewish father
both in their temporary failure.
Our voices meet above the Sultan's Pool
in the valley between us. Neither of us wants
the child or the goat to get caught in the wheels
of the terrible *Had Gadya* machine.

Afterward we found them among the bushes
and our voices came back inside us, laughing and crying.

Searching for a goat or a son
has always been the beginning
of a new religion in these mountains.

CHANA BLOCH

Lying in Wait for Happiness

On the broad steps leading down to the Western Wall
A beautiful woman came up to me: You don't remember me,
I'm Shoshana in Hebrew. Something else in other languages.
All is vanity.

Thus she spoke at twilight standing between the destroyed
And the built, between the light and the dark.
Black birds and white birds changed places
With the great rhythm of breathing.
The flash of tourists' cameras lit my memory too:
What are you doing here between the promised and the forgotten,
Between the hoped for and the imagined?
What are you doing here lying in wait for happiness
With your lovely face a tourist advertisement from God
And your soul rent and torn like mine?

She answered me: My soul is rent and torn like yours
But it is beautiful because of that
Like fine lace.

<div align="right">GLENDA ABRAMSON AND TUDOR PARFITT</div>

The Eternal Mystery

The eternal mystery of oars
that strike back while the boat floats forward,
thus actions and words strike back the past
so the body can move on with the man inside.

Once I was sitting in a barber's chair by the street
and in the large mirror I saw people coming toward me
and suddenly they were cut off and swallowed up in the abyss
beyond the large mirror.

And the eternal mystery of the sun setting in the sea:
even a professor of physics says:
Look, the sun is setting in the sea, red and lovely.

Or the mystery of phrases like
"I could be your father,"
"What was I doing a year ago today?"
and other such words.

<div align="right">GLENDA ABRAMSON AND TUDOR PARFITT</div>

Rain in a Foreign Land

Rain in a foreign land and a journey of two
together who have only
the remembrance of a journey in rain.
You, too, are from another summer,
you, too, are the nakedness of the land,
dry grass in the hair,
juice sticking to the hot thigh,
ointment of silence on the brow
and the scent of thirsty earth
in the hollows of the eyes,

a great sorrow's institute,
head on sloping shoulder, where
you too dream, pointlessly dream.

But now rain in a foreign land
and a journey of two
who will have only
the remembrance of a journey in rain.

ROBERT ALTER

Air Hostess

The air hostess said put out all smoking material,
but she didn't specify, cigarette, cigar or pipe.
I said to her in my heart: you have beautiful love material,
and I didn't specify either.

She told me to fasten and tie myself
to the seat and I said:
I want all the buckles in my life to be shaped like your mouth.

She said: Would you like coffee now or later
or never. And she passed me
tall as the sky.

The small scar high on her arm
showed that she would never have smallpox
and her eyes showed that she would never again fall in love:
she belongs to the conservative party
of those who have only one great love in their life.

GLENDA ABRAMSON AND TUDOR PARFITT

I Don't Know If History Returns

I don't know if history returns
but I know that you—don't.

I remember the city that was divided
not only between Jews and Arabs
but also between you and me
when we were in it together.

We made ourselves a womb from dangers
and built ourselves a home from deadly war,
like the people of the distant north
who build a safe, warm home
from deadly ice.

The city again is united,
but we are no longer in it together.

Now I know
that history does not return
just as I've always known that you—don't.

ROBERT ALTER

A Child Is Something Else Again

A child is something else again. Wakes up
in the afternoon and in an instant he's full of words,
in an instant he's humming, in an instant warm,
instant light, instant darkness.

A child is Job. They've already placed their bets on him
but he doesn't know it. He scratches his body
for pleasure. Nothing hurts yet.
They're training him to be a polite Job,
to say "Thank you" when the Lord has given,
to say "You're welcome" when the Lord has taken away.

A child is vengeance.
A child is a missile into the coming generations.
I launched him: I'm still trembling.

A child is something else again: on a rainy spring day
glimpsing the Garden of Eden through the fence,
kissing him in his sleep,
hearing footsteps in the wet pine needles.
A child delivers you from death.
Child, Garden, Rain, Fate.

CHANA BLOCH

People in the Dark Always See

People in the dark always see those
In the light. This is an ancient truth, since the creation
Of sun and night, people and darkness and electric light.
A truth exploited by warriors
For an easy kill in ambush, a truth that allows the wretched
To see the joyful, and the lonely to see lovers
In a room gloriously alight.

But between darkness and light real life goes on:
"I've locked the door," you said,
An important and fateful phrase. The words are still in my memory,
But I've forgotten on which side of the door they were said,
Inside or out,

And from the one letter I wrote you
I only remember the taste
Of the stamp's bitter glue on my tongue.

GLENDA ABRAMSON AND TUDOR PARFITT

The Rustle of History's Wings, as They Said Then

Not far from the railway track beside the painful post office
I saw a ceramic plaque on an old house, and I knew
That this was the name of the son of someone whose girl I took
Years ago: she left him and came to me
And the young man was born to another woman
And didn't know about all this.

Those were days of great love and great destiny.
The colonial power imposed a curfew on the city and confined us
To sweet love in a room
Guarded by well-armed soldiers.

I paid five shillings and changed my ancestral name
From the Diaspora to a proud Hebrew name to match hers.

That whore fled to America, married someone,
A spice broker, pepper, cinnamon and cardamom,
And left me with my new name and the war.

"The rustle of history's wings," as they said then,
Which almost killed me in battle,
Blew softly over her face.

And with the terrible wisdom of war they told me to carry
My first-aid bandage right over my heart
Over the foolish heart that still loved her
And over the wise heart that would forget.

GLENDA ABRAMSON AND TUDOR PARFITT

A Café in the Old City

I've already lived many years in my city
and the voices looking for me are dwindling,
as in, Come to me, Don't talk like that, Sit down and rest.
And the voices increase in which I'm only included, anonymous:
bells, sirens, and radio announcements.
So I can slip away unnoticed
and sit in a café of glittering games of chance
among excited young people, Jews and Arabs together,
street kids with pale yeshiva students,
and the ringing of their games and the clicking of their chance
are also God's wills and His games.

And Byzantine columns in green oil-based paint
stand there, holding up the arched ceiling.
I have no such obligation.
I have no such known style,
so I get up and go.

ROBERT ALTER

A Tourist

On a great rock by the Jaffa Gate
sat a golden girl from Scandinavia
and oiled herself with suntan oil
as if on the beach.

I told her, don't go into these alleys,
a net of bachelors in heat is spread there,
a snare of lechers. And further inside,
in half-darkness, the groaning trousers
of old men, and unholy lust in the guise of prayer
and grief and seductive chatter in many languages.

Once Hebrew was God's slang
in these streets,
now I use it for
holy desire.

GLENDA ABRAMSON AND TUDOR PARFITT

Join Me on My Last Way

Join me on my last way.
My last way might go on another twenty years
or thirty, for you your first way.

You are young and I am very much older than you,
you're a fresh person and I'm a man from the freezer.

How hard they tried to keep us apart: your father came
at noonday and my mother showed up in a dream at night.
Even the winds sought to tear us asunder,
and the olive trees, the trees of peace,
whipped our days with hard branches.

We traded places, slept outside, without walls,
so that they couldn't write for us
the writing on the wall.

You said: Our pride is that sometimes
we can do what we really want.

I said: We are a new interpretation of the biblical phrase,
"to do what is right," what is most right and shortest.
So join me.

ROBERT ALTER

Return from Ein Gedi

From the green and hidden lushness of Ein Gedi
We returned to the hard city. I called you Rejah
After the Arab name of the wadi
And after the Hebrew word for yearning.
We came back to our empty room already let to others.
On the floor a torn mattress and orange peels
And a sock, a newspaper and other knives for the heart.

What did we learn at Ein Gedi? To make love in the water,
What else? That the mountains are more beautiful as they crumble.

Once more we looked out of the arched window.
Together we saw the same valley, but each of us
Saw a different future, like two fortune-tellers
Who disagree with each other in a serious and silent encounter.

A day after we left, thousands of years had already passed
The piece of paper on which was written "Same place
Tomorrow at seven" had yellowed and crumpled straight away
·Like the face of a child born old.

GLENDA ABRAMSON AND TUDOR PARFITT

A Woman Like That

A woman like that, lovely as the dream-plan
of a modern architect, and elegant, like a clipping
from a fashion magazine for angels.

But a woman forgets and a woman loses things!
And all the things she forgets and loses
are the handwriting of her life
that I still have to learn to read:
and when I finally am able to read it
and raise my head,
she's already far away.

<div align="right">ROBERT ALTER</div>

I Dreamed a Dream

I dreamed a dream: in my dream seven maidens
fat and sleek came up to the meadow
and I made love to them in the meadow.
And seven skinny wind-scorched maidens came up after them
and swallowed up the fat ones with their hungry thighs,
but their stomachs remained flat.
I made love to them too and they swallowed me too.

But she who solved the dream for me,
the one I really loved,
was both fat and thin,
both swallower and swallowed.

And the day after her, I knew
that I would never return to that place.

And the spring after her, they changed the flowers in the field
and the telephone books with all their names.

And in the years after her, war broke out
and I knew I would dream no more.

GLENDA ABRAMSON AND TUDOR PARFITT

Ballad on the Changing Room

They were so lovely, a man and a woman,
that you could paint her head and his
on the door marked "women" and the door marked "men"
in the changing room by the sea.

And the light gave birth to them day after day in pain,
and they were always moist and shining without pain,
and oxygen and nitrogen joined drunken in their breathing,
and they were like a show window for the world's creation.

And she pulled him and he pulled her,
and the earth pulled them both by the law of the earth,
and so they were together in a triple pull,
and if they part, all the laws will break.

And he said to her: man's soul is woman,
and she said to him: woman's soul is always man.
And so we will never be able to part.

And they who were so lovely together on the shore
came in the end to the shore and on the shore to the end,
she went in through the door marked "women" and was never seen
 again,
he went in through the door marked "men" and was never seen
 again.

And now only sand and lilies and a low tamarisk tree
and the scent of seaweed and snails and orange peel
and two closed doors that will never open again,
and on one the image of her head and on the other the image of his.

ROBERT ALTER

289

Jerusalem Is Full of Used Jews

Jerusalem is full of Jews used by history
Secondhand Jews, with small flaws, bargains.
The eye turns always to Zion. And all the eyes
Of the living and the dead are broken like eggs
On the edge of the bowl to make the city
Rich and fat and rise like dough.

Jerusalem is full of tired Jews
Always whipped into memorial days and feasts
Like bears dancing on aching legs.

What does Jerusalem need? It doesn't need a mayor,
It needs a ringmaster with a whip in his hand
To tame prophecies and to train prophets to gallop
Round and round in a circle, and to teach its stones to arrange
 themselves
In a daring and dangerous formation in the final act.

Afterwards they spring to the ground
To the sound of cheers and wars.

And the eye turns to Zion and weeps.

GLENDA ABRAMSON AND TUDOR PARFITT

For Ever and Ever, Sweet Distortions

Pictures of dead Jews on the wall of a room in Petah Tikva,
Like stars that died eons ago
Whose light has only just reached us.

What's Jewish time? God's experimental places
Where he tests new ideas and new weaponry,
Training ground for his angels and demons.
A red flag warns: Firing range!

What's the Jewish people? The quota that can be killed in training,
That's the Jewish people,
Which has not yet grown up, like a child that still uses the
Baby talk of its first years,
And still can't say
God's real name but says *Elokim, Hashem, Adonai,*
Dada, Gaga, Yaya, for ever and ever, sweet distortions.

GLENDA ABRAMSON AND TUDOR PARFITT

Song of Love and Pain

While we were together
We were like a useful pair of scissors.

After we parted we again
Became two sharp knives
Stuck in the world's flesh
Each one in its own place.

GLENDA ABRAMSON AND TUDOR PARFITT

A Young Girl Goes Out in the Morning, Like a Knight

A young girl goes out in the morning
Pony-tailed and swaying as if on horseback.

Dresses and handbags, sunglasses, chain and buckles.
Are like armor on her.
But beneath all this
She's light and slender.

Sometimes at night she's naked and alone.
And sometimes she's naked and not alone.

You can hear the sound of bare feet
Running away: that was death.

And afterwards the sound of a kiss
Like the fluttering of a moth
Caught between two panes of glass.

GLENDA ABRAMSON AND TUDOR PARFITT

Eyes

My eldest son's eyes are like black figs
For he was born at the end of summer.

And my youngest son's eyes are clear
Like orange slices, for he was born in their season.

And the eyes of my little daughter are round
Like the first grapes.

And all are sweet in my worry.

And the eyes of the Lord roam the earth
And my eyes are always looking round my house.

God's in the eye business and the fruit business
I'm in the worry business.

GLENDA ABRAMSON AND TUDOR PARFITT

A Gymnastics Teacher from Petah Tikva

A gym teacher once lived in this deserted house.
Her skin was brown and soft as silk.
She reared a whole generation of hard stomach and leg muscles
for wars in the desert and for love among the orchards.

She herself left the country to live
in Vienna, the city of whipped cream. She left and got fat there.

On this spring evening I stand beside the house.
My knowledge of its imminent destruction
and the house's knowledge
that I will never come there again
together make a perfume stronger
than all the smells of war, and sweeter than the fragrance of
 orchards.

GLENDA ABRAMSON AND TUDOR PARFITT

Peace of Mind, Peace and Mind

"Peace of mind," my parents used to say,
"A person needs to have peace of mind."
Like rich Arabs who spend winters in Jericho
and summers in Ramallah and forget the desert in between,
they too are forgetters of the in-between. Or when you carry
a sleeping child from the place he fell asleep to his bed
without waking him. Or like a man who places a bomb
and goes so far away he can't even hear the echo of his act.

A woman once said to me: I am living in peace
outside history. And I said to her: That's just what Rahab said,
"I'm living on the wall," and look how
she entered history and hasn't come out.

Peace of mind, peace and mind. I want
just once to be inside the room
I see every evening from where I work.
The shade is always drawn and sometimes there's light within.

I've lived long enough to want
just that, and not the kingdom of heaven.

ROBERT ALTER

In the Morning It Was Still Night

In the morning it was still night and lights were burning
When we rose from happiness like those who rise from the dead
And like them we immediately remembered our former lives:
That's why we parted.

You wore a striped shirt of old silk
And a tight skirt, an old-fashioned hostess of partings
And our voices were like loudspeakers
Announcing times and places.

Out of a leather bag, with soft folds like an old woman's cheeks,
You took out lipstick, passport, a letter, sharp as a knife,
You put them on the table
And you put them back.

I said: I'll move back a little like at an
Art exhibition to get a better view
And I haven't stopped moving back a little since.

Time will be light as froth,
The heavy sediment will stay in us.

GLENDA ABRAMSON AND TUDOR PARFITT

Ecology of Jerusalem

The air over Jerusalem is saturated with prayers and dreams
like the air over industrial cities.
It's hard to breathe.

And from time to time a new shipment of history arrives
and the houses and towers are its packing materials.
Later these are discarded and piled up in dumps.

And sometimes candles arrive instead of people,
and then it's quiet.
And sometimes people come instead of candles,
and then there's noise.

And in enclosed gardens heavy with jasmine
foreign consulates,
like wicked brides that have been rejected,
lie in wait for their moment.

CHANA BLOCH

Tourists

1

So condolence visits is what they're here for,
sitting around at the Holocaust Memorial, putting on a serious face
at the Wailing Wall,
laughing behind heavy curtains in hotel rooms.

They get themselves photographed with the important dead
at Rachel's Tomb and Herzl's Tomb, and up on Ammunition Hill.
They weep at the beautiful prowess of our boys,
lust after our tough girls
and hang up their underwear
to dry quickly
in cool blue bathrooms.

2

Once I was sitting on the steps near the gate at David's Citadel and put down my two heavy baskets beside me. A group of tourists stood there around their guide, and I became their point of reference. "You see that man over there with the baskets? A little to the right of his head there's an arch from the Roman period. A little to the right of his head." "But he's moving, he's moving!" I said to myself: Redemption will come only when they are told, "Do you see that arch over there from the Roman period? It doesn't matter, but near it, a little to the left and then down a bit, there's a man who has just bought fruit and vegetables for his family."

<div align="right">CHANA BLOCH</div>

We Traveled to a Sleep Far from Us

We traveled to a sleep far from us,
so that you might know, so that I might know, so that we might
 know.
We traveled at evening, O beloved land.
A school outing wants to reach its resting-place,
welcoming houses are closed all along the way,
fires in the fields were the beginning of a new religion.
By our side sat the prudent man who keeps silent.
Tears rolled down the cheeks
as when a telephone rings in an empty house.

We were close to each other like two
similar languages, Hebrew and Arabic,
English and German.

It was good for us together. But your heart studied
in a different school from your head.

Our meeting was an illusion of red bliss
like the meeting of sun and sea at evening.

ROBERT ALTER

Love of the Land

And the land is divided into regions of memory and districts
 of hope,
and its people are all mixed together,
like those returning from a wedding and from a funeral.

And the land is not divided into war zones and peace zones.
And he who digs a foxhole against shelling
will return to lie in it with his girl,
if he survives for peace.

And the land is lovely.
Even enemies all around adorn it
with weapons shining in the sun
like a necklace round the throat.

And the land is a package:
it is neatly tied up and everything's in it, and it's tied up tightly
and the cords sometimes hurt.

And the land is very small,
and I can hold it within me.
The ground's erosion erodes my rest, too,

and the water level of the Kinneret is always on my mind.
Thus I can feel the whole land
when I close my eyes: sea-valley-mountain.
Thus I can remember what happened there
all at once, as a man remembers his whole life
at the moment of his death.

ROBERT ALTER

Straight from Your Prejudice

Straight from your prejudice you came to me
You hardly managed to get dressed.

I want to Judaize you with my circumcised body
I want to bind you in phylacteries from top to bottom.

I want to dress you in gold and velvet,
Like the Torah scroll, and to hang a Star of David around your neck.

And to kiss your thighs.
Like a mezuzah at the door.

I'll teach you the old custom
Of washing feet with love:

Oh, wash my memories for me,
For I've walked in them so much that I'm tired.

And my eyes are tired of the square letters of my language
I want letters that flow like your body.

I don't want to feel like a prophet of wrath
Or like a prophet of consolation.

I almost
Succeeded.

But when you cried, tears shone in your eyes
Like snow and Christmas trimmings.

GLENDA ABRAMSON AND TUDOR PARFITT

Infinite Poem

Within the brand-new museum
an old synagogue.
Within the old synagogue
me.
Within me
my heart.
Within my heart
a museum,
within the museum
a synagogue,
within it
me,
within me
my heart,
within my heart
a museum.

ROBERT ALTER

End of Summer in the Mountains of Judea

End of summer in the mountains of Judea. The land lies
As last year's rains left it. The firing range on the slope
Is now silent, riddled targets have stayed there
Like people. An old man cries out with gaping mouth
About the loss of land and flesh, and his small grandson puts
A round head on his knees without understanding what it's
 all about.

Further on pretty girls sit on a rock
Like severe lawyers
To protect the summer and administer its legacy.

Further on in a dark cave stands a fig tree,
The big brothel where ripe figs
Couple with hornets
And are split to death.

Laughter not burnt, weeping not dried,
And a great silence in everything.

But a great love sometimes starts here,
With the sound of dry branches breaking in the dead forest.

GLENDA ABRAMSON AND TUDOR PARFITT

A Great Tranquillity:
Questions and Answers

The people in the painfully bright auditorium
spoke about religion
in the life of contemporary man
and about God's place in it.

People spoke in excited voices
as they do at airports.
I walked away from them:
I opened an iron door marked "Emergency"
and entered into
a great tranquillity: Questions and Answers.

CHANA BLOCH

The Hour of Grace

1983

אֵלֶּה הָיוּ יְמֵי חֶסֶד

"אֵלֶּה הָיוּ יְמֵי חֶסֶד", שָׁמַעְתִּי פַּעַם אוֹמְרִים
בִּימֵי יְדִידוּת וָצַעַר בִּרְחוֹב שֶׁל חֹרֶף.
גַּם לִימֵי חֶסֶד צְרִיכִים לְפָחוֹת שְׁנַיִם,
נוֹתֵן הַחֶסֶד וְהַמְקַבֵּל אוֹתוֹ.
כְּשֶׁהֵם נִפְרָדִים גַּם הַחֶסֶד לֹא נִשְׁאָר
אוֹ נִשְׁפָּךְ לָרְחוֹב כְּמוֹ מִשְׁבָּר צִנּוֹר.

דָּתוֹת לֹא עוֹשׂוֹת חֶסֶד, הֵן רַק מַזְכִּירוֹת
זְמַן רֵיק, בְּפַעֲמוֹן, בִּקְרִיאַת מוּאַזִּין,
בְּצוֹפָר וּבְשׁוֹפָר וּבִנְקִישׁוֹת בַּדֶּלֶת
בִּימֵי סְלִיחוֹת: אֶת הָאֱלֹהִים אֵינָן
יְכוֹלוֹת לְהַזְכִּיר וְלֹא אֶת חַסְדּוֹ.

מִיּוֹם שֶׁבָּטְלוּ הַקָּרְבָּנוֹת
נִשְׁאָר כָּל אֶחָד עִם עַצְמוֹ
לְהַקְרִיב.

(TRANSLATION ON PAGE 318)

On Some Other Planet You May Be Right

"On some other planet you may be right,
but not here." In the middle of talking you shifted
to a silent weeping, as people shift from blue to black
in the middle of a letter when a pen goes dry,
or as they used to change horses during a journey.
Talk grew tired, tears
are fresh.

Seeds of summer flew into the room
we were sitting in. In front of the window
there was an almond tree growing black:
one more warrior in the eternal battle
of the sweet against the bitter.

Look, just as time isn't inside clocks
love isn't inside bodies:
bodies only tell the love.

But we will remember this evening
the way swimmers remember the strokes
from one summer to the next. "On some other planet
you may be right, but not here."

CHANA BLOCH

The Scent of the Orange Groves

The scent of the orange groves lingers here
among the houses that have replaced the groves.
Like an amputee who feels his amputated leg,
the pain lingers and the sweet tingling lingers
in the empty places.
And the scent of the orange groves and the spirit of the people
were a single whole,
and words and sprinklers were a single utterance
and night and day were a day-and-night of truth
and the roof of every house a true cover
against the burning summer and the winter rain,
and the souls still walked about in the streets,
and the sky was a couple, man and woman,
who would never part.

Now everything is changed.
The words "forever" and "for all time"
fade away from the mouths of lovers,
and you can hear them in the words of
heads of state and generals.
But beyond the latest conclusions
there is still another land,
fields without remembering, landscape without man.

Oh, genetics of hopes,
merciful Father, mother of all that lives:
the words linger,
to be continued in other days.

<div align="right">ROBERT ALTER</div>

Patisserie Josef

Patisserie Josef in the Old City,
on your walls are painted many waters and dream fish
and Jerusalem and Venice, both
in the colors of an ardent young whore,
and on the fourth wall a snow-covered mountain in the Alps
to cool my eyes burning in the heat of the day.

Sometimes I sit there.
I search through my life for new beginnings
and find only changes. Behind the hope
is always a new hope. That is true despair,
and these walls close me in with the colors of the end of days.

Patisserie Josef, soft-thighed girls
sit in you on hard chairs
and a German couple atones in quiet talk
for a sin from another place.

Keys clinking in my pocket ring
for private prayer. The coins are quiet in my hand.
If life is war,
why do I need life?
Coffee, tea, and hot orchids.
No charge for the tears. Self-service.

<div align="right">ROBERT ALTER</div>

Everyone Needs an Abandoned Garden in His Life

Everyone needs an abandoned garden in his life
or an old house with peeling walls,
everyone needs another forgotten world.

People look with great longing
at a landscape and name it with body parts:
back of the mountain, foot of the mountain, shoulder of the
 mountain.
Men of war, too, designate targets for heavy fire
with gentle words:
the nipple, the hollow, the crotch, the meeting-point.

For everyone needs an abandoned garden in his life
(Adam and Eve knew everyone needs such a garden)
or an old house,
or at least one locked door
that will never open again.

ROBERT ALTER

The Real Hero

The real hero of the Binding of Isaac was the ram,
who didn't know about the collusion between the others.
He was volunteered to die instead of Isaac.
I want to sing a memorial song about him—
about his curly wool and his human eyes,
about the horns that were so silent on his living head,
and how they made those horns into shofars when he was
 slaughtered
to sound their battle cries
or to blare out their obscene joy.

I want to remember the last frame
like a photo in an elegant fashion magazine:
the young man tanned and pampered in his jazzy suit
and beside him the angel, dressed for a formal reception
in a long silk gown,
both of them looking with empty eyes
at two empty places,

and behind them, like a colored backdrop, the ram,
caught in the thicket before the slaughter,
the thicket his last friend.

The angel went home.
Isaac went home.
Abraham and God had gone long before.

But the real hero of the Binding of Isaac
is the ram.

CHANA BLOCH

The Same Embroidery, the Same Pattern

I saw a man wearing a skullcap embroidered
With the pattern of the underwear
Of a woman I loved
A long time ago.

He didn't understand why I looked at him
And why I turned back after he passed,
He shrugged his shoulders and went away.

And I mumbled to myself: the same
Colors, the same embroidery, the same pattern.
The same embroidery, the same pattern.

BENJAMIN AND BARBARA HARSHAV

In the Hotel

The evening wasn't finished. In front of the big windows
lanterns were lit to mark the border
between day and night. In the hotel lobby
dwarf lemon trees in planters.
(In my land they are big and bear fruit.)

The elevator took you from me,
the divine chamber that held you
ascended illuminated
and in its place the guts of the elevator came down,
heavy weights and chains
dripping black oil and sticky pitch
to me.

ROBERT ALTER

Herbal Tea

She poured him herbal tea to calm
him. She told him: "The things you want
are lusts tamed over thousands of years,
you know, like wolves and dogs.
Tonight you'll be like thousands of years ago."

She led him by his hoarse cock
to a white bedroom to find favor
in the eyes of God and the eyes of man.

"You'll be amazed what can be
wings, you'll be amazed; even
heavy thighs, even memories."

She took off her long dress,
the outer soul of her body.
The inner one she left on.

ROBERT ALTER

Everyone Sometimes Needs a Mirror

I once bought a mirror at a time when my world lay in ruins,
now it's broken when my world has again been made whole.
And its shards have been tossed into the garbage.

This spring the first grass sprouts on the slope of the mountain
cut through to make a road.
So words come at once with destruction.
The last who asks, "What was here
under the grass?" will fall silent.

And that which was is that which will be.
Prophecy, too, is archaeology.
At the end of words and time
stands a shard of glass.

ROBERT ALTER

Those Were Days of Grace

"Those were days of grace," once I heard someone say
in days of loneliness and sorrow on a wintry street.
For days of grace one also needs at least two,
the one who grants grace and the one who receives.
When they part, the grace, too, does not remain
or spills into the street as from a broken pipe.

Religions don't offer grace, they only recall
empty time, with bells, with the muezzin's cry,
with siren and shofar and knocking on the door
in the days of penitential prayers; God they cannot
recall, nor His grace.

From the day sacrifice came to an end
everyone is left with himself
to sacrifice.

ROBERT ALTER

Try to Remember Some Details

Try to remember some details. Remember the clothing
of the one you love
so that on the day of disaster you'll be able to say: last seen
wearing such-and-such, brown jacket, white hat.
Try to remember some details. For they have no face
and their soul is hidden and their crying
is the same as their laughter,
and their silence and their shouting rise to one height
and their body temperature is between 98 and 104 degrees
and they have no life outside this narrow space
and they have no graven image, no likeness, no memory
and they have paper cups on the day of their rejoicing
and disposable paper plates.

Try to remember some details. For the world
is filled with people who were torn from their sleep
with no one to mend the tear,
and unlike wild beasts they live
each in his lonely hiding place and they die
together on battlefields
and in hospitals.
And the earth will swallow all of them,
good and evil together, like the followers of Korah,
all of them in their rebellion against death,
their mouths open till the last moment,
and blessing and cursing are a single
howl. Try, try
to remember some details.

CHANA BLOCH

God, My Insulation Is Gone

for Luba

God, my insulation is gone,
the padding is torn, the stuffing is worn,
cold and heat go right through me,
the raw pain is laid bare,
I hear hollow.

I've wasted my last
yes and no.
I have no ammunition,
I will have to surrender.

Don't tell me about psychology!
Tell me about geology.

Strata break up inside me,
ceilings collapse into my love.

Give me fossils—not memories!
God, my insulation is gone,
my death is exposed.

ROBERT ALTER

Four Poems on War and Peace

1
In a little park, not far from my house,
there's a marble plaque and on it the names of dead soldiers
written one beneath the next in neat order
and in clear letters, like the names of tenants at the entrance
of a large and empty building.

2
I think of the red-headed man
who died here, and his hoarse wife.

I think of the hoarse wife
of the man who died here years ago.

And I think of the hoarse wife
who is now a silent wife.

The real abortion is
of those who fall in battle:
against it
no one protests.

3
Once a bomb exploded
by the butcher shop:
the slaughtered meat
was slaughtered again and again,
but there's no pain anymore
and almost no blood.

4
I am a peace racist:
the blue-eyed are murderers,

the black-eyed are killers,
the curly-haired are destroyers,
the straight-haired are bombers,
the brown-skinned tear my flesh,
the pink-skinned shed my blood.

Only the colorless ones,
only the transparent ones are good,
who allow me to sleep at night without terror
and through them to see
the sky.

ROBERT ALTER

A Man in His Life

A man doesn't have time in his life
to have time for everything.
He doesn't have seasons enough to have
a season for every purpose. Ecclesiastes
was wrong about that.

A man needs to love and to hate at the same moment,
to laugh and cry with the same eyes,
with the same hands to throw stones and to gather them,
to make love in war and war in love.

And to hate and forgive and remember and forget,
to arrange and confuse, to eat and to digest
what history
takes years and years to do.

A man doesn't have time.
When he loses he seeks, when he finds
he forgets, when he forgets he loves, when he loves
he begins to forget.

And his soul is seasoned, his soul
is very professional.
Only his body remains forever
an amateur. It tries and it misses,
gets muddled, doesn't learn a thing,
drunk and blind in its pleasures
and in its pains.

He will die as figs die in autumn,
shriveled and full of himself and sweet,
the leaves growing dry on the ground,
the bare branches already pointing to the place
where there's time for everything.

CHANA BLOCH

And the Child Is No More

My son, again you worry me.
From time to time you worry me,
so regularly it should calm me.

I remember once, when you were little,
we saw a fire together in a big hotel.
The flames and the water and the smoke,
the wailing and the shouting and the madly flashing lights,
all these saved me from lots of talk
on what life is. And we stood in silence.

I ask myself where my father hid his fear,
perhaps in a closed closet
or some other place beyond the reach of children,
perhaps deep in his heart.

But now again you worry me.
I'm always looking for you,
this time among the mists of the Upper Galilee.
I am a mist father.
And the child is no more, for he is already grown.

ROBERT ALTER

An Attack of Longing

Anywhere in the world an attack of longing
seizes you like a sudden fever.
O, girl in the passing train car and woman
on the lit and desolate platform.

I think an anonymous woman like her
is like the unknown soldier: both get
more flowers and more longing than those who are known.
And the gates of heaven open and close
very quickly all the time
like nervous eyelids.

Once I saw a lovely woman
in a consulate building come out on the balcony.
She took down the flag from the gilded staff,
she folded the flag
and went inside and closed the door.
She no doubt stripped naked and covered herself
with the foreign flag and lay down happily.
I am on the street below, my toenails broken
from so much longing
as once the heart was broken.

O, woman of the balcony, woman of the bridges,
O, girl of the telephone booth
whose eyes are eyes of rain
or eyes of tears.

ROBERT ALTER

A Man Marked for Death

And a man marked for death in his garden inside the double walls
put his hand on my shoulder and blessed me
with the blessing of those who are marked.
Behind him in the grass the toys of his terribly faraway grandson.
The light was on them, the flowers in the shade.
"Don't forget me." Life passes.
Once I heard soldiers singing in an open truck
crossing over the hills. I didn't see them
but I heard their singing. That's how
life passes. A man needs a waiter's power of memory.
"Don't forget to remember!"

He led me to the entrance of the garden
and took leave of me and went back into the marked house.
The heavy door decorated with ancient carving
slowly closed behind me with the hum of some subtle device,
and turned me into a man from outer space.

ROBERT ALTER

My Wild Children

My wild children: in the morning
they eat my dreams, at evening
they wolf down my memories.
I am their manger.
I feel their rough tongues
on my soul.
I hear their sweet and empty slurping
day and night.

My wild children, my barracudas
sopping up my madness, muting my scream.
I dig into them.

I want to light my eyes
from their eyes,
as on a dark nocturnal street
a man asks for a light
for his last cigarette.

ROBERT ALTER

The Inn of the Sun

The Inn of the Sun in the mountains. We were there
a day or two. People talked by big windows
toward the dark,
high grass wanted us to cry
and in the misty valley tennis players played silently,
as though without a ball.
And the sad-eyed came to the clear-voiced ones
and said: You are living in my house that was
my house. Here a big tree grew. What did you do with it?

The Inn of the Sun. We were there
two or three days.
And in the white rooms—a memory and hope,
night and eternal salvation
for those who will no longer return
and a golden giggle behind the walls.
Planes passed over on high
and above them a camouflage net made of stars
so that we wouldn't see there is no God.

But below, at a heavy table
in smoke and alcohol fumes,
a heavy Christian and a light Jew
work together on a new religion.

The Inn of the Sun. "Light rain has fallen."
That's all that remains of the Inn of the Sun.

<div align="right">ROBERT ALTER</div>

Miracles

From a distance everything looks like a miracle
but up close even a miracle doesn't look like that.
Even someone who crossed the Red Sea when it split
saw only the sweating back
of the man in front of him
and the swaying of his big thighs,
or at best, in a hasty glance to one side,
fish in a riot of colors inside the wall of water,
as in a marine observatory behind panels of glass.

The real miracles happen at the next table
of a restaurant in Albuquerque:
two women sat there, one with a diagonal
zipper, altogether lovely,
and the other said, "I kept it together
and didn't cry."
And after in the red corridors
of the foreign hotel I saw
boys and girls who held in their arms

tiny children born of them,
and they held
sweet little dolls.

ROBERT ALTER

What a Complicated Mess

What a complicated mess in this little country,
what confusion! "The second son of the first husband
is off to fight his third war. The Second Temple
of God the First is destroyed again every year."
My doctor treats the intestines
of the shoemaker who mends the shoes of the man
who defended me in my fourth trial.
In my comb there's hair that's not mine,
and in my handkerchief, someone else's sweat.
Other people's memories cling to me
like dogs, drawn by the smell,
and I have to drive them away
with scolding and a stick.

And each one's infected by the others, and each one
keeps touching the others, leaving
his fingerprints. The Angel of Death
must be an expert detective
to tell them apart.

Once I knew a soldier who was killed in the war.
Three or four women mourned him:
He loved me. I loved him.
I was his. He was mine.

Soltam makes cannons together with cooking pots
and I don't make anything.

CHANA BLOCH

Eye Virgin

There was old pain in the garden planted
just three years ago. On the stone dais musicians
sat and played. I knew the man playing the trumpet
as I knew the old pain,
but the woman with the transparent dog
in the transparent dress I did not know.

And she had large thighs for painters
and long hair for poets
and a forehead for dreamers of bold dreams
and breasts for exhausted heroes.
But her eyes were kept only for her:
she was still an eye virgin.

ROBERT ALTER

A Precise Woman

A precise woman with a short haircut brings order
to my thoughts and my dresser drawers,
moves feelings around like furniture
into a new arrangement.
A woman whose body is cinched at the waist and firmly divided
into upper and lower,
with weather-forecast eyes
of shatterproof glass.
Even her cries of passion follow a certain order,
one after the other:
tame dove, then wild dove,
then peacock, wounded peacock, peacock, peacock,
then wild dove, tame dove, dove dove
thrush, thrush, thrush.

A precise woman: on the bedroom carpet
her shoes always point away from the bed.
(My own shoes point toward it.)

CHANA BLOCH

At the Maritime Museum

I saw clay jars covered with barnacles
that were saved from the ocean bottom,
and thought about the sailors of ancient times
who gave half their lives to sail to those jars,
and the other half to bring them back here.
They did what they had to do, and drowned near the shore.

A woman beside me said, "Aren't they
beautiful!" and was startled by her words and by me.
Then she walked away into her life,
which is also half a setting out
and half a returning.

CHANA BLOCH

Hamadiya

Hamadiya, memory of pleasures. The forties
and love on the threshing floor. The chaff
pricks me even now, though my body
has been washed many times since then and my clothes
have been changed again and again and the girl left for
the fifties and vanished inside the sixties and was lost forever
in the seventies—the chaff pricks me even now,
my throat is hoarse from so much shouting:
Come back one more time you
come back to me come back time come back loquat tree!

Love used to be the raw material of this poor country,
real life and dream, joined to make the climate,
here joy and sorrow were still
weather conditions.
Dangers pounded all around like water-pumps
hidden in orchards, and the voice
that began as a cry for help
became a calming song.

We didn't know then that the debris of joy
is like the debris of any wreckage:
you have to clear it away to start over again.

<div style="text-align: right;">CHANA BLOCH</div>

I See the Faces of Many Others

Children ask me: What are you dreaming?
As my father asked when I was a child, What
are you dreaming? That's what I've come to now.
My hair turning white is a new beginning
or a flag of slow surrender. Talk of
what happened in the past passes like a cloud
and my mother's birth-pangs when she gave birth to me
have passed into me, every day a bit of pain.
And what was on earth is in the heavens and what was
in the heavens is on earth. And what was transparent
has turned opaque and what was opaque is transparent now:
when I look out the window
I see only myself outside,
and when I look in the mirror
I see the faces of many others.

ROBERT ALTER

Almost Rain

To clean the gutters of summer's leavings,
put pitch on the roof, replace a broken tile,
and salute the old worker
with a negligent army salute,
to crack the last vows of summer
like sunflower and watermelon seeds,
to see the sign on which is written
"Data Processing Company"
and laugh out loud,
to hear passing steps
and not to see a face,

and like a judge, to distinguish
between emotion and law, with great effort,
and with sweat of the brow, as in any hard work.
And at night to see the stars,
which are stones that sought to pelt me and stopped
and in their beauty froze on high
till the day of my death.

And then to breathe over and over,
the hills' breathing exercises and mine,
almost rain.

ROBERT ALTER

The Box

Once my salary wasn't transferred from the place where I work to my bank account. I went to the bank and entered the large hall that looks like a gleaming space station. I approached the pretty clerk and she scrolled the letters and the numerals on the computer screen in front of her. And she said, That's right, the money wasn't transferred. So I said, Look, I know that, that's why I came. So she sent me to the floor below her to a large quiet hall more gleaming than the one before. And a clerk more lovely than the one before scrolled the letters and the numerals on a screen that was larger than the one before, and she said to me, That's right, the money wasn't transferred. So I said, But I know that, that's why I came. So she sent me to the cellar of the bank beneath her. And the cellar doesn't gleam, and there are no computers, no pretty clerks, and it is lit by a yellow light like the light in my childhood.

And a soft, aging clerk heard me and went over to the wooden cabinets behind him in which there were many files and cardboard boxes. He searched and took out a cardboard box, put it on the table and took the rubber band off the box. And the rubber band was broad and pink as the elastic on women's underwear when I was young. And he thumbed through the papers in the box, found the paper, made amends for the money that wasn't transferred, closed the box, wound the pink rubber band around it and put it back in the cabinet. And I said to myself: That box is like my innermost heart, and I came up from the cellar and went out into the street.

CHANA BLOCH

From Man You Are
and to Man You Shall Return

1985

עַכְשָׁו הִיא יוֹרֶדֶת

עַכְשָׁו הִיא יוֹרֶדֶת לְתוֹךְ הָאֲדָמָה,
עַכְשָׁו הִיא בְּמִפְלַס קַוֵּי הַטֶּלֶפוֹן וְחוּטֵי הַחַשְׁמַל
וְצִנּוֹרוֹת הַמַּיִם הַטְּהוֹרִים וְצִנּוֹרוֹת הַמַּיִם הַטְּמֵאִים,
עַכְשָׁו הִיא יוֹרֶדֶת לַמְּקוֹמוֹת הַנְּמוּכִים יוֹתֵר,
נְמוּכִים מִתַּחַת לַנְּמוּכִים שֶׁבָּהֶם
הַסִּבּוֹת לְכָל הַזְּרִימָה הַזֹּאת,
עַכְשָׁו הִיא בְּשִׁכְבוֹת הָאֶבֶן וּמֵי הַתְּהוֹם,
שֶׁבֵּין מְנִיעֵי הַמִּלְחָמוֹת וְגוֹרְמֵי הַהִיסְטוֹרְיָה
וְגוֹרָלוֹת הֶעָתִיד שֶׁל עַמִּים וְשֶׁל בְּנֵי-אָדָם,
שֶׁטֶּרֶם נוֹלְדוּ:
אִמִּי חֲלָלִית הַיְשׁוּעָה,
הִיא הוֹפֶכֶת אֶת הָאֲדָמָה
לְשָׁמַיִם אֲמִתִּיִּים.

(TRANSLATION ON PAGE 344)

My Mother on Her Sickbed

My mother on her sickbed with the lightness and hollowness
 of a person
Who has already said goodbye at an airport
In the beautiful and quiet area
Between parting and takeoff.

My mother on her sickbed.
All she had in her life is now
Like empty bottles in front of the door
That will show once more with colored labels
What filled them with joy and sadness.

Her last words, "Take the flowers out of the room,"
She said seven days before her death,
Then she closed herself for seven days,
Like the seven days of mourning.

But even her death created in her room
A warm hominess
With her sleeping face and the cup with its teaspoon
And the towel and the book and the glasses,
And her hand on the blanket, the same
Hand that felt my forehead, in childhood.

BENJAMIN AND BARBARA HARSHAV

Now She's Breathing

Now she's breathing quietly, I said. No, she's
screaming inside because of a great pain, the doctor said.
He asked my permission
to remove the wedding ring from her finger
because it was very swollen. I gave permission in the name of
the pain and in the name of my father
who never left her in his life. We kept turning the ring
like the magic ring in a fairy tale, but
it didn't come off and there was
no miracle. The doctor asked permission to cut
the ring, and he cut it with the gentleness
of careful forceps.

Now she's laughing, practicing the laughter of over there.
Now she's crying, weaning herself
from the crying of here.

The photo on her passport was taken many years ago.
After she came to the land of Israel, she never
went abroad. A death certificate
doesn't need a photo.

<div align="right">CHANA BLOCH</div>

My Mother Died on Shavuot

My mother died on Shavuot, at the end of
the Counting of the Omer.
Her oldest brother died in 1916; he fell in the war.
I almost fell in 1948, and my mother died in 1983.
Everyone dies at the end of some counting, long or short,
everyone falls in a war and deserves
a wreath, a ceremony, an official letter.
When I stand at my mother's grave
it's as if I'm saluting,
and the hard words of the kaddish are like a gun salute
into the bright summer sky.

We buried her in Sanhedria next to my father's grave,
we'd saved a place for her
the way people do on a bus or at the movies:
we left flowers and little stones, so that no one
would take her place.

(Twenty years ago the graveyard
was on the border, facing the enemy positions.
The tombstones were a good defense against tanks.)

But when I was a child, there was a botanical garden here,
all sorts of plants and shabby wooden signs
with names in Hebrew and Latin:
the Common Rose, Mediterranean Sage,
the Common Shriek, the Tufted Lamentation,
the Annual Lamentation, the Perennial Grief,
the Crimson Remembrance, the Sweet Remembrance,
the remembrance and the forgetting.

CHANA BLOCH

Now She Goes Down

Now she goes down into the earth,
now she's at the level of telephone lines and power cables
and the pipes for clean water and the pipes for foul water,
now she goes down to still lower places,
low beneath low, where
the reasons for all this flowing reside,
now she is in the strata of stones and ground water
that contain the motives for wars and the causes of history
and the future fates of peoples and human beings
as yet unborn.
My mother is salvation's spaceship,
she turns earth
into true skies.

ROBERT ALTER

The One and Only Door

She left by the one and only door
through which all the dead leave the world.
It's the one and only door
through which we enter the world.

And her new family name
like that of them all:
Ofblessedmemory.

Her full name from now till the resurrection:
Frieda Ofblessedmemory.

ROBERT ALTER

First Yahrzeit

My mother's first yahrzeit far from Jerusalem
among the green islands of western Canada.
Forgetful water and remembering water
mingle at the shore,
high tide and ebb tide are also a continuous flow,
continuous and eternal life.
An eagle circles above, like a lonely soul,
and my mother never saw an eagle.

Here beneath myriad trees and myriad clouds
that have joined me for a minyan I say kaddish.
One can say kaddish in any place and one can say kaddish
even after the resurrection of the dead.
Even should my mother sit opposite me at the table,
little and bent, I would still mourn her death
before her eyes and say kaddish to her ears.

ROBERT ALTER

I'm in Big Trouble

The carrot grows happily in the ground,
the slaughtered sheep's head in the butcher shop calms me down,
the half-sweet wine
looks for its bitter half,
and I'm in trouble.

The flute vendor plays his flutes to sell them,
the drum vendor beats his drums,
the streetwalker bares her thighs,
and I'm in big trouble.

On the door of the fruit shop fruit is painted,
on the fish restaurant fish are painted,
on the entrance to war a young man is painted,
and I'm in big trouble.

From a man who loses things
I've turned into a lost man.
I am tired of doors,
I want windows, only windows.
I want clothes
that are light and loose on my body
like hands waving goodbye, without pain.

I am anxious about what the past
will do to me in the future.
From the synagogue of my childhood
all that's left is the sky
that I saw through its windows.
God, I'm in big trouble.

ROBERT ALTER

The Great Show That Is Called the Future

The people I'll never see again
sit and eat with me.

The little boy in his bed dreams
he'll be a deep-sea diver or a high-sky flier.

And they're all combed with the same comb
all in the same direction. And the dead sing hallelujah
with a mouth full of dust.
The days hide within a night of grace.

A woman on the radio news tells
in a sweet and gentle voice
what men do to each other in war.

The great show that is called the future
begins.

ROBERT ALTER

My Little Girl Looks

My little girl looks into my eyes
as into the windows of a dark house of mourners.
But inside she sees
grooms and brides preparing for the ceremony.

A little girl filled with food,
a bowl brimming with happiness, a sweet sack.

The great love you put on a girl in her sleep
does not weigh on her. To the contrary:
she gets lighter and lighter.

The little birthmark
will remind her years after my death
that she was born to her father Yehuda and to her mother Hana
on a beautiful summer day.

ROBERT ALTER

End of the School Year in Hadasim

A year blessed with rain
will make many plants grow in the spring
that will build up the fiery flame
to consume them in the summer.

A year blessed with children
will build up the war
when those children grow up
in this time.

Here among the trees whose dark tops
sway like oaths and like vows,
classes of life part from each other
to the accompaniment of a tune, the big windows
lit and open like pages from a picture album.
The big iron gate like wings
in a rustling of open and close.

Wings riveted forever to this earth
and to the fate of its sons in their going and coming,
and the roar of departing planes
foretells what we already knew.

The hands blessing will go far from the blessed
and lips kissing will forget,
like the drinking lips
that will forget the water.

And one way leads to the planted field
and another toward the hills
and the third way isn't there
for it died in my heart.

ROBERT ALTER

Inside the Apple

You visit me inside the apple.
Together we can hear the knife
paring around and around us, carefully,
so the peel won't tear.

You speak to me. I trust your voice
because it has lumps of hard pain in it
the way real honey
has lumps of wax from the honeycomb.

I touch your lips with my fingers:
that too is a prophetic gesture.
And your lips are red, the way a burnt field
is black.
It's all true.

You visit me inside the apple
and you'll stay with me inside the apple
until the knife finishes its work.

CHANA BLOCH

Memory of Love—Opening the Will

I'm still inside the room. Two days from now
I will see it from the outside only,
The closed shutter of your room where we loved one another
And not all mankind.

And we shall turn to our new lives
In the special way of careful preparations
For death, turning to the wall
As in the Bible.

The God above the air we breathe,
The God who made us two eyes and two legs
Made us two souls too.

And we shall open these days
On a day far away from here, as one opens
The will
Years after a death.

BENJAMIN AND BARBARA HARSHAV

From Man You Are and to Man You Shall Return

Death in war begins
with the going down the stairs
of a single man,
a young man.

Death in war begins
with the silent closing of a door,
death in war begins
with opening the window to see.

So, weep not for him who goes,
weep for him who comes down the stairs of his house,
weep for him who puts his key
into his last pocket.
Weep for the photo that remembers instead of us,
weep for the paper that remembers,
weep for the tears that do not remember.

And in this spring
who will rise and say to the dust:
from man you are and to man you shall return.

ROBERT ALTER

Evidence

An abandoned tractor stuck in the mud,
a shirt tossed on the seat and some crushed grass
testify to a great love, nearby
among the thick bushes, oleander and reed.
There is always more evidence than necessary.
I think of what people buy in a store
in different combinations.
I saw soap, a pack of matches, and two apples
in one shopping basket, and some other things
whose combination I can't decipher.

I think about the effort of history
to make connections and to remember,
and about the loneliness of an ancient clay jar
in a glass case in the museum, all lit up,
rescued from forgetting and prevented from death.
I think of the basalt stones in the old Roman bridge:
they too are evidence
for things I don't know.

Round time and square time
travel at the same speed,
but their sound as they pass is different.
And many memorial candles together
make a great joyful light.

CHANA BLOCH

Remembrance of Love: What Will Be

The jasmine blossoms broke the law of darkness,
and the sound of turning sprinklers delayed the end of days.

Thigh, thigh, hand, hand,
thus the lovers' dirge when they are still together.
The sunset shows them
a possibly different life.

Like the clearing between two forests, so their sleep,
bare and empty, and safe from fire
and from sudden fear that may come.

But in the morning, right away, questions instead of greetings,
even cries of excitement are questions:
how goodly, how great are Your works, what will be?

ROBERT ALTER

A Rosebush Hangs over the Wall

A rosebush hangs over the wall, witness to bliss
Of others, in closed gardens that break your heart
With so much yearning,
Plenty and loss, like the last bread
Tossed over the wall of a besieged city,
A sweet seized moment in red ardor
On the faces of prophets of the End of Days,
Death and lust, sleep of the waking, talk
In a dream, and time in vain. A rosebush covers
A letterbox holding the letter of pain:
Between the event at the window
And the event at the door
Sometimes a whole life passes.

A rosebush over the wall.
I know a scholar of hard history
Who sired three soft daughters,
Beauties who grew up and left home.
But a rosebush hangs over the wall.

<div align="right">BENJAMIN AND BARBARA HARSHAV</div>

North of Beersheba

The soil is ploughed up. Inside
has turned into outside now
like a man who's confessed.

And all the crumbling things
are on their way to becoming one again
like the long resounding "One"
at the end of *Shema Yisrael*.

In Jerusalem my children roll over in their sleep
in the direction of my travels
into the past and the future.

Dry riverbeds think I'm water,
a cloud, the shadow of a cloud,
and I think: Don't count on me.

I have two friends left, a geologist
and a biologist.
The terrain between them is mine.

CHANA BLOCH

The Course of a Life

Till eight days like any happy fly,
on the eighth, a Jew
to be circumcised,
to learn pain without words.

In childhood, a Catholic
for the dances of ritual and its games,
the splendor of fear, the glory of sin
and shining things up above,

or a Jew for the commandments of Shalt and Shalt Not.
We begged you, Lord, to divide right from wrong
and instead you divided the waters above the firmament
from those beneath it. We begged
for the knowledge of good and evil, and you gave us
all kinds of rules and regulations
like the rules of soccer
for the permitted and the forbidden, for reward and punishment,
for defeat and victory, for remembering and forgetting.

A young man believes in nothing and loves everything,
worships idols and stars, girls, hope, despair.

A Protestant at the age when toughening sets in,
the cheek and the mouth, wheeling and dealing, upper
and lower jaw, commerce and industry.

But after midnight, everyone's the muezzin
of his own life, calling out from the top of himself
as if from the top of a minaret,
crying parched from the pressure of the desert
about the failure of flesh and of blood,
howling insatiable lusts.

Afterward, a motley crowd, you and I, religions
of oblivion and religions of memory,
hot baths, sunsets and a quiet drunkenness
till the body is soul and the soul, body.

And toward the end, again a Jew,
served up on a white pillow to the *sandak*
after the pain, from him to a good woman
and from one good woman to another,
the taste of sweet wine on his lips, and the taste
of pain between his legs.

And the last eight days without
consciousness, without knowledge, without belief
like any animal, like any stone,
like any happy fly.

CHANA BLOCH

Atlit

Here the ancient harbor still remembers in its ruins
all the ships that came to it. Its remembering is by the measure
 of its size.
And we humans remember by the measure of our
little heads and our silence is the size of our shout
and the vision of the end of days the size of the eye.

And at the shore in the sands, joy and jubilation
over all those not yet drowned.
No one will chant history,
no one will sing the song of the generations.

But the child leaps from the waves back to me,
from the future back to me.
I towel him off and hug him:
time has lost a few moments in my favor.

<div align="right">ROBERT ALTER</div>

End of Summer in the Sharon

End of summer in the Sharon. The first citrus fruit
almost overtakes the last grapes.
In the space between them is a place for my own quiet fruit.
The scent of imminent rain while hearing the name of a man
I'll never see again triggers internal weeping in me,
and internal weeping is stronger than the weeping of the eyes,
almost lethal, like internal bleeding.

A house sometimes breaks before its tenants break
and they go out so as to forget.
And the house over which heirs have quarreled
still stands in the dying orange grove
and the house over which heirs agreed lovingly
is destroyed. And the cypresses planted long years ago
have climbed up, since then,
through layers of love and layers of hate
to stand high above them and free of all things.

In front of an old man's house
I saw the four festival kinds
flung into a single pile with the holiday refuse:
the palm branch, the citron, the myrtle, and the river willow
that grew far from each other
in great longing a whole year
to be together for seven festival days
now bonded in death.

ROBERT ALTER

Late Marriage

I sit in a waiting room with bridegrooms
much younger than me. If I had lived in ancient times
I would be a prophet. But now I wait quietly
to register my name along with the name of my beloved
in the big book of marriages,
and to answer the questions I still
can answer. I've filled my life with words,
I've gathered enough data in my body to supply
the intelligence services of several nations.

With heavy steps I carry light thoughts
as in my youth I carried thoughts heavy with destiny
on light feet that almost danced from so much future.

The pressure of my life brings my date of birth closer
to the date of my death, as in history books
where the pressure of history has brought
those two numbers together next to the name of a dead king
with only a hyphen between them.

I hold onto that hyphen with all my might
like a lifeline, I live on it,
and on my lips the vow not to be alone,
the voice of the bridegroom and the voice of the bride,
the sound of children laughing and shouting
in the streets of Jerusalem
and in the cities of Yehuda.

CHANA BLOCH

Two Poets in Mexico

Claudia is many Jews
from whom a lovely girl in Mexico was made.
Veronica is many rumors.

I want to describe them as in travel books
from the last century
with great love and scant information.

I don't know what words make them happy
and what words make them sad,
what are the landscapes of despair and the landscapes of their hope,
what deep plantations, and what deserts,
what distant snow-capped mountains and what of the night.

Claudia is lovely, like windows open to the sea,
she is a spy for the lands of parting.
Veronica is Trotsky's great-granddaughter,
her lovely hair covers the deep wound in her great-grandfather's
 skull.
She lives in a house with many books and much death.

Recently I saw them together in the holy rite
of photo shoots at the bottom of the steps
among people joining and dispersing.
The trumpet melody that should have been calming
opened old and painful memories.

Claudia will bear on her shoulders
her face fading to oblivion.
Veronica will take with her
the words I do not know,
like the tremor in the skin of a sleeping dog,

my soul yearns for them.
Hand and handle together are lost,
and the bee has drowned in the honey it made.

ROBERT ALTER

At the Swimming Pool

Here I take off my fearful and foolish clothes
and put them in the holy arks of the changing room.
And the metallic smell and the smell of water and rust
are the incense of yearning for distant ports
and for worlds that are gone from the world.

I swim tranquilly from side to side in the pool
in the rhythm of my life and the movements of memory.
On my lips the murmur of my locker's number,
like the recitation of Psalms, like a charm that saves from
 destruction.
And with me the young men and women in zestful swimming
and in a purity greater than all the baths of purification,
lovely and tanned by the sun's desire and gilded by my desire.

I am the son of Meir and Frieda and the son of mortality,
I who am going to die bless those
who will remain after me, like a gladiator in the stadium
before the last combat.
I who lose things describe in passionate words what I'll lose,
I whose house will be razed and whose body will rot
praise the new houses
and the bodies still fresh and filled with love.

I come out of the water, I towel my body
like another man's body, and put on my clothes.
I pronounce the blessing for the pool
and forget, as in a kiss on the brow, the number.

ROBERT ALTER

North of San Francisco

Here the soft hills touch the ocean
like one eternity touching another
and the cows grazing on them
ignore us, like angels.
Even the scent of ripe melon in the cellar
is a prophecy of peace.

The darkness doesn't war against the light,
it carries us forward
to another light, and the only pain
is the pain of not staying.

In my land, called holy,
they won't let eternity be:
they've divided it into little religions,
zoned it for God-zones,
broken it into fragments of history,
sharp and wounding unto death.
And they've turned its tranquil distances
into a closeness convulsing with the pain of the present.

On the beach at Bolinas, at the foot of the wooden steps,
I saw some girls lying in the sand bare-bottomed.
their heads bowed, drunk
on the kingdom everlasting,
their souls like doors
closing and opening,
closing and opening inside them
to the rhythm of the surf.

CHANA BLOCH

The Fist, Too, Was Once an Open Hand and Fingers

1989

שִׁשִּׁים קִילוֹגְרַם שֶׁל אַהֲבָה טְהוֹרָה

שִׁשִּׁים קִילוֹגְרַם שֶׁל אַהֲבָה טְהוֹרָה,
בְּנוּיָה לְתִפְאֶרֶת שֶׁבָּנְתָה עַצְמָהּ
בְּלִי תָּכְנִיּוֹת אַדְרִיכָל, בְּלִי רֵאשִׁית בְּלִי תַּכְלִית.
אֵשֶׁת נָטוֹ סוֹעֶרֶת שֶׁל גֶּנֶטִיקָה טְהוֹרָה עַצְמִית:
תָּא אַהֲבָה מוֹלִיד תָּא אַהֲבָה.

מָה עוֹשָׂה לָךְ הַסְּבִיבָה,
מָה עוֹשִׂים לָךְ שְׁנּוּיִים?
הֵם מְיַפִּים אוֹתָךְ מִחוּץ, כְּמוֹ שְׁקִיעַת שֶׁמֶשׁ
וּמְדַגְדְּגִים אוֹתָךְ בִּפְנִים. אַתְּ צוֹחֶקֶת,
אֲנִי אוֹהֵב אוֹתָךְ.

(TRANSLATION ON PAGE 376)

Ruhama

Here in this wadi we lived during the war.
Many years have passed since then, many victories
and many defeats. I have gathered many consolations in my life
and squandered them, many sorrows
that I spilled in vain. I've said many things, like the waves
of the sea at Ashkelon in the West
that always keep saying the same thing.
But as long as I live, my soul remembers
and my body slowly ripens in the fires of its life story.

The evening sky lowers like a bugle call over us,
and our lips move like the lips of men in prayer
before there was a god in the world.

Here we would lie by day, and at night
we would go to battle.
The smell of the sand is as it was, and the smell
of the eucalyptus leaves
and the smell of the wind.

And I do now what any memory dog does:
I howl quietly
and piss a boundary of remembrance around me
so no one else can enter.

CHANA BLOCH

Huleikat—the Third Poem About Dicky

In these hills even the oil rigs
are already a memory. Here Dicky fell
who was four years older than I and like a father to me
in times of anguish. Now that I'm older than him
by forty years, I remember him like a young son,
and I an old grieving father.

And you who remember only a face,
don't forget the outstretched hands
and the legs that run so easily
and the words.

Remember that even the road to terrible battles
always passes by gardens and windows
and children playing and a barking dog.

Remember the fruit that fell and remind it
of the leaves and the branch,
remind the hard thorns
that they were soft and green in springtime,
and don't forget that the fist, too,
was once the palm of an open hand, and fingers.

CHANA BLOCH

What I Learned in the Wars

What I learned in the wars:
to march with rhythmically swinging arms and legs
like pumps that pump from an empty well.

To march in line, alone in the middle,
to dig into pillows and covers and the beloved woman's body
and to shout "Mama" without her hearing
and to shout "God" without believing in Him
and even if I believed in Him
I wouldn't tell Him about the wars
as one doesn't tell a child about the grown-ups' horrors.

What did I learn. I learned to keep a route of retreat.
When abroad, I book a room in a hotel
by the airport or the train station.
And even in halls of public celebration
always keep in view the little door
on which "exit" is written in red letters.

A battle, too, begins
like rhythmic drums for dancing
and ends with "retreat at dawn." Forbidden loves
and battles both, sometimes, end so.
But above all, I learned the wisdom of camouflage,
that I shouldn't stick out, that I shouldn't be known,
that they shouldn't tell between me and my surroundings,
even between me and my love,
that they should think I was a bush or a lamb,
that I was a tree, that I was a tree's shadow,
that I was a doubt, the shadow of a doubt,
that I was a hedge, a dead stone,
a house, the corner of a house.

Were I a prophet, I would dim the vision's splendor
and darken my faith with black paper
and cover God's chariot with nets.
And when the time comes I shall don the camouflage of my end:
white of clouds and lots of sky blue
and stars beyond number.

ROBERT ALTER

374

But We

The war began far away. But we
sat in the house. The future was close,
it began by the window with no space between.

The future was yellow, the color of acacia blossoms
and purple, the color of bougainvillea, and its voices
were the voices of the two of us.

We made love in the orange grove on the sandy soil,
the grove lent us its strength and we lent it our strength.
And beyond the row of cypresses the train passed by
but we only heard it, we didn't see.
And all the things we spoke between us
began with the words, "But we."

And when we parted after the war's end,
these words parted too: the word "but"
stayed in its place, and the word "we" passed on to another place.

ROBERT ALTER

Sixty Kilos of Pure Love

Sixty kilos of pure love
built with a splendor that built itself
without an architect's plans. Without beginning without end.
A passionate net-weight woman with pure genetics of her own:
love-cell spawning love-cell.

What does the environment do to you,
what do changes do to you?
They make you lovely on the outside, like a sunset,
and tickle you inside. You laugh,
I love you.

ROBERT ALTER

A Lit Window, the Dark Is with Me

The public park became a private garden.
You don't have to return to the garden,
only to touch its gate without going in,
only to touch the gate without looking in,
as one touches a bound packet of letters
without undoing the string, without opening the letters,
without reading,
as one touches with a kiss of the lips or a kiss of the hand
a rolled-up Torah scroll, closed on its history and its wonders.
You don't have to spread it out
and read it but only love
with all your heart and all your soul.

A lit window cuts out light from the dark.
So your body showed me a bit of the world-without-end
of others, of another man, of another woman.
The dark is with me.

ROBERT ALTER

Sorrow and Joy

Sorrow and joy alternating
like water and vapor and ice,
sorrow and joy from the same substance.
We knew.

Love and unlove, two colors
in a single rose, it's wonderful,
an achievement of the rose's cultivator
whose name stays with the rose.

Many years later we met again
without pain, each of us with our own tranquillity.
That was the Garden of Eden
but it was also hell.

<div align="right">

ROBERT ALTER

</div>

Between

Where will we be when these flowers turn into fruit
in the narrow between, when the flower is no longer a flower
and the fruit not yet a fruit. And what a wonderful between we made
for each other between body and body.
A between of eyes, between waking and sleep.
A twilight between light, not day and not night.

How your spring dress so quickly became a flag of summer
that flutters already in the first wind of fall.
How my voice was no longer my voice
but like a prophecy, almost.

What a wonderful between we were, like earth
in the clefts of the wall, a small stubborn earth
for the valiant moss, for the thorny caper bush
whose bitter fruit
sweetened what we ate together.

These are the last days of books.
Next come the last days of words. Some day
you will understand.

ROBERT ALTER

Four Resurrections on Emek Rephaim Street

First Resurrection
A woman resembling my mother sees a man resembling me,
they pass each other without turning around.

Mistakes are wondrous and simple, like life and death,
like a small child's arithmetic book.

In the home for indigent girls, the girls are singing on the balcony
and hanging their clothes out to dry, love's flags.

In the center for fibers they are making rope from fibers
to bind up souls in the bundle of life.

The noon wind blows as though asking,
What did you do, what did you talk about?

Within old stone houses young women do by day
what their mothers' mothers dreamed of by night.

The Armenian church is empty and shut
like a deserted wife whose husband left her for distant places
and was never seen again.

Indigent girls are singing: "The dead will God revive
in His abundant kindness" and folding their clothes now dried.
"Blessed for all time be His praiseworthy name."

Second Resurrection
In the park are cans that once contained plants,
now empty and crushed like castaway wombs.

The children's play structures are like instruments of torture
or like the wings of a great bird or a fallen angel.

And the ancient rite begins,
a father says to his little son:
"I'm going,
and you stay here by yourself."

So summer and winter in their season, so
the changing generations, so those who stay and who go.

Third Resurrection
In a panhandler's pleading voice
I praise the world.

In a voice crying for help from the depths
I acclaim.

A young woman curses her mother,
who passed on to her fat thighs.

I bless her
and her as well.

The sorrow of parted lovers
is empty here and hollow as a drum.

People write on the gate of their house,
"No entry to strangers,"
yet they themselves are strangers within it.

By the wall of the Christian cemetery
a vandalized telephone booth,
the torn wires dangling like veins
and sinews: waiting for their moment.

Fourth Resurrection
I saw the seats of a ruined movie house
laid out in an empty lot
that had been taken from their good dark home
and exposed to the ruthless sun,

fragments of seats with pieces of numbered rows:
24, 26, 28, 30 with 7, 9, 11, 13.

And I asked my soul: Where are the deeds and where are the words
that once were on the screen? Who by fire and who by water
and where are those who sat in these seats,
where is their lament and where their laughter,
where their wanderings and where their vows
and what sights and images do they see
and what are the words they hear now?
Do they still sit in numbered rows
or stand in long lines
and how will they rise from the dead, and where?

ROBERT ALTER

I Am a Penniless Prophet

I am a penniless prophet, like a child who has
only two colors. I paint my life in war
and love, in noise and stillness.

The great prophets threw away half their prophecies
like the half-smoked cigarettes of a nervous smoker.
I pick them up and make them into penniless prophecies.

In the water towers the water is silent,
in empty pipes the un-water wails and growls.

Words soak up "blood, sweat, and tears"
and are thrown into the garbage. Disposable words
like paper tissues. Disposable people,
that is their forever.

Words should have been empty
and narrow and hard, like a watershed,
despair and hope, joy and sorrow, tranquillity and rage
should have flowed to both sides
for a new cycle.

I am a penniless prophet. I live within the hopes of others,
as within a beam of light not meant to light me up,
I cast the shadow of my image, of my likeness,
my body hides the famous lovely view.
I come between the seer and his vision.

I am a penniless prophet who comes home at noon
to eat and rest and, in the evening, sleep.
I get an annual vacation and sabbatical years
and soul insurance and a pension for old age.

I began my life so low.
When I go up high in the drunkenness of my soul,
when I reach the height of my visions,
I find myself with everyday people
who have children and jobs and family cares
and household chores. These are my visions. I am a penniless prophet.

ROBERT ALTER

Summer Evening at the Window with Psalms

Careful inspection of the past.
How my soul yearns within me like the souls
of the nineteenth century before the great wars,
like curtains that want to be free of
the open window and fly.

We console ourselves with short breaths,
as after running, we always recover.
We want to reach death
hale and whole, like a murderer
sentenced to death wounded when he was caught
whose judges want him to heal before execution.

I think, how many still waters
can give a single night of stillness
and how many green pastures, wide as deserts,
can give the tranquillity of a single hour
and how many valleys of the shadow of death we need
to be a pitied shade in the merciless sun.

I look out from the window: a hundred and fifty
psalms pass by through the twilight.
A hundred and fifty psalms big and small.
What a great and splendid fleet sails by!

I say: the window is God
and the door is His prophet.

ROBERT ALTER

Summer Rest and Words

The sprinklers calm the wrath of summer.
The turning sprinkler's sound
and the water's rustle on leaves and grass
are enough for me.
Then the newspaper slips from my hand and becomes again
passing times and paper of wings.
Then I close my eyes,
then I go back to the words of my childhood rabbi
on the synagogue dais: "And grant eternal salvation
to those who have gone to the world of truth." He changed
the words from the prayer a bit, he did not chant
and did not trill and did not sob
and did not flatter his God like the cantors
but said what he had to say in quiet confidence, asked of his God
in a calm voice that has followed me all my life.

I ask myself what he meant by those words,
is salvation just for those who have gone to the world of truth?
And what of our world and what of my world?
Is rest salvation, or perhaps it's something else?
And why did he add eternal to salvation?

Words follow me. Words follow my life
like a melody. Words follow my life
like the words on a movie screen down below, on the margin,
that translate their language into mine.

I recall that when I was young sometimes the translation
lagged behind what was said or jumped ahead of it.
The faces on the screen were sad or even weeping
and the words beneath spoke of joy, or the speakers' faces
beamed and laughed and the words spoke of great sorrow.
Words follow my life.

But the words I myself say
are now like stones I throw
into a well in a field to see
whether it's full or empty
and how deep it is.

ROBERT ALTER

Autumn Is Near and the Memory of My Parents

Soon it will be autumn. The last fruits ripen
and people walk on roads they haven't taken before.
The old house begins to forgive those who live in it.
Trees darken with age and people grow white.
Soon the rains will come. The smell of rust will be fresh
and delight the heart
like the scent of blossoms in spring.

In the northern countries they say, Most of the leaves
are still on the trees. But here we say,
Most of the words are still on the people.
Our fall season makes other things fall.

Soon it will be autumn. The time has come
to remember my parents.
I remember them like the simple toys of my childhood,
turning in little circles,
humming softly, raising a leg,
waving an arm, moving their heads
from side to side slowly, in the same rhythm,
the spring in their belly and the key in their back.
Then suddenly they stop moving and remain
forever in their last position.

And that is how I remember my parents
and that is how I remember
their words.

CHANA BLOCH

Man with Knapsack

Man with knapsack in the marketplace, Brother,
Like you, I am a donkey man, a camel man,
An angel man, I am like you.
Our arms are free like wings.
Compared to us, all who carry full baskets
Are slaves of slaves bound and pulled down.

We exchange coins for fresh vegetables,
And for the forgetting of our lives we buy
Fruit and their memories, memory of field and garden,
Memory of the smell of earth and the buzzing of bees on a hot day.

We saw a woman in a light summer dress
Before a great and heavy love
Which will determine her life. She doesn't know yet
But we do. On our back
We carry fruit from the tree of knowledge.

Man with knapsack, where do you live?
I am like you, we live in the distances
Between reward and punishment.
And how do you live? And how do you sleep at night,
What do you dream of? People you love,
Do they still live in the same places?

Our knapsacks like folded parachutes
On our backs, at night they open wide
So we can jump, hovering
Into the fragrance of remembering and forgetting.

BENJAMIN AND BARBARA HARSHAV

The Greatest Desire

Instead of singing Hallelujah, a certain
fluttering from an open window.
Instead of saying Amen, a door or a shutter closing.
Instead of the Vision of the End of Days
the flapping of banners on an empty street after the holiday.

Reflections slowly take over the house,
whatever glimmers in mirror and wineglass.

I saw broken glass flashing in the sun
in the Judean desert, celebrating a wedding
without bride or bridegroom, a pure celebration.

I saw a big beautiful parade going by in the street,
I saw policemen standing between the spectators and the parade,
their faces toward those who were watching,
their backs to whatever was passing by
with fanfare and joy and flags.
Maybe to live like that.

But the greatest desire of all is to be
in the dream of another person.
To feel a slight pull, like reins tugging. To feel
a heavy pull, like chains.

CHANA BLOCH

First Rain on a Burned Car

The closeness of life to death
near the corpse of a car at the roadside.

You hear the raindrops on the rusty metal
before you feel them on the skin of your face.

The rains have come, redemption after death.
Rust is more eternal than blood, more beautiful
than the color of flames.

The shock absorbers are calmer than the dead
who won't quiet down for a long time.

A wind that is time alternates
with a wind that is place, and God
remains down here like a man who thinks
he's forgotten something, and will stick around
until he remembers.

And at night, like a wondrous melody,
you can hear man and machine
on their slow journey from a red fire
to a black peace and from there to history
to archaeology to the beautiful
strata of geology:
that too is eternity and a deep joy.

Like human sacrifice that became
animal sacrifice, then loud prayer,
then prayer in the heart,
and then no prayer at all.

CHANA BLOCH

With a Suitcase in My Hand in a Foreign Land

The suitcase in my hand is full of things. I want
to bring happiness, be a horn of plenty,
at least bring luck like a coin tossed
into a fountain, be a superstition.

I sit in a restaurant, on the table
flowers that perhaps wanted to be a bride's garland
or to adorn a grave in memoriam.

The waiter turns away from me,
the newspaper vendor goes by me,
even the beggar doesn't come to my table,
and the security man at the airport didn't check me,
didn't frisk me, I'm not even suspect.

I remember my father's prophecy, "When you grow up,
you'll be able to travel alone," and I fulfill it.
I remember, in my childhood in a foreign land
my mother and I were knocked down by a bicycle.
Since then, I've grown up and learned to sing the proud song,
"Though we were knocked down, we were not dismayed," I
 sang with
them all, for I was them-alled, very them-alled, with them all.
And now I'm alone in a foreign land. And what's happened to
 them all?
Some were dismayed, some were knocked down and got up,
 and some
remained fallen. My mother is dead. The witnesses are gone.
I remember only one wheel of the bike still spinning a little,
spinning freed from the hard earth.

ROBERT ALTER

What Kind of Man

"What kind of man are you?" people ask me.
I am a man with a complex network of pipes in my soul,
sophisticated machineries of emotion
and a precisely monitored memory system
of the late twentieth century,
but with an old body from ancient days
and a God more obsolete even than my body.

I am a man for the surface of the earth.
Deep places, pits and holes in the ground
make me nervous. Tall buildings
and mountaintops terrify me.

I am not like a piercing fork
nor a cutting knife nor a scooping spoon
nor a flat, wily spatula that sneaks in from underneath.
At most I'm a heavy and clumsy pestle
that mashes good and evil together
for the sake of a little flavor,
a little fragrance.

Guideposts don't tell me where to go.
I conduct my business quietly, diligently,
as if carrying out a long will that began to be written
the moment I was born.

Now I am standing on the sidewalk,
weary, leaning on a parking meter.
I can stand here for free, my own man.

I'm not a car. I'm a human being,
a man-god, a god-man
whose days are numbered. Hallelujah.

CHANA BLOCH

Summer Evening in the Jerusalem Mountains

An empty soda can on a rock
lit by the last rays of the sun.
The child throws stones at it,
the can falls, the stone falls,
the sun goes down. Among things that go down
and fall, I look like one that rises,
a latter-day Newton who cancels the laws of nature.
My penis like a pine cone
closed on many cells of seed.

I hear the children playing. Wild grapes too
are children and children's children.
The voices too are sons and great-grandsons
of voices forever lost in their joy.

Here in these mountains, hope belongs to the landscape
like the water holes. Even the ones with no water
still belong to the landscape like hope.

So I open my mouth and sing into the world.
I have a mouth, the world doesn't.
It has to use mine if it wants
to sing into me. I am equal to the world,
more than equal.

<div align="right">CHANA BLOCH</div>

Lachish Region

On the gate of the house "welcome" is written
and below is written "no entry."
I must get close to see which came first.

People here grew fruit trees, like children,
to grow and learn history, to know by heart
summer and winter, harvest and planting, war and peace.

In the greenhouses the sheeting is torn
and flaps like flags of forgetting,
and the abandoned schoolhouse in memory of kids
like feathers and fluff and eggshells.
But the water tower is still called a water tower
even when there is no water.

I ask, Where are the people
who lived in these houses, where did they go,
what are their windows and their dreams,
what their lament and their tent in the night?

I don't know. But the search for the answer
turns my life into a dance where one person
pretends to search and covers his eyes, and the other is lost.
This dance calms our lives and gives them a rhythm.

And sometimes remembering comes: cloud's sudden shadow
 on the hill.
Forgetting is the shadow of remembering
and remembering itself the shadow of what really was,
the shadow of a shadow. *So that your days may be long
upon the earth.*

ROBERT ALTER

Equality

I buy a small bag of figs,
I hold the bag with the hand
that's at the end of my arm.

My arm is the bridge
between the bag of sweet figs
and my body.

The bridge belongs to them both.
The bag of figs and my body are equals.

CHANA BLOCH AND CHANA KRONFELD

That's How It Is Now

"That's how it is now, it won't be like this again,
that's how it is now, it won't be the way it was."
Words of this sort are like a curtain with heavy folds
to block the painful light and mute the
noise. That's how it is now.
For we're all refugees of loves, leavings of night's happiness
and remnants of day's happiness, orphans of hope, survivors
 of dreams
and banished from belief. Poor heirs of words.

"Now they have parted for good." These too are words
fluttering through the world like torn decorations
after a holiday or like placards flung
on the ground after a demonstration. That's how it is now.

<div align="right">ROBERT ALTER</div>

Life

Like high mountain climbers who set up a base in the valley at the foot of the mountains and another camp and camp number two and camp number three at various heights on the road to the peak, and in every camp they leave food and provisions and equipment to make their last climb easier and to collect on their way back everything that might help them as they descend, so I leave my childhood and my youth and my adult years in various camps with a flag on every camp. I know I shall never return, but to get to the peak with no weight, light, light!

<div style="text-align: right">BENJAMIN AND BARBARA HARSHAV</div>

Beginning of Autumn in the Hills of Ephraim

At the side of the road that is being paved
a group of workers, huddled together
in the cool of twilight.
The last rays of the sun light up the men
who did what they had to do
with the bulldozer and steamroller that did
what they had to do.
Men and machines together in their faith
that they won't fall off the planet.

Already the squill has come up in the field
and there are still almonds on the almond tree.
The earth is still warm, like the head of a child
under its hair. A first wind of autumn
passes through Jews and Arabs.
Migratory birds call out to one another:
Look, human beings who stay where they are!
And in the great silence before dark
an airplane crosses the sky
and descends at the edge of the West with a gurgle
like good wine in the throat.

CHANA BLOCH

The Akhziv Museum

A big anchor thrust into the courtyard. It will wait forever
for the ship it lost. Its longing makes the world lovely,
its rust is a flag of everything lost that will not return.

And by the gate a pile of cannonballs
from past centuries. All together, the balls that hit
with those that missed. The collector made no distinction.

From the roof you see the Western Galilee,
fecund and green, fat of the land. And the road is sunk
deep within it, like a tight bathing suit's edge in the flesh
of the thighs and the buttocks. A very desired land.

And within the house many things in confusion,
a threshing sledge from an old vision,
a pitchfork from prophecies and dead people's
mills. Many tools to grind
and crush and split and many tools to close and smooth,
tools to build and tools to destroy
as in Ecclesiastes. But above all
handles of lost tools, all that remains.
What can one learn from this about man's soul
and all that remains. What can one learn
about tools that were lost and the hands that held them.

Toward evening the sun goes down into the sea
like someone who's heard of a loved one's death.

A man returns from the sea holding his shoes in his hands
as though holding his soul in his hands.
A newspaper bearing an exact date flies by.
Two battleships pass: one to the north and one to the south.

Day people change places with night people.
I see the changing of the guard by a flashlight's beam.

On the mound, over there, the ancient graves open
at night. The opposite of flowers.

ROBERT ALTER

I Want to Mix Up the Bible

A plane flies over the fig tree
which is over the head of the man under his fig tree.
I am the pilot and I am the man under his fig tree.
I want to mix up the Bible.
I so want to mix up the Bible.

I believe in trees, not as they once believed,
my belief is cut short and soon to expire,
by next spring, by next winter.
I believe in the coming of the rain and the setting of the sun.
Order and justice are mixed up: good and evil
on the table before me, like salt and pepper
the shakers are so alike. I so want
to mix up the Bible. The world is filled
with knowledge of good and evil, the world is filled with learning,
birds learn from the blowing wind
and planes learn from the birds
and the sons of man learn from them all and forget.
The earth is not sad because the dead are buried within it
and my beloved's dress is not glad
that she lives within it.
Ararat is a deep valley
and I don't want to go back to my house
because all evil tidings come to the house
as in the Book of Job.

Abel killed Cain and Moses entered
the Promised Land and the children of Israel stayed in the
 Wilderness.
I ride in Ezekiel's chariot,
and Ezekiel himself dances like Miriam the prophetess
in the Valley of Dry Bones.
Sodom and Gomorrah are booming

and Lot's wife has turned into a pillar of sugar and honey
and David king of Israel is alive and well.
I so want
to mix up the Bible.

ROBERT ALTER

The Land Knows

The land knows from whence came the clouds and from whence
 the hot wind
and from whence hatred and love.
But those who live there are confused, their heart in the east
and their body at the end of the west. Their body in the west, their
 heart in the east,
like migratory birds that have lost summer and winter,
lost beginning and end, and they fly about
day after day, till it hurts.

The land knows how to read and write
and is open-eyed. Better
had it been ignorant and unlettered,
better had it been blind,
groping its children without seeing.

The Greater Land of Israel is like a heavy plump matron
and the State of Israel like a young woman
supple and narrow-waisted.
But in the one and the other as well
Jerusalem is always the nakedness,
it's the nakedness of the land,
it's the insatiable nakedness of the land.
The writhing, shrieking desire
that will never finish till Messiah comes.

ROBERT ALTER

Open Closed Open

1998

TRANSLATED BY CHANA BLOCH AND CHANA KRONFELD

27

אַחֲרֵי אוֹשְׁוִיץ אֵין תֵּאוֹלוֹגְיָה:
מֵאֲרֻבּוֹת הַוָּתִיקָן עוֹלֶה עָשָׁן לָבָן,
סִימָן שֶׁהַקַּרְדִּינָלִים בָּחֲרוּ לָהֶם אַפִּיפְיוֹר.
מִמִּשְׂרְפוֹת אוֹשְׁוִיץ עוֹלֶה עָשָׁן שָׁחֹר
סִימָן שֶׁהָאֱלֹהִים טֶרֶם הֶחְלִיטוּ עַל בְּחִירַת
הָעָם הַנִּבְחָר.
אַחֲרֵי אוֹשְׁוִיץ אֵין תֵּאוֹלוֹגְיָה:
הַמִּסְפָּרִים עַל אַמּוֹת אֲסִירֵי הַהַשְׁמָדָה
הֵם מִסְפְּרֵי הַטֶּלֶפוֹן שֶׁל הָאֱלֹהִים
מִסְפָּרִים שֶׁאֵין מֵהֶם תְּשׁוּבָה
וְעַכְשָׁו הֵם מְנֻתָּקִים, אֶחָד, אֶחָד.

אַחֲרֵי אוֹשְׁוִיץ יֵשׁ תֵּאוֹלוֹגְיָה חֲדָשָׁה:
הַיְּהוּדִים שֶׁמֵּתוּ בַּשּׁוֹאָה
נַעֲשׂוּ עַכְשָׁו דּוֹמִים לֵאלֹהֵיהֶם
שֶׁאֵין לוֹ דְּמוּת הַגּוּף וְאֵין לוֹ גּוּף.
אֵין לָהֶם דְּמוּת הַגּוּף וְאֵין לָהֶם גּוּף.

(TRANSLATION ON PAGE 418)

Gods Change, Prayers Are Here to Stay

1

In the street on a summer evening, I saw a woman writing
on a piece of paper spread out against a locked wooden door.
She folded it, tucked it between door and doorpost, and went
 on her way.
And I didn't see her face, nor the face of the man
who would read what she had written
and I didn't see the words.

On my desk lies a stone with the word "Amen" on it,
a fragment of a tombstone, a remnant from a Jewish graveyard
destroyed a thousand years ago in the town where I was born.
One word, "Amen," carved deep into the stone,
a final hard amen for all that was and never will return,
a soft singing amen, as in prayer:
Amen and amen, may it come to pass.

Tombstones crumble, they say, words tumble, words fade away,
the tongues that spoke them turn to dust,
languages die as people do,
some languages rise again,
gods change up in heaven, gods get replaced,
prayers are here to stay.

2

Jewish theology, Theo, Theo. When I was young I knew a boy
named Theodore, as in Herzl, but his mother called him
home from the playground: Theo, Theo, come home, Theo,
don't stay there with the bad boys,
Theo, Theo, lo! Gee.

I don't want an invisible god. I want a god who is seen
but doesn't see, so I can lead him around

409

and tell him what he doesn't see. And I want
a god who sees and is seen. I want to see
how he covers his eyes, like a child playing blindman's bluff.

I want a god who is like a window I can open
so I'll see the sky even when I'm inside.
I want a god who is like a door that opens out, not in,
but God is like a revolving door, which turns, turns on its hinges
in and out, whirling and turning
without a beginning, without an end.

3
I declare with perfect faith
that prayer preceded God.
Prayer created God,
God created human beings,
human beings create prayers
that create the God that creates human beings.

4
God is a staircase that ascends
to a place that is no longer there, or isn't there yet.
The stairs are my faith, my downfall.
Our father Jacob knew it in his dream.
The angels were just adorning the steps of his ladder
like a fir tree decked out for Christmas,
and the Song of Ascents is a song of praise
to the God of the Stairs.

5
When God packed up and left the country, He left the Torah
with the Jews. They have been looking for Him ever since,
shouting, "Hey, you forgot something, you forgot,"
and other people think shouting is the prayer of the Jews.
Since then, they've been combing the Bible for hints of His
 whereabouts,
as it says: "Seek ye the Lord while He may be found,
call ye upon Him while He is near." But He is far away.

6

Bird tracks in the sand on the seashore
like the handwriting of someone who jotted down
words, names, numbers and places, so he would remember.
Bird tracks in the sand at night
are still there in the daytime, though I've never seen
the bird that left them. That's the way it is
with God.

7

"Our Father, Our King." What does a father do
when his children are orphans and he
is still alive? What will a father do
when his children have died and he becomes
a bereaved father for all eternity? Cry
and not cry, not forget and not remember.
"Our Father, Our King." What does a king do
in the republic of pain? Give them
bread and circuses like any king,
the bread of memory and the circuses of forgetting,
bread and nostalgia. Nostalgia for God-
and-a-better-world. "Our Father, Our King."

8

The God of the Christians is a Jew, a bit of a whiner,
and the God of the Muslims is an Arab Jew from the desert, a
 bit hoarse.
Only the God of the Jews isn't Jewish.
The way Herod the Edomite was brought in to be king of the Jews,
so God was brought back from the infinite future,
an abstract God: neither painting nor graven image nor tree nor stone.

9

The Jewish people read Torah aloud to God
all year long, a portion a week,
like Scheherazade who told stories to save her life.
By the time Simchat Torah rolls around,
God forgets and they can begin again.

10

God is like a tour guide
describing our life and explaining to visitors
and tourists and the sons of God: That's how we live.

11

Eyn ke-loheynu, Eyn ka-adoneynu,
"There is none like our God, There is none like our Lord,"
thus we pray.
Eyn ke-loheynu, Eyn ka-adoneynu, in a loud voice
—no reaction from him. So we amp up our voices and sing,
Mi ke-loheynu, mi ka-adoneynu?
"Who is like our God, who is like our Lord," and he won't budge,
won't turn toward us. And again we redouble the force of our
 pleading,
Atah hu eloheynu, atah hu adoneynu, "Thou art our God, Thou art
 our Lord."
Maybe now he'll remember
us? But he remains unmoved, even
turns to us with cold and alien eyes.
So we stop singing and yelling, and in a whisper
we remind him of something personal, something small:
Atah hu she-hikrivu avoteynu le-fanekha
et ketoret ha-samim. "Thou art the one before whom our forefathers
offered sweet incense"—maybe now he'll remember?
(Like a man who reminds a woman of their old love affair:
Don't you remember how we were buying shoes
in that little shop on the corner, and it poured and poured
outside, and we laughed and laughed?)
And it seems as if something begins to wake up in him, maybe
he'll forget not his own,
but too late: the Jewish people is gone.

12

Even solitary prayer takes two:
one to sway back and forth
and the one who doesn't move is God.
But when my father prayed, he would stand in his place,

erect, motionless, and force God
to sway like a reed and pray to him.

13
Communal prayer: Is it better to ask "Give us peace"
with cries of woe, or to ask calmly, quietly?
But if we ask calmly, God will think
we don't really need peace and quiet.

14
Morning Psalms. Innocence rises from human beings
like steam from hot food ascending on high, a steam
that turns into God and sometimes into other gods.

15
A collection of ritual objects in the museum: spice boxes
with little flags on top like festive troops
and many fragrant generations of sacrifice,
and the memory of many Sabbath nights that did not end in death.
And happy menorahs and weepy menorahs and oil lamps
with the pouting beaks of chicks like children singing,
their mouths wide open in desire and love.
And long metal hands to point out everything
that is no more. The human hands that held them—
long since underground, severed from the bodies.
Seder plates that rotate at the speed of time
so it seems they are standing still, and kiddush cups
in a row on the shelf like soccer trophies
or victory cups from the track and field of generations.
All is gold of grief, silver of longing,
copper of calamity. A collection of ritual objects
like the gaudy toys of a baby god, the gift
of an aged nation, like the strange instruments
of a ghost orchestra, like some odd motionless
bottom fish deep in the waters of time.
A collection of ritual objects donated by Dr. Feuchtwanger,
Jerusalem dentist. And whoever hears this will assume
a delicate smile on his lips, like well-wrought filigree.

16

God is like a magician who performs sleight of hand:
causes Himself to appear, makes doves fly out of His pockets,
pulls rabbits out of His sleeve, saws a woman in two,
splits the Red Sea in two, produces ten plagues
and ten commandments with fire and pillars of smoke,
hovers over the waters and vanishes into the wall.
Everyone wants to catch Him in an off moment
and discover how He does it without really doing it.
And everyone wants not to know, not to discover
how He does it, they would like to believe,
each against each. Nothing to nothing.

17

I believe with perfect faith in the resurrection of the dead.
Just as a man who wishes to return to a place he loves
leaves behind a book, a shopping bag, a snapshot, his glasses,
on purpose, so he has to return, that's how the dead leave
the living behind, and they will return.
Once I stood in the mists of a long-ago autumn
in a Jewish cemetery that was abandoned, though not by its dead.
The groundskeeper was an expert on flowers and seasons of the year
but no expert on buried Jews. And he too said: Night after night
they are training for the resurrection of the dead.

18

The ways of my life are tangled and entangled. I am a knot that cannot
be undone. Like a knot one makes in a handkerchief to remember
something. I don't know of what I'm a reminder, and whom I'm
 reminding
not to forget. Maybe I need to remind God
to make a better world, I don't know.
I am the knot in the handkerchief. That's all there is, and that is
 my life.

19

Whoever put on a tallis when he was young will never forget:
taking it out of the soft velvet bag, opening the folded shawl,

spreading it out, kissing the length of the neckband (embroidered
or trimmed in gold). Then swinging it in a great swoop overhead
like a sky, a wedding canopy, a parachute. And then winding it
around his head as in hide-and-seek, wrapping
his whole body in it, close and slow, snuggling into it like the
 cocoon
of a butterfly, then opening would-be wings to fly.
And why is the tallis striped and not checkered black-and-white
like a chessboard? Because squares are finite and hopeless.
Stripes come from infinity and to infinity they go
like airport runways where angels land and take off.
Whoever has put on a tallis will never forget.
When he comes out of a swimming pool or the sea,
he wraps himself in a large towel, spreads it out again
over his head, and again snuggles into it close and slow,
still shivering a little, and he laughs and blesses.

20

I'm kosher. I chew my soul-cud
from the enclosed dark of every little thing that happened,
so as not to forget it, not to lose it. Yet again "Renew
our days as of old," yet again adding
one more day to make the holiday last.
If you have ever seen cows in a meadow
chewing their cud, ease and delight on their faces
and a memory of green grass on eye and tongue,
you know what true pleasure is.
I am cleft. I have no hoofs but my soul is
split. That split, that cleft, gives me the strength to stand it all,
and I beat myself up as if beating my breast for my sins
on Rosh Hashana, or like a man looking for something
he has lost, poking in his jacket or his pockets to find it.
Maybe I've forgotten what sin I'm beating my breast for.
To the confession "We have sinned, we have betrayed" I
 would add
the words "We have forgotten, we have remembered"—two sins
that cannot be atoned for. They ought to cancel each other out
but instead they reinforce one another. Yes, I'm kosher.

21

Reflections on Seder night, *Mah nishtanah*, we asked,
"How is this night different from all other nights?" "How changed?"
Most of us are grown up now and have stopped asking, but some
go on asking all their lives, the way one asks
How are you, or What time is it, and keep on walking
without waiting for an answer. *Mah nishtanah kol layla*, "How
 changed is every night,"
like an alarm clock whose ticking is soothing and soporific.
Mah nishtanah, ha-kol yishtaneh, "What has changed, all shall be
 changed." Change is God.
Reflections on Seder night. Of four sons does the Torah
speak: one wise, one wicked, one simple, and one
who knows not how to ask. But nothing is said there
about a good one, or a loving one.
And that's a question that has no answer, and if there were an answer
I wouldn't want to know. I who have passed through all the phases
 of the sons
in their changing constellations, I've lived my life, the moon shed
 its light
on me for no reason, the sun went on its way, the Passovers
passed without an answer. *Mah nishtanah*. "What has changed?"
Change is God, Death is his prophet.

22

God's love for His people Israel is an upside-down love.
First crude and physical, with a strong hand and an outstretched arm:
miracles, ten plagues and ten commandments,
almost violent, on a no-name basis.
Then more: more emotion, more soul
but no body, an unrequited ever-longing love
for an invisible god in the high heavens. A hopeless love.

23

We are all children of Abraham
but also the grandchildren of Terah, Abraham's father.
And maybe it's high time the grandchildren
did unto their father as he did unto his

416

when he shattered his idols and images, his religion, his faith.
That too would be the beginning of a new religion.

24

The sound of a drawer closing—the voice of God,
the sound of a drawer opening—the voice of love,
but it could also be the other way around.
Footsteps approaching—the voice of love,
footsteps retreating—the voice of God
who left the country without notice, temporarily forever.
A book that stays open on the table beside a pair of glasses—
God. A closed book and a lamp that stays lit—
love. A key turning in the door without a sound—
God. A key hesitating—love and hope.
But it could also be the other way around.
A sacrifice of a fragrant scent to God,
a sacrifice of the other senses to love:
a sacrifice of touch and caress, of sight and of sound,
a sacrifice of taste.
But it could also be the other way around.

25

I studied love in my childhood in my childhood synagogue
in the women's section with the help of the women behind
 the partition
that locked up my mother with all the other women and girls.
But the partition that locked them up locked me up
on the other side. They were free in their love while I remained
locked up with all the men and boys in my love, my longing.
I wanted to be there with them and to know their secrets
and say with them, "Blessed be He who has made me
according to His will." And the partition—
a lace curtain white and soft as summer dresses, swaying
on its rings and loops of wish and would,
lu-lu loops, lullings of love in the locked room.
And the faces of women like the face of the moon behind the clouds
or the full moon when the curtain parts: an enchanted
cosmic order. At night we said the blessing

over the moon outside, and I
thought about the women.

26

I studied love in the synagogue of my childhood,
I sang "Come, O Sabbath bride" on Friday nights
with a bridegroom's fever, I practiced longing for the days
 of the Messiah,
I conducted yearning drills for the days of yore that will not return.
The cantor serenades his love out of the depths,
Kaddish is recited over lovers who remain together,
the male bird dresses up in a blaze of color.
And we dress the rolled-up Torah scrolls in silken petticoats
and gowns of embroidered velvet
held up by narrow shoulder straps.
And we kiss them as they are passed around the synagogue,
stroking them as they pass, as they pass,
as we pass.

27

After Auschwitz, no theology:
From the chimneys of the Vatican, white smoke rises—
a sign the cardinals have chosen themselves a pope.
From the crematoria of Auschwitz, black smoke rises—
a sign the conclave of Gods has not yet chosen
the Chosen People.
After Auschwitz, no theology:
the numbers on the forearms
of the inmates of extermination
are the telephone numbers of God,
numbers that do not answer
and now are disconnected, one by one.

After Auschwitz, a new theology:
the Jews who died in the Shoah
have now come to be like their God,
who has no likeness of a body and has no body.
They have no likeness of a body and they have no body.

Once I Wrote *Now and in Other Days*:
Thus Glory Passes, Thus Pass the Psalms

1

Once I wrote *Now and in Other Days*.
Now I have arrived at those other days.
When I wrote it, they were at the end of the century;
now they are in the past, in the middle of the century.
But the Now is always with me, wherever I go is the Now,
as in the solar system, past and future and I—
always turning, returning. The Now is the sun,
the Now is eternity. Change is God.
And those other days turned into Otherness. On my desk
is a stone with "Amen" written on it, a fragment of a tombstone
from a Jewish grave destroyed a thousand years ago. On my desk
is a piece of torn shrapnel from an exploded grenade.
My children found it at Tel Gath among the spring flowers.
That twisted shrapnel is the angel that redeems me,
the angel that didn't kill me in battle, in those other days.
Perhaps it killed some other person.
Otherness is God. Otherness killed Him. The truth is,
Otherness killed Ruth.

2

When I was young I believed with all my heart
the Huleh swamp had to be drained.
Then all the bright-colored birds fled for their lives.
Now half a century later they are filling it with water again
because it was all a mistake. Perhaps my entire life
I've been living a mistake.
And the God of my childhood, He too
is a mistake, though He is still called God.
But the perfect mistake makes a perfect life,
like perfect faith. The saying "Mistakes happen"
I've turned into a comforting song, and the verse

"All men are false" I've made into a dance tune by day,
a lullaby at night. Amen.

3
And to this day, I still believe sometimes
the way I used to. When we sang "This is the last battle," I believed,
and when they told me, "This is the last supper" I believed. Since
 then
my life has filled with last battles and last suppers, like the last wish
of a death-row inmate. And when they say Rosh Hashana,
which means "the Head of the Year," I remember
only the head sometimes, not the hand or the swift foot of Time
passing. And the measure of justice and the measure of mercy
 were like
getting measured for shoes—to this day I buy shoes a size too big
so they won't pinch my feet. I have learned why this night differs
from all other nights and how it came to be different. And I have
 learned
who ate my porridge and who's been sleeping in my bed.
They told me "I'll be back" and I am still
waiting, and they told me "I'll never come back"
and I am still waiting. And when they told me "Don't ask,"
I began to ask, and I have not stopped asking since.

4
Oh, the small interrogatives of my life,
hopping, chirping, flitting about,
eluding me since my childhood.
Tiny as birds, light as grasshoppers.
But when I grew up, I made them into heavy affirmatives
like fattened ducks or chickens that come home to roost
and can't rise up and fly:
Whatness, Whyness, Whoness. And birds even heavier than those:
Whereness, Awareness, Whither and Die.

5
Blood turns black when it congeals, grass turns gray and brown
 when it dies.

During a heat wave you have to drink lots of water, in a stone wall
you've got to make little gun slits. All this only
to go on living, to postpone a bit
the hour of death. The way a child leaves
a half-eaten chocolate bar in his pants pocket, to have some
when the other kids have finished all of theirs.

6
As clay jars that sank to the bottom of the sea in ancient times
and are raised from the deep all covered with seaweed,
barnacles and algae, though the shape of the jars remains as
 it was—
so too the story of my life: the tears are still my tears
and the laughter my laughter. Don't try
to scrub them clean. The laughter is heavy and out of the depths,
and the tears are wreathed in dense beautiful layers from the abyss.
That too is change, that too is another place,
and the ships? They are all up in heaven.

7
I ask the ground: What goes around?
I ask my heart: Art, art?
I tell the universe: Verse, verse,
but it won't converse.
I say to hope: Cope, cope,
or else just croak.
To joy I tell: Well, well.
I say to despair: There, there.
To memory: Tee-hee.
And to forgetting: No regretting.
To days gone by: Bye-bye.
And what's to come: Come, come.
To my offspring: Spring off,
but don't go away. Stay with me.
And now for my last magic word:
Adraba, Let it be,
my abracadabra on the count of three.
As in the kaddish: Blessed be, be, be.

8

Now the Memorial Days have passed. The gap between the names
of streets and the people who live on them is growing
and hope gets more distant from those who are hoping.
Ah, those were the days! The flowering squill in the fall
had the fragrance of yeast cake, and the children
had biblical names. Seasons had the look of orange groves
and people were like trees in the Garden of Eden,
knowledge trees, knowing good and evil.
A new generation wields the hope of the one that is gone
like case-hardened tools to crack open the future,
the disappointments of one generation shore up
the latest in longings and illusions,
a creek is still called a creek even when it's dry
and joy still goes by the name of joy.

9

I want to live till even the words in my mouth are nothing
but vowels and consonants, maybe just vowels, soft sounds.
The soul inside me is the last foreign language I'm learning.
I want to live until all the numbers are sacred,
not just one not just seven not just twelve not just three
but all the numbers, the twenty-three fallen in the battle
 of Huleikat,
seventeen kilometers to the enchanted place, thirty-four nights,
one hundred twenty-nine days of grace, three hundred thousand
speed-of-light years, forty-three moments of happiness
(and the number of the years of my life still X). The history
of four thousand years in forty-five minutes of a final at school.
And the days and the nights are without number—but
they too shall be numbered—
even infinity will be sacred, and then
I will find perfect rest.

10

Thus glory passes. Thus they pass, the psalms,
crying singing cursing blessing—verses
from the mouths of worshipers: Happy is the man,

Like a tree planted, Happy are they that dwell
in Thy house, All men are false, Servants of the Lord,
My Rock and Redeemer, David and the sons of Korah, hallelujahs,
green pastures, still waters, dark valleys of death.
Thus they pass, like a parade when the circus comes to town
but won't stop, won't open the big tent, elephants
and other animals, the mea culpa band
drumming their chests, the we-have-sinned tumblers
and the we-have-betrayed dancers, tightrope walkers, acrobats
hopping Holy, Holy, Holy
with sobs and laughter, bitter cries and sweet song.
Thus it all passes—what was, and what never has been.
Thus the children parade on Arbor Day
with seedlings they won't ever plant,
thus they pass, thus glory passes.

11
Thus glory passes, like a long train without
beginning or end, without cause or purpose. I always
stand to one side at the crossing—the barrier is down—
and I take it all in: carloads of passengers and history, carloads
packed full of war, carloads teeming with human beings
for extermination, windows with the faces of parting
men and women, the high spirits of travelers,
birthdays and deathdays, pleading
and pity and plenty of empty echoing boxcars.
Thus my children pass into their future,
thus the Lord passed over Moses in the Great Desert,
and Moses did not see His face, just cried out,
"Lord, O Lord, merciful and gracious, abundant in goodness
and truth." Thus glory passes. Thus the barrier
is down forever, until the end of my days.

The Bible and You, the Bible and You, and Other Midrashim

2

How did Gideon choose his army at the Spring of Harod?
He saw them drinking from the spring,
lapping like dogs or kneeling down, and chose.
But my Gideon went on choosing: What is their way with a woman,
in what position do they make love? And how do they weep,
in a bawling voice or with silent tears,
and how do they eat and how do they sleep, on their belly like a baby,
on their side or on their back, and how do they remember their
 childhood?
And he didn't take those who remember and never forget,
and he didn't take those who forget and never remember.
And one said, I drank from the fountain of longing, and another said,
I've been to the enchanted place, and another said, I've never
 been there,
and another said, I stayed in the dream with the sound of the rolling
 barley cake
and I am still rolling. And my Gideon was left
with no army no battle no glory at the Spring of Harod. And he drank
kneeling down and he drank lapping, and he
drank and remembered and forgot.

3

The Bible and you, the Bible and you.
As the Torah scroll is read aloud each year
from "In the beginning" to "This is the blessing"
and back to the start, so we two roll together
and every year our love gets a new reading.
Torah, Torah, rah rah rah!
Sometimes in one night we go through
what the Torah goes through in an entire year,
and sometimes on a good day
we go on rolling, further and further,

past the Torah, past the death of Moses,
through Kings and Prophets and Writings all the way to
Chronicles, to the Chronicles of Love
and back to Genesis, the creation of light and of the world.
And each day God says: "And it was evening
and it was morning," but He never says
"twilight." Because twilight is for lovers only.

4

The famous French king said, *Après moi, le déluge!*
Noah the Righteous said, Before me, the flood,
and when he left the ark he declared, The flood is behind me.
But I say, I am right in the middle of the flood,
I am the ark and the animals, clean and unclean,
I am two of a kind, male and female,
I am the remembering animals and the forgetting animals,
and I am the seedling of the vine for a good world
though I cannot drink the wine myself.
In the end I'll be a tall Ararat, lonely and dry,
carrying a strange empty ark on my shoulders
with some leftover love inside it, a remnant
of prayer, a bit of hope.

5

Moses saw the face of God just once and then
forgot. He didn't want to see the desert,
not even the Promised Land, only the face of God.
In the fury of his longing he struck the rock,
climbed Mount Sinai and came down again, broke
the Tablets of the Law, made a golden calf, searched through
fire and smoke, but he could remember only
the strong hand of God and His outstretched arm,
not His face. Moses was like a man who tries to recall
the face of someone he loved, but tries in vain.
He composed a police sketch of God's face
and the face of the burning bush and the face of Pharaoh's daughter
leaning over him, a baby in the ark of bulrushes.
He sent that picture to all the tribes of Israel,

up and down the desert, but no one had seen,
no one knew. Only at the end of his life,
on Mount Nebo, did Moses see and die, kissing
the face of God.

6
Three sons had Abraham, not just two.
Three sons had Abraham: Yishma-El, Yitzhak and Yivkeh.
First came Yishma-El, "God will hear,"
next came Yitzhak, "he will laugh,"
and the last was Yivkeh, "he will cry."
No one has ever heard of Yivkeh, for he was the youngest,
the son that Father loved best,
the son who was offered up on Mount Moriah.
Yishma-El was saved by his mother, Hagar,
Yitzhak was saved by the angel,
but Yivkeh no one saved.
When he was just a little boy, his father
would call him tenderly, Yivkeh,
Yivkeleh, my sweet little Yivkie—
but he sacrificed him all the same.
The Torah says the ram, but it was Yivkeh.
Yishma-El never heard from God again,
Yitzhak never laughed again,
Sarah laughed only once, then laughed no more.
Three sons had Abraham,
Yishma, "will hear," Yitzhak, "will laugh," Yivkeh, "will cry."
Yishma-El, Yitzhak-El, Yivkeh-El,
God will hear, God will laugh, God will cry.

7
Isaiah in his vision beheld seraphim standing on high above him,
as it is written: "Six wings, six wings had each,
with twain he covered his face, and with twain he covered his legs,
 and with twain
he did fly." And I prolong his vision and pull it along
down here to my beloved: six wings, six wings,
with twain does she uncover her face and with twain uncover her legs,

with twain she brushes a curl from her brow, with twain
she caresses my head, and with twain she closes my mouth,
with twain she covers the past and with twain the future.
She has no wings left to fly.
She will fly away no more, she is with me.

8
A love song in the biblical style. It is written, "He lifted up his voice
 and said,"
and also "He lifted up his voice and wept." And we two go on lifting
our one voice, raising it up high, higher than the words
and the weeping, to say to each other in that chapter and verse:
 My love.

9
King Saul never learned how to play or to sing
nor was he taught how to be king.
Oh he's got the blues,
he's nothing to lose
but the moody tune
on his gramophone
and David is its name-oh, David is its name,
its name its name its name.
Round and round the record spins,
with a spear for a needle that begins
to pierce the heart
and deaden the hurt
as it deadens the heart.

11
Our father Jacob, on the beaten track,
carries a ladder on his back

like a window washer to the VIPs.
He does God's windows, if you please.

Only the ladder remains of his dream;
the angels finally ran out of steam.

He carries the ladder again every night
back into his dream and out of sight.

At dawn he wrestles a man to the ground.
The man is a woman. They roll round and round,

they roll till they're ravished, till both of them reel,
clutching at chest and crotch and heel,

day after day, by the first morning light,
till Jacob and angel are too weak to fight.

He will climb up that ladder, if ever he dies,
right out of this world and into the skies

until the world vanishes into thin air.
For all that we know, he is still climbing there.

12
Progression in Hannah's prayer: from loud weeping
in the bitterness of her soul over a son she doesn't have, to silent
 weeping
and from silent weeping to spoken prayer, and from spoken prayer
to silent prayer, only her lips moving, and she drunk
on the prayer within her body, and Eli the priest thinking
she was drunk on wine. And a final progression:
she sits and God prays to her. Hannah's Prayer.

13
When Samuel was born she uttered words of thanksgiving:
"For this child I prayed."
And when he grew up, and did what he did with his life,
she asked, "For this child I prayed?"

14
Ruth the Moabite knew all about wheat and wheat fields,
about eyes big with love
and golden stubble after the harvest.

And Naomi, who said, I went out full
and the Lord hath brought me home again empty—
she knew all about the physics of the empty and the full,
about her sons who died, about the stifled cry
of a womb emptying like an accordion
which makes music out of the full and the empty.

15
Moses sent many spies to tour the Promised Land
and not just twelve, as it is written. They toured and snapped
 photos
with their eyes, felt up the trees and springs and stones with their
 hands,
measured the height of hills and houses, took the measure of pretty
 women,
strong men, ripe fruit, girls' thighs.
Twelve spies returned to the desert. Ten brought back
a slander of the land. Two praised the land
and brought back a cluster of gigantic grapes, but they brought no
giants, no pretty women, no grasshoppers.
And the story says nothing about the hundreds of spies who stayed
 behind
deep in the fat of the land of Canaan, who slept with the wives of the
 giants
and ate of the fruit on every high hill and under every green tree.
And they, who came to see the land in her nakedness,
sank into her and forgot the desert.

16
"Devoured, devoured was he!" cried Jacob when they showed him
 Joseph's coat
torn and dipped in blood, and he knew not that Joseph still lived.
"Devoured, devoured," we said on a night of loving,
as our clothes got kicked down to the floor in our deranged desire,

torn pantyhose, torn panties, netherwear
and upperwear at the foot of the bed in that little room
in Jerusalem. The Bible and you, the Bible and you.

17

Sometimes I am all alone like King Saul.
I have to play the music for myself, hurl the spear by myself,
then dodge the spear. And I am also the wall
in which the spear lodges, trembling.

18

Two lovers lie together like Isaac on the altar
and it feels good. They don't think about the knife
or about the burnt offering—
she thinks about the ram and he about the angel.
Another version: He is the ram and she is the thicket.
He will die and she will go on growing wild.
Another version: The two of them get up and disappear
among the revelers.

19

Anyone who rises early in the morning is on his own.
He gets himself over to the altar, he is Abraham,
he is Isaac, he's the donkey, the fire,
the knife, the angel,
he's the ram, he is God.

20

"Take now thy son, thine only son, whom thou lovest,
and offer him up as a burnt offering," thus God to Abraham.

And him we call Abraham our Father. What kind of father
is he to us, so ready to sacrifice his son on the altar!
Another interpretation: God knew not a love for sons,
but he did know a love for mountains,
and of all the mountains he loved Mount Moriah best of all,
his mountain, his only mountain, which he did love, and that's
 why they had

the Binding of Isaac and the two Temples on it.

21
Moses held both his hands up
in the battle against the Amalekites to fortify the resolve of his
 fighting men.
And in our day that's a sign of surrender.

23
The dove brought good tidings
of the end of the flood, an olive leaf
in her mouth, like a man holding a letter in his mouth
as he searches around in his pockets with both his hands,
or like a girl holding pins
in her mouth as she mends her dress.

24
Here is the true story of Jacob the lover:
Seven plus seven years vanished forever

in pain and more pain, just to win him a life
under one roof with Rachel, his wife.

She's no princess bewitched, and he is no knight;
they're no beauty-and-beast; not a dragon in sight

for Jacob to slay, snicker-snack, like a man.
Just years of hard labor. No God at hand.

No wizard, no giant, no foe to defeat,
just sheep and shorn fields. In the dust and the heat.

"By the sweat of your brow," quoth the Holy Writ.
So deep runs his love. Like a bottomless pit.

25
Cain and Abel, a misunderstanding of love:
Cain just wanted to hug him tight
but strangled him. Both of them got it wrong.

26
Samson bound to the pillar in the Philistine temple
prayed in Gaza: "Strengthen me, I pray thee, only this one time."
(And what about next time?)

27
"They that sow in tears shall reap in joy."
Whereas they that joyfully sow human beings in the ground
shall sometimes reap in tears. The next installment is open-ended.

28
How do the visions of the prophets see me?
The burning bush sees me as a man extinguished but alive.
And what does Ezekiel's vision of the chariot say about me?
Look, down there is a man who has no wings,
nor the face of a lion, an ox, or an eagle,
and he can walk only in one direction at a time.
He has no radiance about him, no brightness the color of amber,
just a darkness within. That is his soul.
But if we ever fall from our heights and crash to the ground,
he will pick up the scattered pieces,
and all his life, he will keep trying to put us together again,
to restore us, to raise us back up to the skies.

29
I don't imagine that on the night of the exodus from Egypt,
between midnight and dawn, any couple could lie together
in love. (We could have.) In haste,
blood dripping from lintels and doorposts,
silver and gold dishes clanging in the dark, between the firstborn's
stifled death cry and the shrieking of mothers' wombs
emptying like wineskins. And standing over them, legs wide apart,
the Angel of Death, crotch gaping male and female
like a bloody sun in the thick of frizzled black death.
Sandaled feet slapping against the soft dough of matza
and the flesh of belly and thigh, hard belts
cinched tight at the waist, buckles
scraping against skin, tangled in one another.

To roll like that, locked in eternal love,
with all the rabble from the house of slavery
into the Promised Desert.

30
Waiting rooms. The waiting room of Job
where he waits for the bad news
and his friends sit and talk to him in whispers.
The waiting room of Moses in the desert
where he paces back and forth and doesn't sit still for an instant.
The waiting room of Isaac bound on Mount Moriah, waiting
to go under the knife. The waiting room of Sarah
in the tent before the birth of her son,
and the waiting room of King David up on the roof.
He was waiting for Bathsheba to get out of her bath,
then he sat and waited for Nathan the prophet
to come and curse him. And all of us
wait with them in a rustle of wings
and a flutter of newspapers
and coughs and sighs and whispered conversations—
wait for the door to be opened by the white angel
and behind him the blinding white light.

31
Balaam, Balaam, whose curse turned to blessing and his blessing
 to love.
Lay sleepless all night and at dawn he dashed off to the hills
to survey the tribes of Israel and deliver his oracle.
But the children of Israel had departed in haste during the night,
light on their feet, free of blessing and curse, and all Balaam
 could see
was the abandoned camp, tent pegs, bits of rope and campfire
 embers,
the smell of sheep, the memory of women's perfume, veils
left behind, a dress ripped by hard thistles, broken clay jars,
a bright-colored ribbon and a jackal scrabbling in the garbage,
 howling.
And Balaam went home, as a man returns to his lover's room

the morning after and finds the room empty, only a crumpled letter,
a white stocking, a comb with hair in it—that is how Balaam
 longed for
the children of Israel. That Balaam with his oration, man without
 a nation,
whose curse turned to blessing and blessing to love
and love to longing and longing to a pain that has no end.
From his window he could still see the pillar of fire
and the pillar of smoke on the horizon,
and the two shall never meet.

32

The singer of the Song of Songs sought his beloved so long and hard
that he lost his mind and went looking for her with a simile map
and fell in love with the images he himself had imagined.
He went down to Egypt, for he had written "to a mare among
 Pharaoh's chariots
I compare thee," and he went up to Gilead to see her flowing hair,
for he had written "Thy hair is like a flock of goats flowing down
Mount Gilead," and he went up to the Tower of David, for it says
"Like the Tower of David is thy neck," and he got as far as Lebanon
 and found
no peace, for it says "Thy nose is like the Tower of Lebanon that
 looks out
toward Damascus," and he wept by the waterfalls
of Ein Gedi, for he had written "Many waters cannot extinguish
this love," and he went looking for doves in Bet Guvrin
and got as far as Venice, for he had written "My dove in the clefts
 of the rock."
And he dashed off to the desert, for it says "Who is that rising
from the desert like pillars of smoke." And the Bedouin thought
he was one of the crazy prophets, and he thought
he was King Solomon. And he is still wandering, a fugitive and a
 vagabond
with the mark of Love on his forehead. And sometimes he happens
 upon
the loves of other couples in other times; he even got to our home
with its broken roof on the border between Jerusalem

and Jerusalem. And we never even saw him because we
were in each other's arms. He is still wandering, shouting
"You are beautiful, my bride," as if from within a deep sack
of oblivion. And whoever wrote "Love is as fierce as death"—
he understood his own simile only at the end,
understood and loved and died (the metaphor blew up with its
 meaning).

I Foretell the Days of Yore

1

The flight attendants of the next millennium came to me and said:
You can still get a seat on the third millennium before liftoff.
Come with us, dead or alive, we'll take you along. We have no
 malice,
no defenses, but we're strong and mobile as constellations;
our eyes are closed but we can see.
We are women who glide between life and death.
You with your seat belts and gear belts and buckles that click shut,
you, sir, you with the noise of a door closing,
we with our voices of glide and whisper.
Our belts are not for safety or for holding up our clothes,
they are snakes, they are decoration. Gliding spirals,
we are acrobats looping the loops of wish and would.
You with your warm worries and emotions
heavy as cow dung in the field,
you with the sweat of your death like an afterlife perfume.

2

We are the flight attendants of the next millennium, buoyant brides
with no excess baggage of bridegrooms,
while you are weighed down by the stripes and checks on your
 clothing.
You with the flickering colors of traffic lights, permitted, forbidden—
for us color changes are fluid. You with your strict demarcations
of sacred and profane, outerwear and underwear; for us
everything is like water within water. You with your little excitements
and attachments, your oaths and your vows,
your buttons and snaps, your comb and your qualms,
hairbrush and despairs, you with your loneliness
and the compassion of wombs, of testicles and stiff members.
For us everything is smooth and transparent—pliable glass.
You with your conjunctions and prepositions,

you with your spirit, your respiration and resuscitation,
your distance and intimacy. We are the world to come,
come with us, we'll preserve you like a potsherd, like a symbol,
like a lion of stone, and in the year 2024
we will celebrate your hundredth birthday.

3
I am a prophet of what has already been. I read the past in the palm
of the woman I love, I forecast the winter rains that have fallen,
I am an expert on the snows of yesteryear, I conjure the spirits
of what has always been, I foretell the days of yore,
I draw up the blueprints for a house right after it's torn down,
I prophesy the small room with its few pieces of furniture—
a towel draped over the only chair to dry,
the arch of the high window, curved like our bodies in love.

4
I am a prophet of the past. And how do you see and foresee
the future? As when a man sees a woman with a beautiful body
walking before him in the street
and looks at her with desire, but she doesn't turn
to look back, just smooths her skirt a little,
pulls her blouse tight, fixes the back of her hair, then
without turning toward the man's gaze
quickens her step. That's
what the future is like.

6
Life, I think, is hard work:
As Jacob labored to be with Rachel seven years
plus seven plus seven times seven, I've worked
to be one with my life, like the beloved Rachel
and to be one with my death, like the beloved Rachel.

7
Straight from the fear of loss I plunged into the fear of being lost.
I couldn't stay long enough between them
in the sweet little no man's land of my everlasting

passing days. My hands are the hands of search and test,
hands of hope, hands of gloom,
always fumbling among papers on tables
or in drawers, in closets and in my clothes
which have seen their share of loss.
With hands that search for what is already lost, I caress your face,
and with hands afraid of loss I hold you close
and like a blind man feel my way around your eyes, your mouth,
wandering, wondering, wandering, wondering.
Because hands afraid of loss are the only hands for love.

Once I saw a violinist playing and I thought: Between
his right hand and his left—only the violin,
but what a between, what music!

8
Between the eve of the holiday and the final day
the holiday itself gets squeezed, between
longing for the past and longing for the future
the spirit is ground up as if by two heavy grindstones,
upper and lower. Between "In the East is my heart" and "I dwell
at the end of the West," the sea goes dry. Between the preventive
lament of before and the lament of after, joy shuts down.
Between hanging out flags for the holiday and folding them up again
the wind blows and sweeps everything away.
The song of the turtledove mourning is the song
of the turtledove wooing. With the same body
that stoops to pick up a fallen something from the floor,
I bow down to God. That is my faith, my religion.

9
Counting, counting, I hear them counting
as if out for the count at the end of the fight. When I was born
they counted to ten and they went on counting.
Now the referees and the crowd have gone home,
the lights in the arena are off, I got up long ago and headed
for my life, and they are still counting.
The pleasant evening breeze is only the towel

the trainer waves in my face, believing
I'll keep up the fight. Counting, counting I hear,
sometimes out loud, sometimes in a whisper
or in a woman's voice making love, sometimes counting
like taking inventory, taking a blood count or a pulse.
Sometimes a countdown or a count-up into the future,
in a solo voice or in unison, like a Greek chorus.
And they go on counting, deciphering ciphers before
my death and after it, counting
the spheres of the stars and the uppermost spheres,
those heights so high
the singing can have no end.

10

At times I think life is like a terrible accident,
a car rolling off the road down into the abyss, slow or fast.
I roll and reconcile,
reconcile and roll.

11

Life, I think, is a series of rehearsals
for the real show. In a rehearsal you can still
make changes, cut out a sentence, add a line of dialogue, switch
actors, directors, theaters—up until the real show.
Then there is no changing. And it makes no difference
that you can't make a difference:
The show closes right after opening night.

12

All the motions and the positions in my body—
it's already been done.
I sit on a chair and think like Rodin's Thinker.
Ever since I sat folded up in my mother's belly,
I have carried inside me the wisdom of the folding chair.
My arms are raised like Moses' arms when he raised the Tablets of
the Law,
my arms are raised without holding a thing,
a bit in disbelief, a bit in despair.

I give hugs like King David on the roof, or helpless hugs
like Jesus on the cross, but the palms of my hands
are free, I am free, though everything
has already come to pass. I have learned to swim
in the stream of consciousness, and I know a thing or two
about the difference between wire and wireless, God and
No-God, jet and chopper, a door
that opens and closes with a slam
and a revolving door that keeps revolving.

13
Now after many years of living I begin to see
that I rebelled only a little, and I do observe
all the laws and commandments.
I observe the law of gravity, that is, the law of the earth's attraction,
with all my body and with all my might and with all my love;
I observe the law of equilibrium and the law of the conservation
 of matter:
my body and my body, my soul and my soul, my body and my soul.
I abhor a vacuum in my pain and in my joy
I follow the law of water seeking its own level; past and future
are recycled back to me. I rise and I raise with the law of the lever.
I begin to understand, as I would with an old car,
what makes it work, the action of pistons and brakes,
reward and punishment, be fruitful and multiply,
forget and remember, bolts and springs,
fast and slow, and the laws of history.
Thus spake the years of my life unto the days of my life,
thus spake my soul unto the parts of my body.
This is a sermon in the synagogue, this is a eulogy
for the dead, this is burial and this
is resurrection. Thus spake the man.

David, King of Israel, Is Alive: Thou Art the Man

1

Lately I've been thinking a lot about King David.
Not the one who is alive forever in the song,
and not the one who is dead forever
under the heavy carpets on his tomb that is not really his tomb,
but the one who played and played for Saul
and kept dodging the spear until he became king.
David changed his tune and pretended to be mad to save
his life; as for me, I change my tune and pretend to be sane
to save my life. If he were alive today
he would tell me: No, it's the other way around.
Every nation had a first king once
like a first love. And the other way around.

2

King David loves Bathsheba,
hugs her tight, fondles her with the same hands
that cut off the head of Goliath,
the very same hands. The same man who rent his clothes
and scattered ashes on his head when his son died,
the very same man. When the sun
rose in the east, he rose up over Bathsheba
like the lion on the banner of Jerusalem
and said to her: Thou art the woman.
And she to him: Thou art the man!
Before long, he would hear the very same words
from the prophet: Thou art the man!

3

King David lies with Bathsheba on the rooftop,
they are heavy as a cloud and light as a cloud.
Her untamed black hair and the wild red hair of his beard
entangled. They have never seen each other's ears

441

and never will. He acts weak, weepy, lost, betrayed,
escapes into her body and hides inside it
as in the caves and crevices when he fled
from Saul. She counts his battle scars.
You will be mine, she says,
you will be a tower, a citadel, a city, a street, a hotel,
you will be names, names, and in the end
you will be a wadi for two lovers in the desert in 1965:
Nahal David in Ein Gedi.

4

King David took Bathsheba in the hours
between midnight and dawn.
Those are the best hours for a surprise attack
and the best time for making love.
He declared: "Thou art permitted unto me now—
as of this moment you are a widow, the battle is over
in Rabbah." In their bodies, David and Bathsheba
mimicked the death throes
of Uriah the Hittite in battle. Their cries carried
until Yom Kippur and up to our very own day;
the instruments of their love rang out like the bells of Bethlehem
where he was born. He took her from the west
the way his descendants turn east to pray.

6

King David loves many women. He has an ark of love
full of beautiful women, like a holy ark filled with Torah scrolls
brilliant in their beauty, crammed with commands and prohibitions
of Shalt and Shalt Not, weighted with ornaments,
round and sweet as Sephardi Torah scrolls,
heavy as Ashkenazi scrolls with their massive crowns,
dressed in silk and lace and soft velvet embroidered in many colors,
the breastplate hanging like a pendant, and the slender
hand-shaped pointers of silver inlaid with precious stones.
And on Simchat Torah, the Feast of the Law, which is
the Feast of Love, he takes them all out of the ark,
lines them up, kisses them one by one and hugs them,

makes seven rounds and dances with every one,
even with Michal and Merab who never in their lives
wanted him to dance. Then he puts them back
into the depths of the ark, closes the heavy curtain,
and sits down to write the psalms.

7

And all the women said, He loved me best of all,
but Abishag the Shunamite, the girl who came to him in his old age
to keep him warm, she is the only one who said:
I kept him warm, stroked his battle scars and his love scars,
I anointed him with oil, not for kingship but for cure.
I never heard him play or sing, but I wiped his mouth,
his toothless mouth, when I fed him sweet porridge.
I never saw his hands in battle but I kissed
his old white hands.

I am the poor man's ewe lamb, warm and full of compassion,
I came to him from the pasture
as he came from pasture to kingship.
I am the poor man's ewe lamb that rose out of the parable
and I am yours until death comes between us.

My Parents' Lodging Place

1

I passed the cemetery where my parents are buried—
in a poem Ibn Ezra called it "my parents' lodging place."
I didn't go in, just passed by on the road outside the wall.
I wave to my parents whenever I pass, my soul shaped like a hand.
My soul changes shape: sometimes it's my hair in the wind,
sometimes my aching feet as they walk
or my cheerful feet skipping, sometimes my eyes, my eyelids,
sometimes even my eyelashes—all these are my soul.
Peace to my parents, peace to their dust,
peace to their lodging place in Jerusalem.

2

In their great love my parents saved me from disappointment,
from pain and sorrow. Now I am left with their savings
plus the pain I would like to spare my children.
How all those savings have piled up on me!
My parents always told me, "I'll show you,"
sometimes threatening, sometimes in a voice of sweet love:
I'll show you. Just you wait, I'll show you.
"Someday you'll learn," sternly. "Someday you'll learn,"
in a soothing, reassuring voice.
"Do whatever you want," yelling and screaming,
and "Do what you want, you're a free person,"
like the good angels singing in chorus.
You don't know what you want,
you don't know what you want.

3

My mother was a prophet and didn't know it.
Not like Miriam the prophetess dancing with cymbals and
tambourines,

not like Deborah who sat under the palm tree and judged
 the people,
not like Hulda who foretold the future,
but my own private prophet, silent and stubborn.
I am obliged to fulfill everything she said
and I'm running out of lifetime.
My mother was a prophet when she taught me
the do's and don'ts of everyday, paper verses
for one-time use: You'll be sorry,
you'll get exhausted, that will do you good, you'll feel
like a new person, you'll really love it, you
won't be able, you won't like that, you'll never manage
to close it, I knew you wouldn't remember, wouldn't
forget give take rest, yes you can you can.
And when my mother died, all her little predictions came
 together
in one big prophecy that will last
until the vision of the end of days.

4
My father was God and didn't know it. He gave me
the Ten Commandments not in thunder and not in anger,
not in fire and not in a cloud, but gently
and with love. He added caresses and tender words,
"would you" and "please." And chanted "remember" and "keep"
with the same tune, and pleaded and wept quietly
between one commandment and the next: Thou shalt not
take the name of thy Lord in vain, shalt not take, not in vain,
please don't bear false witness against your neighbor.
And he hugged me tight and whispered in my ear,
Thou shalt not steal, shalt not commit adultery, shalt not kill.
And he lay the palms of his wide-open hands on my head
with the Yom Kippur blessing: Honor, love, that thy days
may be long upon this earth. And the voice of my father—
white as his hair. Then he turned his face to me one last time,
as on the day he died in my arms, and said, I would like to add
two more commandments:

the Eleventh Commandment, "Thou shalt not change,"
and the Twelfth Commandment, "Thou shalt change. You will
 change."
Thus spoke my father, and he turned and walked away
and disappeared into his strange distances.

What Has Always Been

1

The poet Rachel sang "Perhaps none of this has ever been."
I want to sing of what has always been,
what has truly been,
for what has been is what shall ever be, like the sun,
and the word "perhaps" is the moon that refines everything with its
 gentle light.
I want to sing of Russian shirts embroidered in the colors of love
and the colors of death, Russian shirts buttoned up or open at the
 throat
for easy breathing, for singing and hope.
Russian shirts like monarch butterflies or winged angels.
I want to sing for those who had the voice of Jacob
and the hands of Esau, the color of Jacob's eyes and Esau's smell of
 a field.
In the Valley of Jezreel, in the west, near the foothills of the
 Carmel,
I know some people. My cousin from the moshav
was a commanding officer there,
my cousin Asher, who with the pistol in his hand
killed the greatest enemy of his life, the cowardly
cancer that hid inside his body and died with him.

3

Now two generations of forgetting have passed
and the first generation of remembering has come. Woe to us
that we have already come to remember
because memories are the hard shell over an empty heart.
Soon people will walk about the fields and cities
and like nature lovers holding a Field Guide to Plants, they will
 hold
a Field Guide to Human Beings. And they will call out to one
 another:

447

Look, I found it, I wasn't mistaken, here are the distinguishing
 features,
the typical color of eyes and of hair, the characteristic smile, the
 scent
and the name, this one was a friend, a friend of a friend, that one
a woman from long ago, this one is father-shaped,
that one is me-shaped and you-shaped,
when are you in bloom when do you wither, this is the scientific
name, that's the common name among friends and lovers,
this is a name without a man, and this, a man without a name.
And that's the way it was.

4

East of the valley, facing Mount Gilboa,
I know that man Nahum who was our commander
in the battles for the distant Negev. The last time I saw him
he was still healthy, his voice quiet, measured, a voice accustomed
to bereavement, to whatever was and will be,
with a wink to Death in his intelligent eyes.
He sat facing me, and behind him Mount Gilboa.
There he sits, his back to the Gilboa. Mountain back
to mountain back. What has always been,
mountain and memory, "remember" and "keep" in one breath.
Decisions taken at night turned into garden flowers
and those not taken, into wildflowers down the mountainside.
But the Gilboa, but Nahum's mountain back.

5

In the waiting rooms of forgetting
landscapes on the wall turn slowly
into portraits, eyes and nose, forehead and chin,
even as portraits turn into landscapes,
mountain, valley, forest, field.

6

God is like a tour guide
describing our life and explaining to visitors
and tourists and the sons of God: That's how we live.

8

Evening. Between Gath and Galon, on a day of dust and heat,
a young woman walks in the place where we mustered once
for battle on that terrible hill. Between Gath and Galon, between
the harvest festivals of spring and fall,
in a harvested field. Hay and straw are also hallelujah gifts of God.
Joy cannot speak, joy sings from her mouth.
Her body is all seven species—wheat barley grapevine and fig
pomegranate olive and date, all seven species.
Her shorts are short and her legs long, and her face looks like
 our hopes
and her eyes are the color of our chances, and the color of sunset
 is like
the color of her new love. (And when was the last time
she cried?) The way she moves between past and future,
between it-was-good and it-may-yet-be, between doubt and certainty,
sways in her hips and thighs like a dance.
(And when will she cry again?) Peace to the doubt that propels
 our lives,
peace to the words that will not come back to our mouths,
words like migratory birds that have no Europe, no Africa,
only the Here with this young woman between Gath
and Galon. Here and now and in other days.

9

I went looking for the grave of a man called Menachem, whose name
means consolation, but he died in one place and was buried
in another, far from where he was born.
Years ago we two sat huddled in that dangerous trench,
packing dynamite—its odor nearly choked us,
its almond smell of spring and summer turned into the smell of death.
I went looking for the grave at his kibbutz among the streams of
 the Galilee.
Again I crossed that temporary bridge—each time a vehicle passed
it sounded like metal clanking. But now the bridge is permanent
and quiet, makes not a sound. The dead man, too,
is permanent and quiet. Only I, the living one, I am still
temporary, I make the sounds of life passing.

And with the consolation of his name, Menachem
took preventive measures against death.

10
I ask myself at what speed the force of things past
reaches me. At the speed of melting snows
that flow from Mount Hermon all the way down to the Dead Sea
or of a heavy slow stream of lava from an erupting volcano
or of stalactites dripping in a cavern.
I don't know. On my desk is a broken stone
with "Amen" carved on it, a stone from a Jewish grave of a thousand
 years ago.
It's on my desk now, weighing down papers so they won't fly away.
There it lies—a thing of beauty, a toy of history and fate.
On my desk is a fragment of a hand grenade
that didn't kill me, and there it is—free as a butterfly.

11
Flowing waters always try to teach us something.
Back then we didn't know what they were teaching, but we learned.
Near the water, wild birds in a bush.
Now they all have precise new names
but they go on flying and blossoming and being called
"pretty bird," "sweet-smelling bush." And decisions taken,
and those not taken, are flowing waters:
waters flowing from what has always been
to what will always be.

12
Nineteen forty-eight—that was the year.
Now everything is different here.

Israeli Travel: Otherness Is All, Otherness Is Love

1
The vineyard in ruins at Petach Tikvah, near the bus co-op
they called "United Fruit of the Land." The fruit was united
and the land was sweet when we were alive and young.
But now the vineyard is old and in ruins, like the vineyards of
 long ago
where they would tread the grapes to make wine,
and the vineyard wall is just a whitewashed wall for mourning
and forgetting. (Enchanted places are the opiates of my life.)
Nearby there was a big orchard that two of us entered.
The two of us. We came out two others:
he-other and she-other together,
he-lover and she-lover together. And I said to myself,
Otherness is all. Otherness is love.

2
Twilight in Ein HaShofet, "Wellspring of the Judge."
Is Hanan here? Is he still around?
No, he's not. He's gone. Someone else is here. Some other man.
But he was here with me, a scrawny fellow, tall, a chronic cougher,
and when someone coughs you don't say "Bless you!"—you say
 nothing at all.
And where is the wellspring? Dried up like the dead judge,
like Hanan's throat.
And now begins the fanfare about the great mistake.
Which mistake? About Hanan, the wellspring, the judge,
the mistake about sundown. The sun doesn't go down,
we do.

3
A night drive to Ein Yahav in the Arava Desert,
a drive in the rain. Yes, in the rain.
There I met people who grow date palms,

there I saw tamarisk trees and risk trees,
there I saw hope barbed as barbed wire.
And I said to myself: That's true, hope needs to be
like barbed wire to keep out despair,
hope must be a minefield.

8

A picture in color of plowman and horse from the turn
 of the century
in one of those early settlements in Palestine
hanging on the wall of a summer home in a land far across the sea.
And outside, a luxurious lawn
surrounded by flowers, and on the lawn an empty chair.
And I said to myself: Sit down in this chair, sit here and remember,
sit here and judge—if not, someone else will sit in this chair
to remember and judge. What took place an hour ago
had its place, and what took place on that farm at the turn
 of the century
had its place, and there were trees whose leaves blustered in the wind
and trees that stood by in silence. And the wind
the same wind. In the trees, the bluster and the silence.
And what was and what might have been are as if they never were.
But the wind is the same wind,
the chair is the same chair for remembering and judging,
and the plowman in the picture goes on plowing
what has always been, and sowing
what never will be.

9

I'm the chimp of chance, the champ of chance, I'm a chum
 of chance
and a chump of chance. When I took off my clothes at night
a coin slipped from my pants pocket onto the floor,
and I didn't know that ringing coin would determine
my fate, perhaps, and the course of my life.
I am the dice in a game of chance, my face up or
my face down. By the way I fall I determine
my own fate and the fate of others.

And I didn't know that my features and the lines on my face
would become a map for someone's travels, or for wars, perhaps,
long after my time.
And he? He won't know either.

10

I remember a problem in a math book
about a train that leaves from place A and another train
that leaves from place B. When will they meet?
No one ever asked what happens when they meet:
Will they stop, or pass each other, or collide?
None of the problems was about a man who leaves from place A
and a woman who leaves from place B. When will they meet,
will they meet at all, and for how long?
As for that math book: Now I've reached
the final pages with the answers.
Back then it was forbidden to look.
Now it is permitted. Now I check
where I was right and where I went wrong,
and know what I did well and what I did not do. Amen.

11

I passed by the school where I studied as a boy
and said in my heart: Here I learned certain things
and not others. All my life I have loved in vain
the things I didn't learn. I am filled with knowledge,
I am an expert on the botany of the tree of knowledge,
good and evil, I know all about its flowering,
the shape of its leaves, the function of its root system, its pests
 and parasites.
I am still studying good and evil, and will go on studying till the day
 I die.
I stood near the school building. This is the room
where we sat and studied. Classroom windows always open
to the future, but in our innocence we thought it was landscape
we were seeing through the window.
The schoolyard was narrow, paved with large stones.
I remember the brief tumult of the two of us

near the rickety steps, the tumult
that was the beginning of a first great love.
Now it outlives us, as if in a museum,
like everything else in Jerusalem.

12

People were always telling me: "You've got to live
in the real world." I heard it from parents and teachers.
To live in the real world, like a verdict. What terrible sin
could these souls have committed
that their lives in this world should begin with a verdict:
You are sentenced to reality for life.
With no possibility of parole.
The parole is death.

13

Here in this field, wild oats used to grow. Up above,
clouds like bags under the eyes of the sleepless,
the lust-weary. Millions of years from now,
heavy clouds and heavy bags under the eyes
will be one and the same.
The poet of the psalms said: "The dead praise not the Lord,"
but I say only the dead praise the Lord.
What have we gained? The known becomes the unknown,
and the unknown is known,
a barter economy that has no end. Human beings
disseminating seed with their shoes as they walk,
playing the role of the wind, of the birds and the bees,
without knowing it. So what have we gained?
The psalms of thanksgiving and praise.

14

In Kfar Blum, between the hills of Golan and the hills of Galilee,
my friend told me: "These hills once were seashore,
we are standing on what once was the floor of the sea."
What does that require of us? To be quieter,
more transparent, to turn inward like fossil shells,
to be light and floating as seaweed.

Then we came to Menachemiya, "God Consoles,"
which lived up to its name and consoled us.
We spoke softly, like the soft hills this spring
near the quiet Jordan, under the sign "No One's Here."
Then we headed south. That waterfall on the Jordan River
soothes as it falls. Unlike a human being.
I thought about the power of dammed-up water
and the power of water falling in a torrent,
the power of weeping and the power of restraint,
the power of a woman's hair pulled back like a dancer's
and the power of a woman's hair bursting free and open like
 a dancer's.
I thought about it all, and when I got home,
I told my children.

15
Yad Mordechai. Those who fell here
still look out the windows like sick children
who are not allowed outside to play.
And on the hillside, the battle is reenacted
for the benefit of hikers and tourists. Soldiers of thin sheet iron
rise and fall and rise again. The sheet iron dead and those sheet
 iron lives,
their voices all—sheet iron. And the resurrection of the dead,
sheet iron that clangs and clangs.

And I said to myself: Everyone is attached to his own lament
as to a parachute. Slowly he descends and slowly hovers
till he touches the hard place.

16
The ancient aqueduct in the Western Galilee and I
do one and the same thing: conduct and convey that which
 is not ours
from one place to another. Thus pass the waters, thus the days,
thus my soul. Thus the road paved blue where those who go
toward their future walk together with those who go toward
 their past,

that too is a conducting and a conveying without beginning,
 without end.
Like God. But back near Gesher Haziv, between the road
and the abandoned railway tracks, which also conduct longings,
stand headstones in a closed circle
that turns, turns on its circuits, in memory of the Palmach boys
who were killed here. They were taken straight from basic training
to blow up the bridge. And they returned to their military
 maneuvers
deep in the ground in the training of the dead for the resurrection.

17

I returned to Bat Gallim, on the outskirts of Haifa. Years ago
I visited that neighborhood; now I don't know a soul there.
A death notice with its black border was posted on the wall:
name of dead man and time of funeral—
gone, like him. I saw a notice about the same
dead man on the wall of a kiosk and the trunk of a eucalyptus
I remembered from that time. (The tree itself has forgotten
its homeland, Australia.) By now I am quite familiar with
the dead man's name and the name of his wife and children,
his workplace that sends condolences, and his burial place.
If I linger another day or two in Bat Gallim,
I'll discover that we're related, I'll become
someone else. And then I passed the crumbling casino,
its pleasures scattered, love affairs grown old.
And the swimming pool—such young archaeology—
its plaster like dried-up tears, and cracked like lips.
I went on down to the harbor, thinking: I'm a lucky man—
I will never have to set sail again.

Evening Promenade on Valley of the Ghosts Street

1

Evening promenade on Valley of the Ghosts Street, German Colony.
Weariness gives way to the pomp of parading
up and down the street—a ritual, almost. The music I hear
from a house I don't know is inside me now
and words not intended for me are the winds I ride
for the rest of my journey, like a sailboat.
In this house, here, my good friend once lived.
Now he's no longer my friend. We grew apart, distant
beyond recognition, like a landscape
that flattens into a map. But the house is still standing
and the door is the same door that opened for me, then closed.
That's how, with some trepidation, a new religion takes shape.
And in this Jerusalem of ours they quickly shush it up,
as adults do when a child speaks among them unawares.

2

People waiting for someone begin to resemble
those who are not waiting anymore. Silence
covers them all. Despair is a lullaby.
And while they are sleeping at night, God violates
the ban of Rabbi Gershom and opens
their souls to read what is written there,
like a letter. In the morning God tucks the letter back in
and licks the envelope shut.
They will never know He has read every word because
He seals the envelope with an artist's hand,
like the military censor.

3

Here is Hulda's house that knew nights of revelry.
The sound of music playing, feet dancing, mouths filled with song.
All those sounds poured out the windows into the quiet night

and swirled around the windowsills
like a river pouring into a great black sea.
In the corners of the rooms, people stood
and jotted down names, addresses, telephone numbers for each other
on memo pads and memorial pads.
They didn't know that what they were writing
was like numbers and names and places carved
onto gravestones, never to be erased. Never to see each other again.
On the door a sign said "Welcome"
in glorious color. It would never say
"Farewell." For how well would they ever fare?

4
The dancers and the danced have all gone now,
the photographers along with the photographed.
The cameras are hidden away in the gloom of closets
and rolls of undeveloped film will remain forever
in the darkrooms of the world. The last to leave
greet the first to pray at dawn—some at the synagogue,
others at the prayer houses of remembering and forgetting.
They have all gone on to their better worlds, not only the dead.
A few remain standing at the crossroads of empty streets
like windsocks at the airport. But each one
is blown a different way, each in the direction of his flight
by his own wind, his own spirit.
Who could have known back then? They were all going
on the same flight, they thought—one way, one destination.

5
Hulda's house still stands in the same place.
But the sounds of holiday parties have since drifted up
and were lost in the heavenly heights, like holy men in Jerusalem
who ascended on high, promised a second coming and never came.
The welcome sign on the door yellows and darkens like autumn
 leaves.
Names keep changing, names and souls that once were one.
People bound by a pledge or a solemn vow
are bound no longer, and the pledges and vows are free now

to look for new pledgers and vowers.
As for truth and lies, in time
even an old lie yellows and fades like an ancient relic
and looks more reliable than a shiny new truth
with its wet paint.

6
Hulda's house knew plenty in its day and forgot plenty.
To the east, the power station, now without power,
its engines quiet as people, and to the south
the stately convent of silent nuns
not far from the railroad tracks.
Once a day the train still passes, like a conjured spirit.

Summer and the Far End of Prophecy

1

It's summer again at Akhziv Beach and
here we are again. We know how much is required of us
who are heavier than air, heavier than water.
And how much is asked of the birds: They must sing
courtship songs for the silent fish too, and what a burden on beasts
who must roar out the joy of human couples
in one another's arms. And how much is expected of two people
like us, who in their loving must keep and preserve
those who have never been together
or are now apart.

3

Through the window that is not there, we see our children
searching the old ruin for toys they lost yesterday
and turning up broken clay jars from centuries ago.
The chasm between generations fills up with dust and sand,
human bones, animal bones, a multitude of broken vessels.
Broken jars speak the truth. A new jar is the lie of beauty.

5

Twilight sobs down the side of the gray house
and is consoled. The olive trees show each other
the color of their leaves, green and silver, that's all they have.
A wind comes up from the sea and blows through the empty chairs,
turns, turns, doesn't whirl about but blows from one there to another.
"So help us God"—He will help us, help us to more of
the good and the bad, the light and the dark.
The sun changes colors at sunset, like someone
shifting from one language to another, or from song
to speech and from speech to murmurs, then whispers, then silence.
And from the distance, like the sound of a ping-pong game:
belief in one God and blasphemy rally with each other.

6

Two lie together in love on one air mattress
they have inflated together with their own breath. Amen.

7

Oh, the calendar's blank prophecy on the first of the year.
Oh, the memory of beach chairs folded and stacked
in winter, shackled together with an iron chain
like galley slaves in ancient days. Slaves of memory.
Swimmers' strokes preserve the memory of swimming
and of last summer too, of all the summers that were,
swimmers' strokes proceed from love
and unto love they shall return. Oh, the great prophecy
of what is past or what is yet to come.
And there, at the far end of prophecy,
a swimsuit spread out to dry.

8

On the way back to Jerusalem we stopped at Aqua Bella,
the valley of beautiful waters. We sat in the shade of a Crusader
 fortress,
but it was not a fortress, it was a convent
whose nuns donated their love to us. How can we rest
with this burden weighing on our love?
The flowers near the water are pledges and vows
that grace our lives with their colors
and their desperate perfume. And in the rush of the beautiful waters
the vows come undone, undone, undone.

9

And how we loved in the Forest of Remembrance for the Shoah dead,
but remembered only ourselves from the night before.
The forest remembered for us and let us love.
You remember how we took off our clothes in our deranged desire;
the upperwear flew like heavy birds to the branches of the trees
and the netherwear remained on the forest floor
and got caught in the thorny brushwood like snakeskins.
And our shoes nearby, their mouths gaping in a psalm of praise.

10

The memorial forest where we made love
burned down in a great conflagration

but the two of us stayed alive and in love
in memory of the burnt forest
and in memory of the burnt ones the forest remembered.

Houses (Plural); Love (Singular)

1
Sheltered by good news,
sheltered even by the bad, now we are at home.
But we remain as we were then, before we had a home,
when we were in the wadis of Ein Gedi. We are still
like those wadis, you the Rejeh, I the Sideir, even now,
sheltered in our home in Jerusalem. At our door
the two eunuchs, Time and Fate, stand guard,
and the mezuzah on our doorpost says:
And thou, man, shalt love;
and thou, woman, shalt love.

2
We lived in many houses and left remnants of memory
in every one of them: a newspaper, a book facedown, a
 crumpled map
of some faraway land, a forgotten toothbrush standing sentinel
 in a cup—
that too is a memorial candle, an eternal light.

3
And in those days before we made a home for ourselves,
we made the whole country into homes.
Even the beach at Caesarea
where we piled our clothes onto a solemn mound,
sandals and shirts and towels and pants, yours and mine,
jumbled together, like us, and then went into the water.
I said to myself: If we'd lived in ancient times and made love
in the mountains or the desert, we'd have piled stone on stone
and called upon the name of the Lord and gone on our way,
but we made love by the sea, our clothes
a mound of witness in the sand,
and we called upon the name of our love.

Passersby thought we might have drowned in the sea.
But we did not drown in the sea, we drowned in all the years
after that chapter, still wrapped up
in each other, like our clothes on that mound on the shore.

4

We lived in the Valley of Gehenna in no man's land in the divided
 Jerusalem.
Our roof was hit, our walls wounded by bullets and shrapnel.
We propped up the broken leg of the bed with a pile of books.
(I don't know if we ever read them again.) The stone steps
were like the ladder the angels left behind when they fled
Jacob's dream, a ladder for us to climb up and down.
In Hebrew, no man's land is called "the zone of abandon."
When we lived there, we were a man and a woman earnest
 in our loving,
we were not abandoned. And if we have not died, we are loving still.

5

And if we have died, we will be first in line at the resurrection
that Ezekiel prophesied in his vision:
bones coming together, bone to bone, skin over flesh and sinew—
Ezekiel didn't go into detail. But the two of us continued his vision:
hips for hugging, soft inner thighs for stroking, twin buttocks, upper
and nether hair, eyes to open and close, lips chiseled, the tongue
 precise.
And we fleshed out his vision even further:
two people talking, a summer dress, underwear hung out to dry, a
 windowsill.
We will be ourselves, we will be ebb and flow, changing weathers,
seasons of the year, we will go on being,
we will go on and on.

7

And how will they use our love. How will they copy the line of
 your thighs
and the line of my arm on their maps to mark boundaries between
 lands

we didn't know existed. How the color of your eyes and the color
 of my eyes
will coexist in the flags of new nations in the future of the world.
And the words we spoke to one another at night will serve as secret
 documents
and proclamations of independence and treaties of surrender and
 victory.
How they will use us! From our positions of loving
they will invent newfangled sophisticated machinery for the coming
 century,
and from our movements of loving, someone may map out a great
military action, hug-and-embrace, grasp-and-pincers, rocket
 trajectories.
And from the lulls in our loving they will calculate the Apocalypse
and visions of a calm happy End of Days
in eternal stillness and everlasting love.

8
"Thy breasts are fashioned and thine hair is grown, whereas thou
 wast naked and bare,"
thus shouted the prophet Ezekiel thousands of years ago,
thus shouted an epileptic drunk in the fury of his lust.
He thought you were a parable and didn't know that he was
 prophesying you for my sake
now. "Thy breasts are fashioned and thine hair is grown," almost
 an agricultural prophecy,
fields readied for sowing, for growing and ripening of grain.
"Whereas thou wast naked and bare": thus years ago,
but now prepared for this life, in our time.
No longer black pantyhose ripped in lust,
but dressed in a serious striped suit, white stripes on black,
over pantyhose pulled taut.
But under all these, you remained naked and bare and wild
as you were back then, in the little house near the Valley of the
 Cross,
just as the prophet, in the desperation of his love, prophesied you
 and didn't know it.

9

We divided the language between us: you took the vowels
and I the consonants, and together we were of one language
and many words. Listen, man, listen, woman:
our life is one, of deaths there are many, and gods not a few,
our life is one and our love is one.

10

About a dead man they say, he went to his world,
and we are alive and we went, you to my world
and I to yours. Over a dead man they say Kaddish
and we say Kaddish every day, Kaddish in its capacity as
thanksgiving and praise and joy and strength and a song of love.
For the dead praise not the Lord.
Kaddish like the Kiddushin of betrothal. Behold, man, thou art;
 behold, woman, thou art:
behold us, behold the world, behold our world.

The Language of Love and
Tea with Roasted Almonds

1

Layla, night, the most feminine of all things, is masculine
in Hebrew, but it is also the name of a woman.
Sun is masculine and sunset feminine,
the memory of the masculine in the feminine, and the yearning
of a woman in a man. That is to say: the two of us, that is to say: we.
And why is *Elohim,* God, in the plural? Because All of Him
are sitting in the shade under a canopy of vines in Akko,
playing cards. And we sat at a table nearby and I held your hand
and you held mine instead of cards, and we too
were masculine and feminine, plural and singular,
and we drank tea with roasted almonds, two tastes
that didn't know each other and became one in our mouth.
And over the café door, next to the sky, it said:
"Not Responsible for Items Forgotten or Lost."

2

Near the cemetery you always find stonecutters and gardeners.
Near the courthouse, lawyers' offices and phone booths.
Near hope, plenty of despair, and around the train station, hotels.
And in the neighborhood of love, words like "I love you,"
"I love you too," more binding than any marriage vow.
It's not enough to say "Behold, thou art fair, my love,"
you have to say "I love" seven times,
just as you say "The Lord is God" seven times
in the prayer of Closing the Gates on Yom Kippur
and when the gates of life are closing.
And there's all that talk about Till death do us part,
Even death will not part us, it will bind us
somewhere in the universe
in a new encounter that has no end.

3

Lovers leave fingerprints on each other,
plenty of physical evidence, words without end, testimonies, a wrinkled
pair of pants, a newspaper with the exact date, and two watches, his and hers.
Every morning they trace each other's contours
the way the police mark the location of the body on the road
with chalk. Lovers surrender each other,
lovers reserve the right to remain silent.
If and when they are separated,
they compose a police sketch of their faces and a lineup
so they can say: He's the one! She's the one!

5

I know a man who assembled an ideal woman
from all his desires: the hair he took
from a woman in the window of a passing bus,
the forehead from a cousin who died young, the hands
from a teacher he had as a boy, the cheeks from a little girl,
his childhood love, the mouth from a woman he noticed
in a phone booth, the thighs from a woman lying on the beach,
the alluring gaze from this one, the eyes from that one,
the waistline from a newspaper ad. From all these he assembled
a woman he truly loved. And when he died, they came,
all the women—legs chopped off, eyes plucked out, faces slashed in half,
hands severed, hair ripped out, a gash where a mouth used to be,
and demanded what was theirs, theirs, theirs,
dismembered his body, tore his flesh, and left him
only his misbegotten soul.

6

Now they will begin to tell the things we've done together
and the places we've been, as compared with the places
we haven't, the things we have not done and will never do.
A two-part harmony will accompany us
like two different choirs on each side of our lives,

or like the two camps that assembled—one on the Mount
 of Blessings
and one on the Mount of Curses. Sometimes even
in a quiet conversation between two people at the next table,
or in the way names and times and places are announced at
 the airport.
And sometimes the voices are within us
like a confession: Yes, we were, yes, we did,
yes, we lingered for a while, no, we were not, we did not.
Like a confession trilled out on Yom Kippur. And that
is all of eternity that we shall know.

7

Like the fowl of the air and the beasts of the field, that's how I want
to love you. That's how I want you to love me.
What in the Bible was an accursed unhappy ending, for us was love.
"Devoured, devoured was he," Jacob howled when they brought him
the coat of his son Joseph, torn and dripping blood.
"An evil beast hath devoured him"—and all for love, all for love!

8

Imagine that when you and I are driving in this car,
the entire factory rides along: engineers
and workers, the assembly line, the noise of the machines,
oil wells down in their depths, geologic faults,
even the formation of planet earth.
Now that's the way to love!

9

The way a photographer, when he sets up
a shot of sea or desert out to the edge of the horizon,
has to get something large and close up into the picture—
a branch, a chair, a boulder, the corner of a house,
to get a sense of the infinite, and he forgets about the sea
and the desert—that's how I love you, your hand,
your face, your hair, your nearby voice,
and I forget the everlasting distance and the endless endings.
And when we die, again there will be only sea and desert

and the God we so loved to look at from the window.
Peace, peace to the far and the near, to the true Gods, peace.

10
Thus have lovers preeminence above all others:
others may say "Take my place"
but lovers actually keep their word.
Now I am in your place, and you in mine. You are me, I am you.
Everything has changed; nothing has changed. Only the places.
The others. Sometimes people argue "You're
just using me," "you're taking advantage."
But lovers say the very same words with joy, with passion:
"I want it, take advantage of me," "I
want it too—use me
up."

11
In the faint light on the balcony of an old house in Barcelona
one summer night, I saw a man and a woman.
In the room behind them, a white bed shining in the bright light.
Downstairs, their names in the dark, near the gate, like mezuzahs,
and ancient names whispered over their sleek taut skin, like a breeze.

12
Every woman in love has the face of the Virgin Mary, mother of
 Jesus,
in the pietàs. She remembers what happened to another woman
in another time, she remembers even what has not
happened yet, the future already belongs
to her memory. Pain and joy yoked together.
She knows about the death of the dead man as he lies in her arms,
and she knows about the resurrection of the dead in her arms.
She too is the precision of pain and the blurriness of joy.

13
What shall we do with the wonderfully sly story
of David and Jonathan? "Behold, the arrows are beyond thee,"
said Jonathan. But where? Over there,

there, a bit to the left. But where exactly? As in a children's game:
cold, colder, getting warm, warmer, hot, right there.
What shall we do with that old story now, in our own day?
One generation handed it down to the next in the synagogue
 reading
on the Sabbath before the new moon—"Tomorrow is the feast
of the new moon," said Jonathan. Handed it down like a beautiful
sad glass dome with David and Jonathan inside
till it fell from empty hands and shattered.
Ours is the age of the mender, the healer and the restorer,
but it is the two of us, you and I,
who will fill in the missing pieces when we love.

14

Every woman in love is like our mother Sarah,
lying in wait behind the door while the men inside
discuss the beauty of her body and her future.
She laughs into her palm, her hollow palm, as into a womb,
ocarina of a future, like the light cough of a clever fox.
Every woman making love is Rachel and Leah trading off
body and soul between them, seasons and dresses, kohl
 and perfumes,
the tastes of day flavored with the spices of night,
night stirrings with day sounds, thighs and breasts, to become
 one body,
Rachel and Leah, Racheleah. It's as if Jacob were in bed with
 two women,
one stormy and fiery, knowing she will die soon in childbirth,
the other placid and soft and heavy, down the generations
till me. And the face of every woman when she's loving
is like the face of the moon in its cycle,
full-face in the door as it opens and half-face by the window.
And every loving woman is like Rebecca at the well, saying
"Drink, and thy camels also." But in our day Rebecca says:
"The towels are on the top shelf in the white closet
across from the front door."

The Precision of Pain and the Blurriness of Joy:
The Touch of Longing Is Everywhere

1

I sit in my friends' garden on a chair made of hollow
bamboo reeds. Other reeds were turned into flutes to be played
in other places. I sit at ease, I sit shiva for time lost
and time that will be lost, and my heart is calm and quiet.
The spirits of the dead visit me in the light of day
and the spirits of the living haunt my nights.
I sit on a chair made of bamboo reeds
that wanted to be flutes, just as the flutes would have liked
to be calm and quiet in a chair. I think about bamboo reeds
that grow near the water. There's longing everywhere.
The precision of pain and the blurriness of joy.

2

On my desk there is a stone with the word "Amen" on it,
a triangular fragment of stone from a Jewish graveyard destroyed
many generations ago. The other fragments, hundreds upon
 hundreds,
were scattered helter-skelter, and a great yearning,
a longing without end, fills them all:
first name in search of family name, date of death seeks
dead man's birthplace, son's name wishes to locate
name of father, date of birth seeks reunion with soul
that wishes to rest in peace. And until they have found
one another, they will not find perfect rest.
Only this stone lies calmly on my desk and says "Amen."
But now the fragments are gathered up in loving-kindness
by a sad good man. He cleanses them of every blemish,
photographs them one by one, arranges them on the floor
in the great hall, makes each gravestone whole again,
one again: fragment to fragment,
like the resurrection of the dead, a mosaic,
a jigsaw puzzle. Child's play.

3

In my garden I saw jasmine blossoms carried by the autumn wind,
clinging to the bougainvillea. Oh, what a mistake, what a waste,
what a loss to no end. I saw a sun setting in the sea,
I saw God, what a mistake, what a hope!
I saw two birds caught in the lofty halls
of an airport. In despair they flew over the chaos below.
Oh, what a mistake, what a flight, what a desperate love,
what a way out without an out, what a vision of the Shekhinah's
 wings!
And high up, above it all, a plane is circling. I'm trying, it says,
I'm trying again. Try, they tell it
from the control tower. Try again, try again.

4

Each year the melons are sweeter than the year before.
Is it forgetting last summer that makes me say this
or some great weariness? When a voice gets worn out
it grows sweeter. Even hoarseness is like white sugar,
and seedless melons are the sweetest of all.
"Let not the eunuch say, Behold, I am a dry tree"—thus
 the prophet,
long ago, consoled those who have no offspring
and never will. Even seed spilled on the ground
may one day sow a human being.
Comfort ye, comfort ye, Er and Onan, you will be resurrected yet.

5

I saw a yellowing photo of Jaffa, from the time
before I was born, and in the photo a tower
and on the tower a clock, and on the clock: quarter to six.
The tower was precise and the time precise.
O, dirges of the hours, weep ye for all the seven o'clocks that will
 not return,
grieve for the lost half past twos, woe for the six o'clocks
that were gathered unto the hours in their prime,
in my prime, a bitter wailing for all the hours that have passed away,
an elegy for the good times, a hallelujah howling for the bad.

Mourn ye quarter to six. Mourn quarter past six. Even half hours
and quarter hours will find perfect rest
in the ascension of ordained times and memorials
under the wings of forgetting.

6
To erect a monument in the wrong place, like the Tomb of Rachel,
to call someone by the wrong name, to say words that were not
 meant
to miss or to hit, to move things from one spot to another,
stones from the quarry to the construction site,
to pump water into pipes, to surprise, to change—
these are the true longings.
When a window curtain wants to be a flag outside,
when the past wants to be the future,
when tears yearn not for laughter, nor for the eyes
that wept them, nor for the cheeks they wet,
but for the sea, for the salt in the sea—these are the true longings.

7
At a pay phone, I saw a woman making a call,
and crouching at her feet, a large musical instrument in a black case,
 like a dog.

8
I think about the joy of clothing in the store window
that no one has bought, and the joy
of furniture that has not been sold,
but I also think about the sadness of the clothes and the furniture
and about their longing to be inside rooms with human beings
to sense the warmth of their bodies.

9
We remember the past
and God remembers the future.
Then we forget the past,
God forgets the future,
and the world returns to chaos.

10

Sometimes my soul wants to get out of my body for a little run,
like a dog, and return calmer to the body. But it worries
that it won't find the way back.

12

Godforsaken people meet godforsaking people;
people who forsake their childhood love those who remember.
Both have straps of every kind on their clothing, straps fastened tight
to support them and their souls on their journeys.

13

I saw a man reading about a place in a tourist travel book,
and all the while he was sitting in that very place. Then he closed
 the book
and went off to some other place.

14

King Saul fell upon his sword in the last battle on Mount Gilboa
and died at once. So too we fall upon
our sharp-edged souls when we are born,
but we die only seventy or eighty years later.
All those years, life writhes within us, every motion
and emotion pierces deep, but we grow used to the pain.
Sometimes we call it feeling alive, even joy.
The soul that quickens us kills us in the end
and lodges there, like the sword.

15

When the sun sets in the west, the hope of the night rises red in me.
So too, with the security of a seesaw, we tell about the things we did,
the places we saw. Even wars and loves
steady us and give us that seesaw security, the up-down
of whatever was.

16

In a Jerusalem courtyard I saw seeds
spread on a cloth to dry in the sun, and I said:

Let me be their historian and tell them about the watermelons
and pumpkins they came from. I insist that the sand
remember the stone, that the stone remember the great rock
and the rock—the lava and the fire.
And I myself forget what took place last summer,
even what took place yesterday, which happened to be
a Wednesday. But I remember
the psalm the Levites would sing each week
in the Temple on Wednesday.

17

Ga'agu'im, longings, are masculine plural in Hebrew, like
 Elohim, God.
Erga and *kmiha*, yearning, are both feminine, a woman with no
 memory of the masculine.
I saw a man slip a letter under a locked door,
saw him pass by on the following day and the letter was still
a white strip shining under the door. And I saw him return
once more, twice more, and the white strip still
peeping out like a white strip of underwear of the woman he loved.
The touch of longings is everywhere. The grass growing beside
 the door
is perhaps a prophet of destruction, perhaps a prophet of consolation.
And the word "longings" comes from the long lowing of the heifer's
 tongue
that gave its long lowing voice to human beings.

18

Longings are the fruit.
Words and deeds that truly happen
are the flowers of the field that wither and fade.
The fruit remains a while longer, bearing the seeds of longings
 to come.
The root lasts, deep in the ground.

19

And all the while messengers keep running back and forth
to my childhood to retrieve what I forgot or left behind

as if from a house that is about to be demolished,
or like Robinson Crusoe, from the slowly sinking ship
to the island—so I salvage from my childhood provisions and
 memories
for the next installment of my life.

20

The precision of pain and the blurriness of joy. I'm thinking
how precise people are when they describe their pain in a doctor's
 office.
Even those who haven't learned to read and write are precise:
"This one's a throbbing pain, that one's a wrenching pain,
this one gnaws, that one burns, this is a sharp pain
and that—a dull one. Right here. Precisely here,
yes, yes." Joy blurs everything. I've heard people say
after nights of love and feasting, "It was great,
I was in seventh heaven." Even the spaceman who floated
in outer space, tethered to a spaceship, could say only, "Great,
wonderful, I have no words."
The blurriness of joy and the precision of pain—
I want to describe, with a sharp pain's precision, happiness
and blurry joy. I learned to speak among the pains.

In My Life, on My Life

1

All my life I played chess with myself and with others
and the days of my life were chess pieces, good and bad—I and me,
I and he, war and love, hope and despair,
black pieces and white. Now they're all jumbled together,
colorless, and the chessboard has no squares,
it's a smooth surface blending into night and into day.
The game is calm and has no end, no winners,
no losers, the hollow rules
clang in the wind. I listen. And I am quiet.
In my life and in my death.

2

When I was a boy I said the bedtime prayer
every night. I remember the verse
"The angel who delivers me from all danger."
I never prayed after that, not on my bed,
not in the hills, not in war, not by day and not by night,
but the delivering angel stayed by my side and became
a loving angel. That loving angel will turn into the Angel of Death
when the hour comes, but it is always the same angel
who delivers me from all danger.

3

I always have to revisit the sands of Ashdod
where I had a little bit of courage in that battle, that war,
soft hero in the soft sand. My few scraps of heroism I squandered
 then,
that's why I always revisit the sands of Ashdod. Now they've become
vacation sands—swimmers, children at play,
warning flags, a lifeguard. In those days
there were no warning flags, no guard, no one to save us.

5

I always have to revisit the ticklings of my childhood,
the ticklings I used to get from my aunts back when it was
an act of grace, true grace. For the sheer joy of living.
Since then, tickling has become a serious business, no longer
the ringing
laughter of a child: a tickle verging on pain, new skin healing
the breach
between good and evil, a tickle of wild passion and resurrection.
Sometimes I send my hand all the way up to my scalp to scratch
like a rocket launched into light-years of space—my head at the edge
of the galaxy.
Sometimes in the morning I rub my eyes lightly, toward my nose,
toward the soothing, saving work of memory.
That motion conjures spirits from the magic-trick-bag
of the body, the generations of tickles. And best of all,
that sensation when my thigh grows indifferent and goes to sleep,
then suddenly jerks awake with a million exquisite pins and needles.
Thus a new religion begins after an age of apathy:
out of the blue a new tickle, a new faith. Amen selah.

6

I know how slight are the threads that tie me to my joy
but from those slight threads I have woven strong clothing,
a kind of soft armor, the warp and weft of joy
to help me cover my nakedness and protect me.
But sometimes it seems to me my life isn't worth
the skin of my body that wraps around it, not even
these fingernails with which I hang on to my life.
I am like a man who holds his wrist up
to catch a glimpse of Time, even when he isn't wearing a watch.
And sometimes the gurgling of the last waters
draining from the bathtub
is a nightingale's song to my ear.

7

The world is filled with remembering and forgetting
like sea and dry land. Sometimes memory

is the solid ground we stand on,
sometimes memory is the sea that covers all things
like the Flood. And forgetting is the dry land that saves, like Ararat.

8

I want my brain not to be inside my head
but in some other part of my body—my feet, my belly,
my buttocks, an intense little cerebellum in my navel.
Or even outside my body—let my brain be a hollow
scooped in the sand, where donkeys, dogs and children
roll around, tumble and squeal with delight.
On my life, I swear it: that's what I want in my life, on my life!

9

And every person is a dam between past and future.
When he dies the dam bursts, the past breaks into the future,
and there is no before or after. All time becomes one time
like our God: our Time is One.
Blessed be the memory of the dam.

10

Life is called life as the west wind is called
west, though it blows toward the east.
The way death is called death, though it blows toward life.
In a cemetery we remember the living, and outside it—
the dead. As the past leads to the future
though it's called past, as you to me and I to you in love
though I'm called by my name and you by yours.
As spring provides for summer, as summer beds down into fall.
As my thoughts will be till the end of my life. That is the banner of
 my God.

11

When a man dies, they say "He was gathered unto his fathers."
As long as he is alive, his fathers are gathered within him,
each cell of his body and soul a delegate from one of his
thousands of fathers since the beginning of time.

12

Each day now I hear the circles of my life closing,
the click of buckles, like kisses
of conciliation and love. And these lend a rhythm
to the latest version of my life. Things that were lost long ago
find their places now, like billiard balls, each one into its pocket.
Contracts and prophecies are fulfilled, prophecies true and false.
I come upon the missing lids of pots and pans that stayed uncovered,
I find the matching pieces, like an ancient contract of clay
broken into two parts, unequal but fitting together.
Like a mosaic, like a jigsaw puzzle, children searching
for the missing pieces. When the game is over,
the picture will be whole. Complete.

13

I, may I rest in peace—I, who am still living, say,
May I have peace in the rest of my life.
I want peace right now while I'm still alive.
I don't want to wait like that pious man who wished for one leg
of the golden chair of Paradise, I want a four-legged chair
right here, a plain wooden chair. I want the rest of my peace now.
I have lived out my life in wars of every kind: battles without
and within, close combat, face-to-face, the faces always
my own, my lover-face, my enemy-face.
Wars with the old weapons—sticks and stones, blunt axe, words,
dull ripping knife, love and hate,
and wars with newfangled weapons—machine gun, missile,
words, land mines exploding, love and hate.
I don't want to fulfill my parents' prophecy that life is war.
I want peace with all my body and all my soul.
Rest me in peace.

14

When I die, I want only women to handle me in the Chevra Kadisha
and to do with my body as they please: cleanse my ears of the last
words I heard, wipe my lips of the last words I said,
erase the sights I saw from my eyes, smooth my brow of worries

and fold my arms across my chest like the sleeves of a shirt after
 ironing.
Let them salve my flesh with perfumed oil to anoint me King
 of Death
for a day, and arrange in my pelvic basin as in a fruit bowl
testes and penis, navel and frizzy hair—like an ornate still life
from some past century, a very still life on a ground of dark velvet,
and then with a feather tickle my mouth-hole and asshole to check
if I'm still alive. Let them laugh and cry by turns
and administer a last massage that passes from their hands
 through me
to the entire world till the End of Days.
And one of them will sing God Full of Mercy,
will sing in a sweet voice God Full of Womb,
to remind God that mercy is born of the womb, true mercy,
true womb, true love, true grace. On my life, I swear it,
that's what I want in my death, in my life.

Jewish Travel: Change Is God and
Death Is His Prophet

1

Jewish travel. As it is written, "I will lift up mine eyes unto the hills,
from whence cometh my help": not a hike to see a tall mountain in
 all its glory,
nor a climb to rejoice in the vistas of Nature,
but a hike with a purpose, to seek help from the high heavens.
And how to interpret "I will lift up mine eyes"? Heavy Jewish eyes
that need lifting. And it is written, "Who shall ascend the mountain
 of the Lord?"
Not hikers singing, knapsacks on their shoulders, but rather
a congregation praying with "clean hands and a pure heart,"
not strong bodies and sturdy legs. And fertile valleys
are simply good places for prayer: as it says, "Out of the depths
have I cried unto thee, O Lord." Even "green pastures"
and "still waters" are not about resting and eating in the shade
 of a tree
or camping near a stream in the scorch of summer,
but about praising the Lord, since right after that it says
"the Valley of the Shadow of Death"—
the shadow of death overshadows everything. Jewish travel.
Even Moses climbed Mount Sinai not as mountaineers do,
but to receive the Tablets of the Law. And he went up Mount Nebo
not to come down again but to die.

2

Yehuda Halevi wrote, "In the East is my heart, and I dwell at the
 end of the West."
That's Jewish travel, that's the Jewish game of hearts between east
 and west,
between self and heart, to and fro, to without fro, fro without to,
fugitive and vagabond without sin. An endless journey, like the trip
Freud the Jew took, wandering between body and mind, between
mind and mind, only to die between the two.

Oh, what a world this is, where the heart is in one place and the body
in another (almost like a heart torn from a body and transplanted).
I think about people who are named for a place where they have
 never been
and will never be. Or about an artist who draws a man's face
from a photograph because the man is gone. Or about the migration
 of Jews,
who do not follow summer and winter, life and death
as birds do, but instead obey the longings of the heart. That's why
they are so dead, and why they call their God *Makom*, "Place."
And now that they have returned to their place, the Lord has taken up
wandering to different places, and His name will no longer be Place
but Places, Lord of the Places.
Even the resurrection of the dead is a long journey.
What remains? The suitcases on top of the closet,
that's what remains.

3
Moses standing on Mount Nebo was the first
to say in his heart, "In the West is my heart, and I
am at the end of the East," but he also said,
"In the East is my heart, and I am at the end of the West."
Thus began the long voyage, the great Jewish journey.
Mount Nebo was the watershed where his longings divided.
He yearned for the land of Canaan he would never see,
but he turned east, toward the desert of those forty years,
and wrote the Torah as a travel book,
a memoir, every chapter with something very personal
that was his alone—like Pharaoh's daughter, like his sister Miriam,
his brother Aaron, his black wife, the Ten Commandments.

4
Moses went into training in preparation for the long trek in
 the desert.
He staged a reconnaissance mission to the burning bush,
trained the pillar of fire and the pillar of smoke, then returned
 to Egypt
to arrange a dress rehearsal for the exodus. He practiced each move

like an acrobat, till the miracle rod felt natural in his hands.
In maneuvers with live ammunition, people sometimes get killed.
There are those who consult a map before a long march
and those who check later: "This is where I walked,
that's where I was." And there is the grief before, and the grief after.
And Jesus the Jew staged a reconnaissance mission to Golgotha,
to the Valley of Gethsemane and up the Via Dolorosa.
He inspected his Jewish burial place, measured it,
tested the weight of the gravestones, what the weather was like,
and how deep the pit from which he would rise, a Christ.

5
Every year our father Abraham would take his sons to Mount
 Moriah
the way I take my children to the Negev hills where I once had
 a war.
Abraham hiked around with his sons. "This is where I left
the servants behind, that's where I tied the donkey to a tree
at the foot of the mountain, and here, right here, Isaac my son,
 you asked:
Behold the fire and the wood, but where is the lamb for a burnt
 offering?
Then, up a little further, you asked for the second time."
When they reached the mountaintop, they rested a bit, ate
 and drank,
and he showed them the thicket where the ram was caught by
 its horns.
After Abraham died, Isaac started taking his sons to the same place.
"Here I lifted the wood, this is where I got out of breath,
here I asked, and my father answered: God will see to the lamb
for the offering. Over there, I already knew it was me."
And when Isaac's eyes were dim with age, his children
led him to that same spot on Mount Moriah, and recounted for him
all that had come to pass, all that he might have forgotten.

6
We no longer ask: Where has the sun disappeared to, whence
does the moon rise, where did my father go, where is God,

whither is thy beloved gone. Our questions are cunning and concealed
like baited fishhooks: Where is that man who was here a moment ago,
when do the latitudes cross the longitudes—all a nudge and a wink
at death. Where is Palmach Street. Where is the street
that used to be Palmach Street. Where is the Palmach
they turned into a street, and the street they turned into a crossroad.
What remains? Move and countermove.
When they meet, they create turbulence. East and west will never meet,
like the two halves of a tunnel that is badly planned.
What remains? The sense of expansion and the sense of contraction,
expansion like a night of stars,
contraction like a mouth puckering at the taste of lemon.
What was and what might have been.
Deeds and the empty gestures of deeds along the roadside
like rows of trees lining the boulevard.

7
In the museum in St. Petersburg, they found a Jewish marriage
 contract
from the seventeenth century. It had a golden border
of peacocks and doves, not an image of bride and groom. The lettering
has not faded, nor have the illuminations; today that ketubah
is more valuable than the memory of the couple.
The voice of the bridegroom and the voice of the bride
were silenced and forgotten in the smoke-and-mirror halls of time.
Did he tell her "I love you" before
he said "Behold, thou art sanctified unto me"
or after? And what is in the space between "I love"
and "Behold, thou art"? What grows there, what rustles and hums,
what is whispered, what remains, what of the night?
The suitcases on top of the closet, that's what remains,
like empty coffins.

8
Jewish travel of another kind: with my wife and children
I went to the remote German village where my grandmother
was born. The house with its red roof is still there,
the stream at the edge of the garden still streaming,

the fertile flower beds between house and stream.
In those flower beds I would have liked to plant choirs of children,
mouths open like snapdragons for a mournful song.
Here grandmother the girl picked mulberries and raspberries.
Someday, in another faraway time, these may be new names
for new children: Mulberry, Mulberella, Raspberry, Raspberitte.
Then shall the song of that mournful choir be thanksgiving
 and praise.
And my grandmother is buried on the cruel dry Mount of Olives
from which the olives have retreated—it is a stone mountain,
a grave-mountain. There she lies buried
and the memory of the streaming water and the mulberries
lies buried with her.

9

On a little hill amid fertile fields lies a small cemetery,
a Jewish cemetery behind a rusty gate, hidden by shrubs,
abandoned and forgotten. Neither the sound of prayer
nor the voice of lamentation is heard there,
for the dead praise not the Lord.
Only the voices of our children ring out, seeking graves and cheering
each time they find one—like mushooms in the forest, like wild
 strawberries.
Here's another grave! There's the name of my mother's
mothers, and a name from the last century. And here's a name,
and there! And as I was about to brush the moss from the name—
Look! an open hand engraved on the tombstone, the grave
 of a kohen,
his fingers splayed in a spasm of holiness and blessing,
and here's a grave concealed by a thicket of berries
that has to be brushed aside like a shock of hair
from the face of a beautiful beloved woman.

10

Then we came to a ritual bath in ruins. A good man led us to it
as if it were one of those hidden shrines in the jungles of Burma or
 Mexico.
For fifty years that ruined mikveh lay covered with a thicket of thorns,

not a soul to uproot it. The rain
that once gathered into a pool of purifying waters
has not stopped falling, but there is no pool now, no purifying.
Where a mirror once hung on the wall, there is a raspberry bush,
and in place of the Jewish woman who gazed into that mirror, ferns
grow wild. And where vapors rose from the pools of water
and from the skin of the women immersing themselves, the nettle
 grows
and the ivy, the vapors became witnesses of death, the women
died in the cycle of impurity and purity and fire, in the cycle of change
and Otherness. Speak O my soul, Change is God.
The cycle is all: the cycle of blood in the body, the cycle of water,
of prayers for the holy days. Speak O my soul, sing
O my soul, to the God who is Himself part of the cycle
of praise and lament, curse and blessing.
Speak O my soul, sing O my soul, Change is God
and death is His prophet.

11

And at dusk, in the last light of day, we saw
a small soccer field in a forest clearing:
the chalk lines had long since faded, and there were no boundaries,
 no rules,
no regulations. Dead soccer players were playing, invisible,
and the whistle shrieked like keening women.
The goalposts were the Gate of Justice at one end
and the Gate of Mercy at the other. The nets were torn,
the souls of the dead slipped through.
And in the middle of the field, a soccer ball, black and white,
was the only real thing in the grass, as if left there from those
 other days.

12

At night I walked again along the row of weeping willows
whose branches reach down. I sat on the same bench
where I waited many years ago, when I was a little boy.
Two generations of remembering have passed,
now the first generation of forgetting has come. The circle

was closed, the circle was broken. But there I was again, sitting
 and waiting
near the weeping willows, sitting and waiting for the man, for
 the other.
Tears drew silver threads from the streetlight to my eyes.
If there are weeping willows there ought to be
joyful willows and hoping willows too, whose branches reach up.
(And when was the last time you cried?) Rings in a tree trunk reveal
how old the tree is, as tears tell the length of a human life.
And when was the last time you cried?

13
He stepped out of the car. I offered him water.
Where had he come from, I asked, and where was he going this time,
did all of this really need to be. He answered, his voice
unsteady, "I am in transit, I have been traveling, I am in the cycle
of departure and return, I come from those other days
and I am headed toward those other days. But the Now is always
 with me."
He took a sip, handed me the cup, and said: "They have built
a small temple where the great old synagogue used to be.
The new temple is modern and shiny, air-conditioned, the seats
are comfortable, the partition of the women's section
is made of expensive fabric, an artistic design, but there is no
minyan for prayer and no women in the women's section.
Nor should you forget the red memorial light, the eternal
flame—that incurable inflammation of the Jewish people.
Now they have built a modern mikveh on the ruins of the old one,
and the walls are made of marble, the faucets solid-gold-plate,
with sweat rooms and fitness corners. But there are
hardly any women left, and those who remain
have no need of a mikveh. Their cycle is over. Finished."

14
"And now I must leave again. I must return
to the cycle of remembering and forgetting. Farewell. We will meet
someday." Thus he spoke and turned away from me.
I followed him to the black car, the car

drove off. He drove off, he was gone.
What remains? The suitcases on top of the closet—
they are all that remains, like suitcases
floating on the water after a ship goes down.
Until they too—

15
Once I said, Death is God and change is His prophet.
Now I have calmed down, and I say:
Change is God and death is His prophet.

I Wasn't One of the Six Million:
And What Is My Life Span? Open Closed Open

1

I wasn't one of the six million who died in the Shoah,
I wasn't even among the survivors.
And I wasn't one of the six hundred thousand who went out
 of Egypt.
I came to the Promised Land by sea.
No, I was not in that number, though I still have the fire and
 the smoke
within me, pillars of fire and pillars of smoke that guide me
by night and by day. I still have inside me the mad search
for emergency exits, for soft places, for the nakedness
of the land, for the escape into weakness and hope,
I still have within me the lust to search for living water
with quiet talk to the rock or with frenzied blows.
Afterwards, silence: no questions, no answers.
Jewish history and world history
grind me between them like two grindstones, sometimes
to a powder. And the solar year and the lunar year
get ahead of each other or fall behind,
leaping, they set my life in perpetual motion.
Sometimes I fall into the gap between them to hide,
or to sink all the way down.

2

I've never been in those places where I've never been
and never will be, I have no share in the infinity of light-years and
 dark-years,
but the darkness is mine, and the light, and my time
is my own. The sand on the seashore—those infinite grains
are the same sand where I made love in Akhziv and Caesarea.
The years of my life I have broken into hours, and the hours
 into minutes
and seconds and fractions of seconds. These, only these,

491

are the stars above me
that cannot be numbered.

3

And what is my life span? I'm like a man gone out of Egypt:
the Red Sea parts, I cross on dry land,
two walls of water, on my right hand and on my left.
Pharaoh's army and his horsemen behind me. Before me the desert,
perhaps the Promised Land, too. That is my life span.

4

Open closed open. Before we are born, everything is open
in the universe without us. For as long as we live, everything
 is closed
within us. And when we die, everything is open again.
Open closed open. That's all we are.

5

What then is my life span? Like shooting a self-portrait.
I set up the camera a few feet away on something stable
(the one thing that's stable in this world),
I decide on a good place to stand, near a tree,
run back to the camera, press the timer,
run back again to that place near the tree,
and I hear the ticking of time, the whirring
like a distant prayer, the click of the shutter like an execution.
That is my life span. God develops the picture
in His big darkroom. And here is the picture:
white hair on my head, eyes tired and heavy,
eyebrows black, like the charred lintels
above the windows in a house that burned down.
My life span is over.

6

My life is the gardener of my body. The brain—a hothouse closed
 tight
with its flowers and plants, alien and odd
in their sensitivity, their terror of becoming extinct.

The face—a formal French garden of symmetrical contours
and circular paths of marble with statues and places to rest,
places to touch and smell, to look out from, to lose yourself
in a green maze, and Keep Off and Don't Pick the Flowers.
The upper body above the navel—an English park
pretending to be free, no angles, no paving stones, naturelike,
humanlike, in our image, after our likeness,
its arms linking up with the big night all around.
And my lower body, beneath the navel—sometimes a nature
 preserve,
wild, frightening, amazing, an unpreserved preserve,
and sometimes a Japanese garden, concentrated, full of
forethought. And the penis and testes are smooth
polished stones with dark vegetation between them,
precise paths fraught with meaning
and calm reflection. And the teachings of my father
and the commandments of my mother
are birds of chirp and song. And the woman I love
is seasons and changing weather, and the children at play
are my children. And the life my life.

7
I believe with perfect faith that at this very moment
millions of human beings are standing at crossroads
and intersections, in jungles and deserts,
showing each other where to turn, what the right way is,
which direction. They explain exactly where to go,
what is the quickest way to get there, when to stop
and ask again. There, over there. The second
turnoff, not the first, and from there left or right,
near the white house, by the oak tree.
They explain with excited voices, with a wave of the hand
and a nod of the head: There, over there, not *that* there, the
 other there,
as in some ancient rite. This too is a new religion.
I believe with perfect faith that at this very moment.

Names, Names, in Other Days and in Our Time

1

My name is Yehúda. The stress on the *hu*,
Yehu, yoo-hoo—a mother's voice calling her little boy in from play,
who who, a voice that crieth from the wilderness, who who,
a voice that crieth unto the wilderness. A surprising *yoo* and a
 surprised *hoo*,
a long-drawn-out who of the loves of my life.
My name is Yehudá, the stress on the *da*,
Yehudá like "thank you" in Hebrew, *todá*, a Yehudean pride,
relic of the heroics of Judah the Maccabee.
Yehudá like a resounding oud—a dull echo
like a string wrapped around a pack of letters,
or a sharp echo like an elastic band snapping
at a woman's waist. *Da da*, no Yehu, no Yahweh,
but a daring plunge with a wide-open parachute into a wedding,
down through the atmospheric layers of my life.

2

My name is Yehuda, but those who love me call me Yuda
as old Jews used to be called, like Grandpa's brother.
Yuda. *Yoo-yoo* a child calls out from his hiding place,
yoo of longings, *yoo-yoo* a ship's foghorn,
yoo yowling or *hoo* hailing Hallelujah, *yoo-yah* Hallelujah.
Yoo from the depths and *hoo* from the heights,
you and who together in the chambers of love.

3

My name is Yehuda, and it comes from
the storehouse of names. The penis is mine,
the erection is mine, but the sperm comes from the semen-silo
that has no end, that returns through my offspring
to the Great Sea.

6

Meir Mindlin divorced his name three times,
went back to his first name and left the country. In his empty flat
many years ago I loved a great love
because a flat cannot tolerate a void: *horror vacui.*
I don't remember in which war I first met him
and in which history, public or private.
He knew five languages, but when the stroke hit him
he was paralyzed, struck dumb in all five tongues.
I want to cleanse his death notice of all the other news on the page
the way archaeologists scrub a clay pot, or the way
a dead body is cleansed of every impurity.
I want to advertise his life—false advertising
for an item that's out of stock, you can't get it anymore.
I want rites of mourning, rending of clothes, shoes slipped off
lightly, easily, like cursing, because curses are light.
It's the blessings that weigh you down.

7

Tova's brother, whom I carried wounded from the battle at
 Tel Gath,
recovered and was forgotten because he recovered, and died
in a car crash a few years later, and was forgotten
because he died. And even if my bloodied hands
had been prophets then, my eyes saw not
and my feet knew not what the grain in the field knows,
that green wheat ripens yellow.
That's the life prophecy of a field of wheat.

I howl *Hoshana*, O save us! I weep, I implore on Hoshana Rabba.
That howl ripens into beautiful music—in the church choir
it is almost a psalm of praise, Hosanna, Hallelujah,
praise the Lord who did not save.
But I go back to a weepy pleading *Hoshana*
that turns my mouth into a gaping wound
and may soothe me yet, like an infant crying itself to sleep.

8

Abraham Rubinstein arrived at our school in Jerusalem
in 1937, a quiet dark-eyed boy from Lithuania. We
had a party for him when he came. That same year
our voices began to change like the seasons, like a summer
 and winter
that will never return in the cycle of voices,
back when first loves stirred up a first disorder in our souls
like the mess in the closet or on the table.
In 1938 he returned with his family to Lithuania and we had
 a party
for him when he left, fun and games, as we did when he came.
If he had stayed in Jerusalem, he would have changed his old
 Jewish name
to a proud Hebrew name: Rubinstein would have turned into
Ruby, Stone, Diamond, Sapphire,
any gem would do, no matter what color, any name is a good name.
But he went back to Lithuania and I never heard his adult voice,
whole, final, howling in the death camp.
He didn't get to the enchanted places, in life or in death.
And now they come together—what might have been
and whatever was—and the two become one,
like the long-drawn-out "one" at the end
of *Shema Yisrael*. Hear O Israel: The End.

9

Dan Omer—a rebel in life and in death. Even his pitch-black beard
was a rebel, never soft or submissive, never resigned to its fate.
In the end, his own heart rose up against him and killed him
 from within.
A man of many new beginnings. But even a multitude
of new beginnings comes to a single end. He died
in a hospital called Gates of Justice. All his life he tried to storm
the gates of justice. (Now that old hospital building has also
fallen into decay.) Sometimes I see his aged father still walking
the streets of Jerusalem, head erect, meticulously dressed,
in his hand a dignified walking stick, not just a cane to lean on.
He swings it with the elegance of a Europe gone by.

Inside that walking stick is the soul of his dead son Dan,
like a narrow saber concealed in the cane of a secret agent,
and he doesn't even know it. I am the only one who knows,
because Dan was my friend.

10

Paul Celan. Toward the end, the words grew
fewer inside you, each word
so heavy in your body
that God set you down like a heavy load
for a moment, perhaps, to catch
His breath and wipe His brow.
Then He left you and picked up a lighter load,
another poet. But the last bubbles
that rose from your drowning mouth
were the final concentration, the frothy concentrate
of the heaviness of your life.

12

Louis Rappaport died of a heart attack.
The best father in the world to his four children.
Father of the little girl who sang in the school chorus,
her mouth wide open like a chick in the nest
for the food that Papa would bring, and out came a song
wonderfully sweet.

Then one day that good father suddenly died
and now he's become a cautionary tale, the moral of a story
for less perfect children of less perfect fathers:
"Don't upset Papa, you'll give him a heart attack."
But Louis Rappaport was the best father of all.

And from now on we'll need a dispensation to rejoice
like the dispensation to pray on Yom Kippur:
Our sorrow is no sorrow, our weeping no weeping,
our dead are not dead, our despair is no despair.
We permit ourselves to rejoice with the joyous,
to love with the lovers, and to pass with those who pass away.

13

One man's parents gave him an old-fashioned name from the
 Diaspora.
These days only very old, very praying Jews still go by such a name.
His friends gave him a wild name, because he grew up
to be a big brave paratrooper, raised horses
out in the world and came back to raise them in the hills of Galilee.
His parents own a shop of women's undergarments, corsets for the
 stout ones,
lightweight bras and little silk panties for the lean ones.
And whoever laughs at the story of a generation gap like that,
whoever even cracks a smile, doesn't know a thing about
wild horses or the names of the land of Canaan or Diaspora names
or the hills of Galilee or women
or women's garments, either under or over,
or the land of Israel, or the history of the people of Israel.

14

Ruth Ruth Ruth, little girl from my youth—
now she's a stand-in for Otherness.
Otherness is death, death is Otherness.
Will you come back to me the way the dead sometimes
come back to the living, as if they were born again?
Does the arrow celebrate its return to the bow, and what about
the ball that returns from the wall to the hands of the child at play?

Oh, names without people, people without names,
all those secondhand names. I sometimes think about
the difference between borrowing a book and borrowing money.
In the one case, you must return the same thing.
In the other, you just give back
something of equal value,
like small change.

15

All those names, cleansed and purified, recycled
in the cycle, in the big mixer of names,
the name for its own sake and the name taken in vain,

names from over there and names
for over there, names of silence,
names of welter and waste.

Ruth Ruth, who died in my youth, now the two giants, Yitgadal
 and Yitkadash,
Magnified and Sanctified,
will watch over your death
in place of the two other giants, May He Bless and May He Keep,
who failed to watch over your life.
Ruth Ruth, thy hallowed name
magnified and sanctified,
His hallowed name, thy name.

16
Oh, the names of God, Blessed be His Name,
the Speakable Name and the Unspeakable Name.
Oh, family names for the dominion of day
and first names for the dominion of night,
names whispered in the dark.

In a piazza in Rome, I once saw a woman waiting
at a corner. I don't know how long
she stood there, or whether the one who hadn't come
did come in the end, or not. But after her death, God
will gently pry open her head, as He always does,
to look for the name of the one she truly loved.
And it won't be His name, it won't be His.

Jerusalem, Jerusalem, Why Jerusalem?

1

Jerusalem is forever changing her ways, like King David
who put on a crazy face to escape from death. The dead
 pretend
to be resurrected, the living to be dead,
peace puts on a scary mask of war, and war
changes its ways to peace. And we who dwell within her
are displayed in the shop windows of history with a wardrobe
of peculiar fashions and frozen gestures,
a heavenly expression on our faces for pilgrims and tourists
and the exalted angels. But what we really wanted
was to go wild in dark storerooms with an untrammeled joy
as in the Garden of Eden: "They were naked and were not
 ashamed."
And the saints who ascended on high in the distant past
and the astronauts who will ascend from Jerusalem in the distant
 future—
it's as if they are running away from her to heaven.
For compared to Jerusalem, even the outer space of infinity
is safe and protected, like a true home.

2

A city that has a wall, as Jerusalem has,
is like children who have a father,
and neither wall nor father can protect them any longer.
We cannot be fooled. I have seen people standing in a crowded
 bus
with weary extinguished eyes in their flaming faces
or flaming eyes in their weary extinguished faces.
And those who are standing raise their arms to hold on
as if rising in silent prayer, and they read the ads,
the writing on the wall above the bus windows: No Smoking,
Buy, Buy, Emergency Exit, just Buy, Buy!
Yes, we can be fooled.

3

Jerusalem sits in mourning, she's sitting shiva,
and those who come to visit and comfort
give her no peace, day or night. In their solicitude
they don't mention the name of the dead or the dead one's life,
they chat with her about world affairs and the daily grind.
With all the comings and goings, she has no time to mourn,
still unaware it is she who is both the mourned
and the mourner. They will not let her sit alone
so she keeps watch over the old houses of worship
the way a mother keeps the room of her son who died in the war
and will not change a thing in it. Will not even open the curtain.

4

The trees in Jerusalem try really hard to rustle like the sea,
and so do those who pray from their depths, and the lovers
 in their beds,
but we cannot be fooled.
Yes, we can be fooled.

5

Jerusalem is like an Atlantis that sank into the sea:
everything there is submerged and sunken.
This is not the heavenly Jerusalem, but the one down below,
way down below. And from the sea floor, they dredge up ruined walls
and fragments of faiths, like rust-covered vessels from sunken
prophecy ships. That's not rust, it's blood that has never dried.
And clay jars covered with seaweed, the corals of time and the fury
 of time
and coins from days gone by, the negotiable currency of the past.
But some very young memories are down there too:
a love-memory from last night, see-through memories
quick as glamour fish caught in a net, thrashing and splashing.
Come, let's throw them back into Jerusalem!

6

Jerusalem is a merry-go-round-and-round
from the Old City through all the neighborhoods and back
 to the Old.

And you can't get off. Whoever jumps off puts his life on the line
and whoever gets off at the final round has to pay again
to get back on for the rounds that have no end.
And instead of elephants and painted horses to ride,
there are religions that go up and down and turn on their axis
to the music of oily tunes from the houses of prayer.
Jerusalem is a seesaw: sometimes I dip down
into past generations, sometimes I rise up to the skies and then
I shriek like a child, feet swinging on high:
I want down, Daddy, I want down,
Daddy, get me down.
And that's how the saints all ascend to heaven,
like a child screaming, Daddy, I want to stay up here,
Daddy, don't get me down, Our Father Our King,
leave us up here, Our Father Our King!

7

In Jerusalem, everything is a symbol. Even two lovers there
become a symbol like the lion, the golden dome, the gates
 of the city.
Sometimes they make love on too soft a symbolism
and sometimes the symbols are hard as a rock, sharp as nails.
That's why they make love on a mattress of six hundred thirteen
 springs,
like the number of precepts, the commandments of Shalt and
 Shalt Not,
oh yes, do that, darling, no, not that—all for love
and its pleasures. They speak with bells in their voices
and with the wailing call of the muezzin, and at their bedside, empty
 shoes
as at the entrance of a mosque. And on the doorpost of their house
 it says,
"Ye shall love each other with all your hearts and with all your
 souls."

8

Why, of all places, Jerusalem? Why not New York
with her buildings on high and burrows down below

and tunnels and lower depths from which to call out:
O Lord, out of the depths have I cried unto thee.
Why Jerusalem, why me,
why not Athens, Egypt, Mexico,
India, Burma—the temples are already there,
the domes gilded, the pillars in place.

9

Why is Jerusalem, Yerushalayim, always two, the Heavenly and
 the Earthly?
I want to live in an in-between Jerusalem,
without banging my head up above or gashing my feet down below.
And why is Yerushalayim in the dual form, like hands, *yadayim*,
 and feet, *raglayim*?
I want to live in Jerusal, singular,
because I am just I, singular, not an I-im.

10

And there are days here when everything is sails and more sails,
even though there's no sea in Jerusalem, not even a river.
Everything is sails: the flags, the prayer shawls, the black coats,
the monks' robes, the kaftans and kaffiyehs,
young women's dresses and headdresses,
Torah mantles and prayer rugs, feelings that swell in the wind
and hopes that set them sailing in other directions.
Even my father's hands, spread out in blessing,
my mother's broad face and Ruth's faraway death
are sails, all of them sails in the splendid regatta
on the two seas of Jerusalem:
the sea of memory and the sea of forgetting.

11

Why, of all places, Jerusalem? Why not Babylon
with her Tower of Babel and her babbling tongues,
why not Petersburg with the mystery
of her white nights, white as priestly robes,
and her name changes: St. Peter, St. Lenin.
Why not Rome with her catacombs,

why not Mecca with her Black Stone,
why not Vancouver with her salmon
that ascend to her from the sea, crawling
on their bellies up the hard mountain slope
like atoning pilgrims, kosher pilgrims of fin and scale
that arrive at the blue heights, spawn, and die.

12
Shirts and dresses hung up to dry—right away you know
it's a holiday. White panties and undershirts mean peace and quiet.
But when flags are flying, you never can tell if it's a sign of peace
or of war, if they are left over from a festival
or a memorial for the dead. War and peace look the same
from a distance, as galaxies of new-formed stars look like
old stars that imploded and died.
We can be fooled. No, we cannot be fooled.
What summons us to prayer? The wail
of the fire engine, the police car, the ambulance.
And when prayers ascend on high, they fall
back down like shrapnel from anti-aircraft shells
that have missed their target. Then once again, a siren
summons us to prayer.

13
"How doth the city sit solitary," the prophet lamented over
 Jerusalem.
If Jerusalem is a woman, does she know desire?
When she cries out, is it from pleasure
or pain? What is the secret of her appeal?
When does she open her gates willingly and when is it rape?
All her lovers abandon her, leaving her
with the wages of love—necklaces, earrings,
towers and houses of prayer
in the English, Italian, Russian, Greek, Arab styles,
wood and stone, turrets and gables, wrought-iron gates,
rings of gold and silver, riots of color. They all give her
something to remember them by, then abandon her.
I would have liked to talk to her again, but I lost her
among the dancers. Dance is total abandon.

Jerusalem sees only the skies above her
and whoever sees only the skies above—
not the face of her lover—truly does lie solitary,
sit solitary, stand solitary, and dance all alone.

14
And there are days here when everything is gut, full gut or empty gut,
gut that ends up as violin strings or as sausage casing, the gut
of Jeremiah griping about the writhing in his gut,
a blind gut or a gut with vision that prophesies,
gut of history and gut of hysteria, the gut that links nothing
to nothing—no mouth, no way out, no body,
nothing but gut. All is gut.
All is vanity, all inanity, all is pain.

15
Why, of all places, Jerusalem? Why not London
with its gardens and palaces and towers and the chiming
from the top of Big Ben. Big Ben, a big old boy,
Big God, great God in the mists of holiness.

16
There are days here when all is mouth: fish mouth, mouth
of slaughtered lamb, blabbermouth, the mouth of a well,
of cantor and choir, pretty mouth, mouth of keyhole,
asshole, gaping mouth of the abyss,
mouth pious or profane, double-edged mouth, the mouth
of the ass that spake unto Balaam, the mouth of a camel baring
 its teeth.
And my mouth shall proclaim Thy glory.

17
In Jerusalem, hope springs eternal. Hope is like a faithful dog.
Sometimes she runs ahead of me to check the future, to sniff it out,
and then I call her: Hope, Hope, come here, and she
comes to me. I pet her, she eats out of my hand.
And sometimes she stays behind, near some other hope,
maybe to sniff out whatever was. Then I call her my Despair,
I call out to her: Hey, my little Despair, come here,

and she comes and snuggles up, and again
I call her Hope.

18
Two lovers talking to each other in Jerusalem
with the excitement of tour guides, pointing,
touching, explaining: These are my father's eyes you see
in my face, these are the sleek thighs I inherited from a distant
 mother
in the Middle Ages, this is my voice which traveled
all the way here from three thousand years ago,
this is the color of my eyes, the mosaic of my spirit,
the archaeological layers of my soul. We are holy places.
In ancient caves we can hide and write secret scrolls
and lie together in the dark.
Once in Ein Kerem in an abandoned cave I saw
rooster feathers and the torn dress of a woman
and I was filled with fury, my wrath was almost biblical.
In the courtyard of the orphanage, in the convent beside that cave,
there was suddenly a wild commotion and a rushing about
of young girls and nuns, a crazy she-goat, barking dogs.
Then stillness and a worn brown wall.

19
Sometimes Jerusalem is a city of knives.
Even the hopes for peace are sharp, to cut through
the hard reality. After a while, they grow blunt or brittle.
Church bells keep trying to ring out a calm round tone
but they grow heavy, like a pestle in a mortar pounding
artillery shells—muffled, leaden, trampling sounds.
The cantor and the muezzin want to sweeten their tune
but in the end, a piercing wail cuts through the din:
The Lord God of us all, the Lord is
one, one, one.

20
I always have to go in the opposite direction to whatever
is passing and past. That's how I know I live in Jerusalem:

I go against the tide of pilgrims parading in the Old City,
brush by them, rub up against them, feel the weave of their clothes,
breathe in their smell, hear their talk and their song
as they fly past my cheeks like beautiful clouds.
Sometimes I get tangled in a funeral procession
and emerge at the other end, heading toward the good life.
And sometimes I'm held captive by the joy-parades and I raise
 my arm
like a swimmer against the stream, or as if to say: Go in peace,
go, go away, and I head for the other side, toward
my griefs and my peace. I go against the longings and the prayers
to feel their warm breath on my face,
the buzz and rustle of the stuff of longing and prayer.
This could be the start of a new religion,
like striking a match to make fire, like the friction
that sparks electricity.

21
There are days when everyone says, I was there,
I'm ready to testify, I stood a few feet from the accident,
from the bomb, from the crucifixion, I almost got hit, almost got
 crucified.
I saw the faces of bride and groom under the wedding canopy
 and almost
rejoiced. When David lay with Bathsheba I was the voyeur,
I happened to be there on the roof fixing the pipes, taking down
 a flag.
With my own eyes I saw the Chanukah miracle in the Temple,
I saw General Allenby entering Jaffa Gate,
I saw God.
And then there are days when everything is an alibi: wasn't there,
 didn't hear,
heard the explosion only from a distance and ran away, saw smoke but
was reading a newspaper, was staying in some other place.
I didn't see God, I've got witnesses.
And the God of Jerusalem is the eternal alibi God,
wasn't there didn't see didn't hear
was in some other place. Was some Place, some Other.

22

Why Jerusalem? Why not the sublime San Francisco?
After all, she already bears the name of that bird-loving saint,
and she has a golden gate, ascents and descents and ascents,
and a rumbling in the depths always ready to burst forth in fire
and pillars of smoke, as when God gave the Torah on Mount Sinai,
and an earth that opens its mouth wide, as in the Bible.

23

Why Jerusalem, why not Paris with her squares
and boulevards, arches of glory for the King of Glory,
her broad bridges over the narrow world.

25

There are days in this city when no one is himself
but somebody else's son. And they are called *Ibn, Ben,*
Son, Sohn. He is not he and you are not you
and I am not I but the son of I, Ibn Ezra and Ibn Musa,
Ben Abraham, Ibn Allah, Son of God.
And all of them gospeling what will be, even those
who cannot remember go around reminding the others,
and even Love laments the destruction of the Temple,
the rocking motions of the body in lament and in love are one.
And then there are days when everyone is somebody's father,
and they are all called *Abu*: Abu This, Abu That,
Father of Progeny, Father of Orphans, Father of Pains,
Father of Mercies, Abu-of-Us-All, Our Father Our King.

26

Longing for Jerusalem, for childhood in Jerusalem, in another
 faraway time:
the children of the Levites longing, now that they are old, in exile
by the waters of Babylon. They still remember singing
in the Temple when their voices had just begun to change.
At night they remind one another of their childhood:
Remember how we played hide-and-seek behind
the Holy of Holies, among the urns of frankincense,
near those drainage ditches around the altar, in the shadow

of the embroidered mantle on the Holy Ark,
between the cherubim?

27

And there are days when all is thighs in Jerusalem, the thighs of
 slaughtered cows
hanging upside down in the butcher shop, and the thighs of tourists,
and the thighs of heavy-laden donkeys.
And round pillars and even the mezuzahs on the two sides of
 the gates
are thighs, and the hard thighs of chairs and the soft thighs
and the honeymoon thighs and the thighs of a bride and the hairy
 thighs of bridegrooms.
All is thighs.

28

Why Jerusalem, why me?
Why not another city, another person?
Once I stood at the Western Wall
when suddenly a flock of startled birds soared up,
shrieking and flapping their wings like bits of paper
with wishes scribbled on them, wishes
that flew out from between the massive stones
and ascended on high.

Conferences, Conferences:
Malignant Words, Benign Speech

1

Above the hotel gate, I saw a sign:
"International Conference on Inflammations of the Eye"
for those who have cried too much or not cried enough.
All of them with name tags on their lapels
like temporary nameplates in a cemetery or markers
in a botanical garden.
They approach one another as if sniffing, as if checking,
Who are you where are you from and when
was the last time you cried.
The subject of the morning session is "Sobbing:
The End of Crying or the Way It Begins." Sobbing
as soul-stuttering and griefstones. Sobbing
as a valve or a loop that links cry to cry,
a loop that unravels easily, like a hair ribbon,
and the crying—hair that fans out in profusion, glorious.
Or a loop that pulls into an impossible knot—
sobbing like an oath, a testimony, a cure.
Back in their cubicles, the women translators are busy
translating fate to fate, cry to cry. At night they come home,
scrub the words from their lips, and with sobs of happiness
they start loving, their eyes aflame with joy.

2

A conference on inflammations of the eye. Tears are always delegates
from a big salty sea, they never come from fresh water,
a flowing stream, a placid lake. And when was the last time
you cried? The translators sit and recycle it all to another
recycling plan that has no end, and the spirit of God
hovers above with the whirring wing-blades of a giant fan
whipping the air, the words whipped over and over like foam.
The closing session: "He cried like a dog.
The dog cried like a human being." That is the final meeting,

the undoing of all doctrines, the end of all conferences.
And above the door a sign, "Emergency Exit," lit by an eternal
red light. An eye inflammation of the cosmos
that has no cure.

3

A conference on language: colloquial, baroquial, poetic, pathetic.
And the chance for a new language of war and peace:
Just as nouns and verbs in Hebrew change in the masculine and
 feminine
by adding a syllable or changing a vowel, making the sound longer
or shorter, so will it be with the language of war and, once again,
the language of war. And the final conference,
just me and myself: a panel of my body parts
addressing my soul, each with its set topic
and its allotted time—hands, feet, kidneys, heart,
intestines, reproductive organ, joy and pain.
And the close of the conference: reconvening inside to confer
with myself—no name tags, no translators, only words.
O my words, the good and the bad,
the changing and the changed. O my words—
the malignant words, the benign speech.

4

Conferences and symposia, too numerous to count.
A conference on the import and export
of one religion to another, exporting Torah from Zion and babies
into the world, importing the dead. Or a major conference on Job:
dermatologists on skin diseases, anthropologists
on pain and suffering, legal scholars on justice and injustice,
God on the nature of Satan, and Satan on the notion of the divine.
Job's three friends, Bildad, Eliphaz, and Zophar, on the psychology
of suicide, the science of suicidology.
Zoologists on "The Leviathan: from Job to Paradise,"
and ceramicists on the type of potsherd Job used
to scratch himself. Scratching as a solution,
speech as a scratching in the throat or a scratching unto death,
till death do them part, the scratcher and the good potsherd.

And the translators translate pain to another kind of pain,
remembering to forgetting, forgetting to remembering,
curse to blessing and blessing to curse.
Sometimes they fall asleep in their cubicles like newborns
in their bassinets in the maternity ward.

5
A lecture on the soul. Live testimony. An animated lecture.
In the British Museum I saw a bird with the claws of a lion,
and a lion with a human head, and winged oxen.
I asked them: Why, what do you need that for,
isn't it enough that you are a lion, a bird, an ox?
And they answered: You soul-sotted creatures,
isn't it enough that you are human, of clay and humus made?
Why do you need these tacked-on souls
and a God that doesn't fit you, and emotions, besides?

6
The translators flee their burning cubicles,
run out into the streets, crying "Help!"
and make their way to other, calmer conferences.

7
A conference open to the public. The soul is formed before the body
like an infrastructure—a five-lane highway, straight and wide,
 tucked into
the landscape, so you can get from one place to another quickly, easily.
No: The soul is revealed only when the life of the body recedes,
like the narrow winding paths in the Judean Desert
that become visible only after many generations
of sheep and their barefoot shepherds.
A nocturnal conference: The soul is a search, the soul is a dance
of searches for whatever is lost. I frisk myself
and my clothes, patting softly then harder, looking for
an envelope, some ID, keys, small change, an important note.
I stand up, bend over, shake myself out,
reach my fingers deep into my pockets,
poke at my skin, my flesh.

People think I'm scratching myself. The soul is
an itch. Scratching reveals it, calms it down.

8

Morning session: The body is a heavy stone that has dropped
into still waters. The soul is the ripple. The soul consists
of soft centrifugal rings that grow wider and wider.
A counter-session at noon: The body consists of waves
that ripple inward in centripetal circles,
smaller and smaller, closer and heavier,
to form the heavy soul at the bottom.

9

The body is the workplace of the soul,
the body is the laboratory for experiments, inventions, innovations.

10

The body wants to lock up the soul as if in a safe,
not to be opened until the will is read.
The will is the soul. The body is the safe,
the key is in God's hands. Or simply lost.

11

An afternoon session: "God and the Soul."
A Jew thanks God every day for restoring his soul.
But what would happen if one morning the body decided
it would like a different soul?

12

God in His mercy and thrift may decide to grant
a single soul to a number of human bodies.
Like a streetlight that illuminates several houses,
or a locomotive that pulls all the cars of a train?

13

Evening session: to lie on your belly in the dark,
bury your head in the pillow and, with your eyes closed,
to see stars more colorful, more lovely than those in the sky.

14

The translators, men and women, sit in their cells
and make honey, like bees, from all the buzz and babble:
a cultured honey behind their eyes,
a wild honey under their pubic hair.

My Son Was Drafted

1

My son was drafted. We brought him
to the station along with the other boys.
Now his face has joined the faces of those who say goodbye to me
from the passing windows of the buses and trains of my life,
faces in the streaming rain, faces
squinting in the sun. And now his face.
In the corner of the window, like a stamp on an envelope.

2

In a piazza in Rome near the Colosseum I wash my hands at a
 public faucet
and drink from my cupped palm, and meanwhile a red-haired
 woman
in a white dress who was sitting on a folding chair near a closed gate
is gone. When I lift my wet face
she is no more, flown away like a feather placed on the world
to check if the world is still breathing. The world
is still breathing, the world is alive,
the woman is still alive. We are alive, my son is still alive,
the white feather is still flying and living.
I want my son to be a soldier in the Italian army
with a crest of colorful feathers on his cap,
happily dashing around with no enemies, no camouflage.

3

I want to give him some advice: Listen, my son, don't change.
Remember: Thou art what thou art. On a hot day,
drink a lot of water—chug it down and change.
And another piece of advice I remember from my own wars:
When you go out for a night patrol, fill your canteen to the top
so the water won't make a sloshing sound and give you away.

That's how your soul ought to be in your body, large and full
 and silent.
(When you make love, make all the noise you want.)
And don't forget the window in your room that became
a window in the bus. At the end of all windows, there's a door.
The door giveth and the door taketh away.
And above all, don't forget the wisdom of the folding chair,
the joy of the colorful feathers,
the prophecy of the flying white feather.
And the vision of an old Italian city
where, at the end of tangled alleys, there's always
a piazza of sunlight and talk.

4
Birds know where to build their nests,
fish know where to spawn,
jasmine fills the air with its fragrance only at night,
a sea painted on a wall looks out
on the sea framed by a window.
(Have I ever mentioned that my father knew
the art of tying packages tight for transport?)
I want my son to be a soldier in the Vatican's Swiss Guard
with their coats of many colors, their sashes and blunt lances
glittering in the sun.

5
I would like to add two more commandments to the ten:
the Eleventh Commandment, "Thou shalt not change,"
and the Twelfth Commandment, "Thou shalt change. You will
 change,"
My dead father added those for me.

6
My son was drafted. We visited him at the army base, in the desert,
the desolation that tents with their ropes and tent pegs
try to make us forget. The whitewashed stones along the path
so blinding white-hot I covered my eyes
like a Jewish woman lighting the Sabbath candles.

I sat down on a stone near an empty can, and the music
of the wind in that empty can was all that had ever happened,
all that ever would. From the distant sand dunes I heard scattered
 shots
like a nervous, insistent thumbing through the Book of Life
 and Death.
My son's barefoot steps when he was a baby were louder
than his heavy boots in the fine mealy Negev sand.
I want my son to be a soldier in the British army,
guarding a palace in the rain. A tall fur hat on his head,
everyone staring at him while, without moving a muscle,
he is laughing inside.

7

My children grew and flourished around tears and laughter
like fruit, like houses, but the tears and the laughter
stayed inside the kernel, just as they were. Our Father, Our King!
That's all for today on fathers and kings.
Go, my children whom I begot: Get yourselves into the next century,
where the tears and the laughter will continue, just as they were.
I remember giving them a stern warning:
"Never, never stick your hand out the window of a moving bus."
Once we were on a bus and my little girl piped up, "Daddy, that man
stuck his hand into the outside!"

That's the way to live: to stick your hand into the world's
infinite outside, turn the outside inside out,
the world into a room and God into a little soul
inside the infinite body.

8

I taught them how to walk and now they are walking away from me.
I taught them how to speak to the world
and now they are teaching me to speak to my own heart.
I taught them to sleep, and taught myself to stay awake at night.
I am a camel with a hump of emotions, I'm a worrybear, the worries
are stored inside me in a layer of fat and hair. I'm a kangaroo
whose pouch emptied out. On my soul there's a place marked for pain

as on a form marked with a dotted line: "Cut here and return."
My head is a womb and my heart a garage and my hands
superfluous. Changes like that happen to me from time to time,
changing roles, changing places—change and exchange.
I am an expert on brittle yearnings
and blunted desires. If I were an angel, before I turned around
I would be too weary to fly with my wings.

9

My daughter looks more like my mother than like me or my wife.
Those daring magnificent leaps in the Genetic Games
that have no winners, or those sideways jumps
of the knight in chess—a phantom prophecy that snags us
with its hooks and lines into past and future.
Yes, my son was drafted. When he comes home for the night
he is silent, then he sleeps, and my daughter sleeps too.
There they are, sleeping in my house near the wall
of the Old City of Jerusalem, and I know
that a father is an illusion, just like that wall.
Neither one can protect. Can only love, and worry.

10

Children collect small hopes and the small change of charity
for cancer patients, heart patients, the blind
and God alone knows what else.
They come to the door and knock gently—like a heartbeat:
We've come . . . We've come . . . We've come . . .
Once I checked out the world with my children.
They were my Geiger counters, my depth gauges,
the thermometers and frigometers I used to seek, to check, to find.
Now they use me to probe the world that was and the world to come.

11

"The end of the matter: all has been heard." Now my daughter too
has been drafted. Now her face too is in the window
of the bus that slowly pulls out of the station. Now her face too
in the corner of the window like a stamp on an envelope. Like her
 brother.

Oh, those stamps, those letters sent off into the world,
those letters we send. Those names, addresses, numbers,
those colorful stamps, those faces.
And the thud of the censor's seal like the hammerblow of fate.

12
Now her face too, now she too,
and I want to give her some advice:
Don't forget the tremendous power of hair that fans out free
 and open,
and the tremendous power of hair pulled back, coiled tight
like a dancer's.

13
As for that piazza in Rome, the water goes on streaming from
 the faucet,
and the flags are out for a feast day,
and the song of the fife and drum is heard in the land;
as for the woman who vanished, and as for the feathers,
they go on vanishing and flying in the world of time.
And the illusion of walls in Rome and Jerusalem
goes on deluding, along with all the other questions and chimeras.
And as for my children and their journeys away from life,
may the two Kaddish giants Yitgadal and Yitkadash
protect them as they protected my father and mother—
my children in their lives, my parents in their deaths.

Autumn, Love, Commercials

1

End of summer. After extreme torture by the last *hamsin*,
summer confesses its guilt and I say: The dry tree is regal, the thorn
glorious, the thistles that give themselves over to their hardness
are marvelous. The parasite ivy is more beautiful than the host,
and the dry tendrils of the vine cling to the bramble in love.
White feathers at the mouth of a cave tell of a brutal death
but also of the beauty of great wings beating.
The fissures and cracks in the tormented earth will be the map
of my life. From here on, bird-watchers will determine history,
geologists will plot out the future, meteorologists
will read the palm of God's hand, and botanists
will be experts in the tree of knowledge, good and evil.

2

With a squeeze of my fingers, like a lover's pinch, I check
if the figs are ripe. I will never know what counts as death
to figs, being left on the tree or rotting on the ground,
what their inferno is and their Eden, what their salvation
and what their resurrection. The mouth that eats them—
is it heaven's gate or the mouth of hell? Once upon a time,
trees were the gods of human beings. Now perhaps we
are gods to the trees and their fruit.
The turtledove calls out in love to its brothers the carob trees;
it knows nothing of the eons of evolution
that lie between them, it calls and calls and calls.

3

The upturned gaze to see if clouds—
what does it light upon along its way: walls, balconies,
the laundry of longings hung out to dry, wistful windows, rooftops,
sky. The open hand stretched out to see if raindrops—
that is the most innocent hand of all,

the most believing, more prayerful
than all the worshipers in all the houses of prayer.

4

In the airplane in the sky, those who are returning home
sit beside those who are leaving, and their faces are the same.
Atmospheric currents of longing form the rain that's about to fall.
In the Crusader ruins, the autumn squill blooms long after
its leaves come up in the spring, but it knows what happened
in the long dry summer between. Its brief eternity.
The water towers in Yad Mordechai and Negba were kept in ruins
as a remembrance. What an autumn nation we are,
to celebrate the fall of Masada and its suicides,
the ruin of Jotapata and Betar and the destruction of Jerusalem
at the Western Wall. Remnant of remnants. Like someone who keeps
shoes that are falling apart, a torn sock, tattered letters as
 remembrances.
All this only to postpone a little the hour of death.
And all our lives, everything that happens in them, that stirs and
 swarms inside them,
is a hedge around life. And death too is a hedge around life.

5

I want to sing a psalm of praise to all that remains
here with us and doesn't leave, doesn't wander off like migratory
 birds,
will not flee to the north or the south, will not sing "In the East
 is my heart,
and I dwell at the end of the West." I want to sing to the trees
that do not shed their leaves and that suffer
the searing summer heat and the cold of winter,
and to human beings who do not shed their memories
and who suffer more than those who shed everything.
But above all, I want to sing a psalm of praise
to the lovers who stay together for joy, for sorrow and for joy.
To make a home, to make babies, now and in other seasons.

6

I saw a tree in fall whose hardened seeds rattled and clacked
inside their pods. A man's seed streams and slithers out, sticky,
and is swallowed up without a sound.
Thus hath the seed of a tree preeminence
over the seed of a man:
it is like a cheerful toy rattle, and that is its love song.

7

For love must be spoken, not whispered, that it may be
seen and heard. It must be without camouflage,
conspicuous, noisy, like a raucous laugh.
It must be a kitschy commercial for "Be fruitful and multiply":
a perky amazing "Be fruitful" and a hard-edged, tortured "multiply"
of the human species—sweet frosting for a bitter life.
Love is words and flowers that attract insects and butterflies
in the field, but also the floral pattern on a woman's dress.
It's the delicate skin of the inner thigh, it's underwear
down to the bottoms of the soul and overwear up to the heavens,
it's public relations, the pull of earth dwellers to earth,
Newton's law of gravity
and the law of levity of the divine. Hallelujah.

And Who Will Remember the Rememberers?

1

Verses for Memorial Day, a psalm of remembering
for the war dead. The generation of memory-veterans
is dying out. Half at a ripe old age, half at a rotten old age.
And who will remember the rememberers?

2

How does a monument come into being? A car goes up in a
 red blaze
at Sha'ar HaGay. A car burnt black. The skeleton of a car.
And next to it, the skeleton of some other car, charred in a traffic
 accident
on some other road. The skeletons are painted with anti-rust
 paint, red
like the red of that flame. Near one skeleton, a wreath of flowers,
now dry. From dry flowers you make a memorial wreath,
and from dry bones, a vision of resurrected bones.
And somewhere else, far away, hidden among the bushes,
a cracked marble plaque with names on it. An oleander branch,
like a shock of hair on a beloved face, hides most of them.
But once a year the branch is cut back and the names are read,
while up above, a flag at half mast waves as cheerfully
as a flag at the top of the flagpole, light and easy,
happy with its colors and breezes.
And who will remember the rememberers?

3

What is the correct way to stand at a memorial ceremony?
Erect or stooped, pulled taut as a tent or in the slumped posture
of mourning, head bowed like the guilty or held high
in a collective protest against death,
eyes gaping frozen like the eyes of the dead
or shut tight, to see stars inside?

And what is the best time for remembering? At noon
when shadows are hidden beneath our feet, or at twilight
when shadows lengthen like longings
that have no beginning, no end, like God?

5
And what should our lament be? David's lament over Saul and
 Jonathan:
"Swifter than eagles, stronger than lions," that is what our lament
 should be.

Had they really been swifter than eagles
they would have soared high above the war
and would not have been hurt. From down here, we would have
 seen them
and said: "There go the eagles! There is my son, my husband, my
 brother."

And had they really been stronger than lions
they would have stayed like lions, not died like human beings.
They would have eaten out of our hands,
we would have stroked their golden manes,
we would have tamed them in our homes, with love:
My son, my husband, my brother, my husband, my son.

8
No one has ever heard of the fruit of the jasmine,
no poet has sung its praises,
they all sing drunken odes to the jasmine flower,
its heady scent, its color, white against dark leaves,
the vigor of its blossoming and the force of its short life—
a butterfly's life or the life of a star.
No one has ever heard of the fruit of the jasmine.
And who will remember the rememberers?

9
No one praises the blossoms of the vine, everyone praises
the fruit of the vine, and blesses the wine.

Have I mentioned that my father, in the wisdom of his hands,
knew how to prepare parcels for transport,
packed tight and sealed tight
so they wouldn't come undone along the way like me?
So much death in everything, so much packing and transport,
so much open that will never close again, so much closed
that will never open.

10
And who will remember? And what do you use to preserve memory?
How do you preserve anything in this world?
You preserve it with salt and with sugar, high heat and deep freeze,
vacuum sealers, dehydrators, mummifiers.
But the best way to preserve memory is to conserve it inside
 forgetting
so not even a single act of remembering will seep in
and disturb memory's eternal rest.

11
Seeking roots in the Warsaw cemetery
Here it is the roots that are seeking. They burst
from the ground, overturn gravestones,
and clasp the broken fragments in search
of names and dates, in search
of what was and will never be again.
The roots are seeking their trees that were burned to the ground.

12
Forgotten, remembered, forgotten.
Open, closed, open.

The Jewish Time Bomb

On my desk is a stone with "Amen" carved on it, one survivor
 fragment
of the thousands upon thousands of bits of broken tombstones
in Jewish graveyards. I know all these broken pieces
now fill the great Jewish time bomb
along with the other fragments and shrapnel, broken Tablets
 of the Law
broken altars broken crosses rusty crucifixion nails
broken houseware and holyware and broken bones
eyeglasses shoes prostheses false teeth
empty cans of lethal poison. All these broken pieces
fill the Jewish time bomb until the end of days.
And though I know about all this, and about the end of days,
the stone on my desk gives me peace.
It is the touchstone no one touches, more philosophical
than any philosopher's stone, broken stone from a broken tomb
more whole than any wholeness,
a stone of witness to what has always been
and what will always be, a stone of amen and love.
Amen, amen, and may it come to pass.

NOTES

ABOUT THE TRANSLATORS

INDEX OF TITLES AND
FIRST LINES

Notes

THE SMELL OF GASOLINE IN MY NOSE
11 line 3. *etrog*. The etrog, or citron, a fruit used in the ritual for the fall holiday of Sukkot, is kept in soft cotton to protect it from damage, which would make it ritually unfit.

YEHUDA HA-LEVI
14 Ha-Levi (ca. 1075–1141), often thought of as the greatest of the medieval Spanish-Hebrew poets, is especially known for his poems expressing an intense longing for Zion, to which he traveled and where he died very soon after his arrival.

IBN GABIROL
15 Shlomo Ibn Gabirol (ca. 1021–ca. 1055), another of the four greatest of the medieval Spanish-Hebrew poets, had a strong mystical bent and, lonely and tormented, suffered from a painful skin disease, as the first line of the poem suggests.

GOD FULL OF MERCY
26 The poem's opening words are the first words of the traditional prayer for the dead.

NOT LIKE A CYPRESS
30 line 19. *shofar-blasts*. The shofar is the ram's horn that is sounded during the services for the Jewish New Year and at the end of the Day of Atonement, together referred to in Hebrew as the Days of Awe (line 17). The shofar will play an important role in the long poem "The Travels of the Last Benjamin of Tudela."

HALF THE PEOPLE IN THE WORLD
32 line 25. *the appalling stations*. The "stations," enumerated in the next two lines, appear in "Had Gadya," the song sung during the Passover seder that enumerates a chain of destruction from the only kid (the meaning of the title) to the Angel of Death.

I WANT TO DIE IN MY BED
34 line 9. *O sun, stand still at Gibeon*. Joshua 10:12.

KING SAUL AND I

Poem 1

39 line 5. *He rehearsed the tearing of oxen.* See 1 Samuel 11:6–7.

Poem 2

39 line 8. *Only the asses bare their yellow teeth.* See 1 Samuel 9:3.

JERUSALEM

60 The poem evokes the divided city before 1967, when from many vantage points one could see the eastern half of the city in Jordanian hands on the other side of the border.

TO THE FULL SEVERITY OF COMPASSION

75 line 2. *Yes, you can count them.* This is a direct rejoinder to God's words to Abram in Genesis 13:16 that his seed will be so numerous that no one will be able to count them.

75 lines 15–16. *the terrible handwriting on the wall.* The allusion is to the dire prophecy that appears during Belshazar's feast in Daniel 5.

AND LET US NOT GET EXCITED

77 line 10. whatever belongeth to me, or belongeth not. These words appear in the ritual formula for cleaning out leavened substances on the evening before Passover.

JERUSALEM, 1967

Poem 1

81 line 6. My heart. Myself. East. West. These words allude to the opening line of Yehuda Ha-Levi's most famous poem: "My heart is in the East and I at the end of the West." Amichai invokes this line in several other poems.

Poem 3

82 lines 12–13. MENE MENE TEKEL UPHARSIN. These are the words written on the wall in Daniel 5.

Poem 4

82 line 7. *You lift up your eyes unto the hills.* Psalm 121:1: "I lift my eyes to the mountains—from where will my help come?"

Poem 5

83 line 13. *the Closing of the Gates prayer.* This is the prayer recited at sunset, just before the end of the Day of Atonement.

Poem 20
88 line 10. *Else Lasker-Schüler.* Lasker-Schüler (1869–1945) a German-Jewish poet, admired by Amichai, ended her days wandering through the streets of Jerusalem as a pathetic figure.

LULLABY
102 line 19. *Trumpeldor.* Joseph Trumpeldor (1880–1920) lost an arm fighting in the czarist army and later became a hero of the Zionist settlement in Palestine, perishing in an Arab attack.

I AM THEIR LAST
103 line 11. *"while he was yet speaking" and "there came another."* These words occur in the messengers' report of the disasters befalling Job's servants and children, Job 1:16 and 18.
103 line 12. *my full unspoken name.* The Hebrew term used is the one for the ineffable name of God.
103 line 17. *Machpelah.* This is the cave where Abraham buried Sarah.

THE TRAVELS OF THE LAST BENJAMIN OF TUDELA
109 The first Benjamin of Tudela wrote a celebrated Hebrew account of his far-flung travels in the second half of the twelfth century. Two nineteenth-century books, one a travel journal and the other a satiric novel, used "The Travels of Benjamin II, III," respectively, as their titles. Amichai, the "last" Benjamin, whose travels are his autobiography, was living on a street in Jerusalem named after the medieval traveler when he wrote this poem.

You went to a Montessori kindergarten
110 line 8. *You have sinned. You have transgressed.* These words are part of the confession of sin (recited in the first-person plural) in the service for Yom Kippur, the Day of Atonement.

On Fridays they stitched my handkerchief
111 line 3. *On festivals priests blessed me.* The kohanim, or descendants of the ancient priestly tribe, bless the congregation while covering their heads with prayer shawls and extending their hands with parted fingers. The congregants are not supposed to look at them during the blessing.

You came via Haifa. The harbor was new. The child was new.
112 line 10. *a mezuzah.* The mezuzah is a small receptacle containing verses from the Torah on parchment that is nailed to the doorposts of Jewish homes. Pious Jews kiss their hand and then touch it to the mezuzah as they pass in and out.

On Yom Kippur, in tennis shoes, you ran.
116 line 1. *in tennis shoes.* The wearing of leather is prohibited on Yom Kippur.

116 line 2. *with Holy Holy Holy, you jumped up high.* It is a traditional custom to stretch up on one's toes while reciting these words.

116 line 4. *Simchat Torah.* The fall holiday celebrating the completion of the annual reading of the Torah. The scroll is then rolled back to the beginning. On this festival of Rejoicing in the Law, congregants dance in circles, holding scrolls of the Torah.

The prayers of your childhood
116 lines 12–13. *a double bed the double cave.* The punning reference is again to the Machpelah cave acquired by Abraham as a burial site. The name of the cave suggests "double" in Hebrew.

Not one finger of God but ten
117 line 11. *the appearance of the High Priest is like the sun.* This line and the next borrow from a liturgical poem in the Yom Kippur service that reenacts the ancient priestly celebration of this sacred day.

117 line 13. *Urim and Thummim.* These are biblical divinatory devices.

Bialik, bald knight among olive trees
125 Haim Nahman Bialik (1873–1934) flourished in Odessa around the turn of the twentieth century and settled in Palestine in his last decade. He is generally regarded as the greatest Hebrew poet of his era.

The lion heart of Richard peers forth and
125 line 14. *its guests ask for milk, get a bottle of dynamite.* This plays on Judges 5:25, a line from the Song of Deborah. The blowing up of a wing of the King David Hotel in Jerusalem was carried out by a Jewish extremist group in 1946.

Yehuda Halevi is bound in his books, caught
126 line 6. *Shmuel Hanagid.* Hanagid (993–1056), one of the great Hebrew poets of Andalusia and Amichai's favorite among them, was vizier of the city-state of Granada and commander of its army.

I lived for two months in quiet Abu Tor.
126 line 16. *double too.* Some Torah readings involve two extended portions of the text. The reading referred to here on leprosy and related matters is Leviticus 12–14.

I live in the German Colony
127 line 2. *the Valley of Ghosts.* This is the literal translation of Emek Rephaim Street, the main street in this quarter of Jerusalem.

Joseph Flavius, son of Matityahu, son of the dead like me
128 line 1. Commonly referred to as Josephus (ca. 37–ca. 95), he was a general who surrendered to the Romans in 68 at Yodfat, the fortress he commanded, which is mentioned later in this poem.

I chose you, I was King Ahasuerus
132 line 1. *King Ahasuerus.* He is the Persian emperor in the Book of Esther.
132 line 12. *a bull for Kippurim.* That is, a bull of atonement.

Tanks from America, fighter planes from France, Russian
133 line 5. *Masada won't fall again.* This Zionist slogan refers to the desert fortress
where, according to Josephus, the besieged warriors committed suicide rather
than surrender to the Romans.

Last spring my child began
137 line 21. *Don't go to the ant, sluggard.* Proverbs 6:6.

Oh world, that everyone fills
138 line 12. Tekiah gedolah. Literally, "great blast," this is the long last blast on the
ram's horn sounded at the end of the shofar ceremony. The sequence of ram's
horn blasts is invoked several times earlier.

JEWS IN THE LAND OF ISRAEL
176 line 9. *as in the Bible story of Shechem.* Genesis 34.

THREE COMMENTARIES
182 line 1. *"And no longer shall your name be called Abram."* Genesis 17:5.
182 line 6. *"The guardian of Israel will not slumber or sleep."* Psalm 121:4.
182 line 11. *"Do not cast us aside in the season of our old age"* This sentence is from
the penitential prayer for the High Holidays.

LEAH GOLDBERG DIED
185 line 1. Leah Goldberg (1911–70) was an important Hebrew poet in the genera-
tion before Amichai.

FROM SONGS OF ZION THE BEAUTIFUL

Poem 14
206 line 4. A. D. Gordon (1856–1922), influenced by Tolstoy, was the great ideo-
logue of the so-called religion of labor in the early Zionist movement.

Poem 27
209 line 8. *a Havdoleh box for cheap spices.* This little box containing aromatic
spices, which is often of filigreed silver, is used in the havdalah (in the older
European accent, "havdoleh") ceremony marking the end of the Sabbath.

TIME

Poem 1
235 line 3. *the black crow people from Meah She'arim.* Meah She'arim is a neighborhood of the ultra-Orthodox in Jerusalem. The men there would be dressed in black suits and black hats.

Poem 49
255 line 1. *I am a man "planted beside streams of water."* Psalm 1:3.

Poem 67
259 lines 1–2. *We walked together . . . like Abraham and his son Isaac.* Genesis 22:6.

AN ARAB SHEPHERD IS SEARCHING FOR HIS GOAT
ON MOUNT ZION
274 line 9. *the terrible* Had Gadya *machine.* This song from the Passover seder, "An Only Kid," reports in a structure like that of "The House That Jack Built" how a cat bit the kid, dog bit the cat, a stick hit the dog, and so forth, all the way to the Angel of Death.

I DREAMED A DREAM
288 lines 1–2, 4. *in my dream seven maidens fat and sleek came up to the meadow . . . And seven skinny, wind-scorched maidens.* All this is based on Pharaoh's dream of antithetical sets of seven cows coming up from the Nile (Genesis 41:2–7).

FOR EVER AND EVER, SWEET DISTORTIONS
291 lines 12–13. *And still can't say God's real name.* Orthodox Jews avoid pronouncing the ineffable name of God, reconstructed by scholars as "Yahweh." The three Hebrew terms here are pious substitutions for that name.

PEACE OF MIND, PEACE AND MIND
296 line 10. *Rahab.* She is the whore in Joshua 2 who has a house in the city wall of Jericho, where she hides the two spies sent by Joshua.

THE REAL HERO
313 line 1. *The Binding of Isaac.* The story is told in Genesis 22.

TRY TO REMEMBER SOME DETAILS
319 The Hebrew sentence for the title and the first line recalls an idiom for introducing a mnemonic device for the Ten Plagues in the Passover seder.

319 line 22. *the followers of Korah*. The story of this rebellion against Moses and Aaron is recounted in Numbers 16.

WHAT A COMPLICATED MESS
331 line 23. *Soltam*. Soltam is a leading Israeli manufacturer of steel products.

MY MOTHER DIED ON SHAVUOT
343 line 1. *Shavuot*. This is the late-spring festival, associated with the giving of the Torah, more or less parallel to the Christian Pentecost, which occurs seven weeks after Passover. The Counting of the Omer (sheaf of grain) in the next line is the counting of each day of the seven weeks that begins on the second night of Passover.
343 line 12. *Sanhedria*. The Sanhedria is an old burial district in Jerusalem.

FIRST YAHRZEIT
346 The yarhzeit is the anniversary of the death of the departed, observed by close relatives by the public recitation of the kaddish prayer.

FROM MAN YOU ARE AND TO MAN YOU SHALL RETURN
354 The line used as a title plays on "From dust you are and to dust you shall return." Genesis 3:19.

REMEMBRANCE OF LOVE: WHAT WILL BE
356 line 12. *how goodly*. Balaam's blessing on Israel, Numbers 24:5.
356 line 12. *how great are Your works*. Psalm 92:6.

NORTH OF BEERSHEBA
358 line 7. Shema Yisrael. "Hear, O Israel" (Deuteronomy 6:4), the Hebrew declaration of faith, ends with the word *ehad*, "one," referring to God's oneness, and it is the traditional practice to draw out the pronunciation of this word as it is recited.

THE COURSE OF A LIFE
360 line 34. sandak. The *sandak* is the godfather who holds the male infant on a cushion during the circumcision ceremony.

END OF SUMMER IN THE SHARON
362 line 18. *the four festival kinds*. The festival is the fall harvest festival of Sukkot, and the four agricultural kinds enumerated in the next line are held together and used in the synagogue ritual.

LATE MARRIAGE

363 lines 21–24. *the voice of the bridegroom and the voice of the bride* . . . This full quotation of Jeremiah 7:34 is part of the traditional wedding ceremony. Although translations of the Bible render the concluding phrase as "the cities of Judah," this translator has used the Hebrew form "Yehuda" in order to convey the poet's pun on his own name.

AT THE SWIMMING POOL

366 line 24. *forget, as in a kiss on the brow.* This phrase recalls the rabbinic legend that before birth the soul knows the entire Torah but forgets it when an angel touches the infant on the chin.

WHAT I LEARNED IN THE WARS

374 line 32. *God's chariot.* The term refers to the vision of the divine chariot in Ezekiel 1.

FOUR RESURRECTIONS ON EMEK REPHAIM STREET

380 The name of the street, an actual street in Jerusalem, means, as noted above, "Ghost Valley Street."

First Resurrection

380 lines 16–18. *"The dead will God revive . . ."* The words these Orthodox girls sing here are the concluding line of "Yigdal," a hymn celebrating the thirteen articles of faith as enumerated by Maimonides that is sung at the end of holiday services.

Fourth Resurrection

381 This entire poem invokes—at times, virtually line by line—a remarkable *ubi sunt* poem by the great eleventh-century Hebrew poet Shmuel Hanagid. In Hanagid's poem it is a ruined citadel that he, as general of Granada's army, comes upon and contemplates. Amichai transforms the citadel into a ruined movie house. Here is Hanagid's poem in a literal prose translation: "I billeted a large force at a stronghold destroyed in times of yore by warrior-princes / who slept on top of it and by its side, and beneath it slept its first inhabitants. / And I said to my heart: Where are the throngs and peoples who once dwelled here? / Where the builders and the wreckers and the nobles and the poor and the slaves and the masters, / and the begetters and the bereaved, and the sons and the mourners and the bridegrooms, / and the many who were born after others in days gone by after days and years? / And they who lodged upon the earth today in the depths of earth are lodged, / who passed from palaces to graves, from lovely courts to dust? / And should they raise their heads and come forth now, they would despoil us of our lives and pleasures. / In truth, my soul, in truth, like them tomorrow shall I be and all these troops."

SUMMER REST AND WORDS
386 lines 25–26. *sometimes the translation lagged behind what was said.* In the Palestine of Amichai's adolescence, subtitles were often mechanically cranked with a handle as the film was projected and did not always keep pace with the spoken words.

WITH A SUITCASE IN MY HAND IN A FOREIGN LAND
392 line 18. *"Though we were knocked down, we were not dismayed."* These defiant words are part of a rousing song once sung in Zionist youth movements.

LACHISH REGION
396 lines 24–25. So that your days may be long upon the earth. Exodus 20:12.

GODS CHANGE, PRAYERS ARE HERE TO STAY

Poem 15
413 line 12. *kiddush cups.* These are wine cups, often made of silver, used in the ceremony inaugurating the Sabbath on Friday evening.

Poem 19
414 line 1. *tallis.* Prayer shawl.

Poem 25
417 lines 8–9. *"Blessed be He who made me according to His will."* This is the blessing women recite at the beginning of the morning service. A man, by contrast, recites a more affirmative blessing that thanks God for making him a man.

Poem 27
418 line 16. *who has no likeness of a body and has no body.* This is a quotation from the "Yigdal" hymn sung at the end of festival services, which is a versification of Maimonides's thirteen articles of faith.

ONCE I WROTE *NOW AND IN OTHER DAYS*

Poem 1
419 line 18. *Ruth.* She is the childhood friend of Amichai's from his hometown in Germany who perished in a concentration camp. He brooded over her terrible fate throughout his life.

THE BIBLE AND YOU, THE BIBLE AND YOU, AND OTHER MIDRASHIM

Poem 2
424 line 1. *How did Gideon choose his army.* See Judges 7:4–8.
424 line 13. *barley cake.* Judges 7:13.

Poem 31
433 line 1. *Balaam.* See Numbers 22–24.

DAVID, KING OF ISRAEL, IS ALIVE: THOU ART THE MAN

Poem 6
443 line 14. *Michal and Merab.* These are Saul's two daughters, the second one promised to David and the first actually given to him as wife. For Michal's objection to David's dancing, see 2 Samuel 6:20–23.

MY PARENTS' LODGING PLACE

Poem 1
444 line 2. *Ibn Ezra.* Abraham Ibn Ezra (1092–1167), a prominent Spanish-Hebrew poet.

WHAT HAS ALWAYS BEEN

Poem 1
447 line 1. *the poet Rachel.* Rachel Bluvstein (1890–1931), a popular Hebrew poet of the 1920s, many of whose poems were set to music, such as the one from which a line is quoted here.
447 line 13. *moshav.* A collective agricultural settlement.

EVENING PROMENADE ON VALLEY OF THE GHOSTS STREET

Poem 1
457 line 1. *Valley of the Ghosts Street, German Colony.* This is the literal translation of Emek Rephaim Street, the main street in the German Colony, a residential neighborhood in West Jerusalem.

Poem 2
457 line 5. *the ban of Rabbi Gershom.* An influential rabbi in the Rhineland in the tenth century, he promulgated a ban on opening the mail of others.

THE LANGUAGE OF LOVE AND TEA WITH ROASTED ALMONDS

Poem 6
469 lines 6–7. *the Mount of Blessings . . . the Mount of Curses.* See Deuteronomy 11:26–32.

Poem 13
470 line 2. *"Behold, the arrows are beyond thee."* See 1 Samuel 20:37.

THE PRECISION OF PAIN AND THE BLURRINESS OF JOY

Poem 3
473 line 8. *the Shekhinah's wings.* The Shekhinah is the Divine Presence in its feminine aspect and is typically imagined with sheltering wings.

Poem 4
473 line 6. *"Let not the eunuch say . . ."* Isaiah 56:3.
473 line 10. *Er and Onan.* See Genesis 38:6–10.

Poem 5
474 lines 11 and 13. *perfect rest . . . under the wings of forgetting.* This is a quotation from the prayer for the dead, where the phrase is "under the wings of the Shekhinah."

IN MY LIFE, ON MY LIFE

Poem 14
481 line 1. *Chevra Kadisha.* Literally "holy association," this is the burial society entrusted with washing the body, keeping vigil over it, and burying it. Traditionally, the Chevra Kadisha would have been exclusively male.

JEWISH TRAVEL

Poem 9
487 line 11. *kohen.* Someone descended from the ancient priestly tribe. When the priests pronounce their blessing in the synagogue, they extend their hands, with a space spread in the middle of the four central fingers.

NAMES, NAMES, IN OTHER DAYS AND IN OUR TIME

Poem 7
495 line 9. *Hoshana Rabba.* This day marks the end of the fall festival of Sukkot. Congregants circle the synagogue chanting *hoshia-na*, save us, please.

Poem 12

497 line 14. *Our sorrow is no sorrow* . . . These words and the ones that follow mimic the language of the Kol Nidrei prayer recited at the beginning of Yom Kippur—"our vows are no vows, our oaths are no oaths."

JERUSALEM, JERUSALEM, WHY JERUSALEM?

Poem 1

500 lines 1–2. *like King David who put on a crazy face.* See 1 Samuel 21:11–16.

Poem 21

507 line 8. *General Allenby.* Edmund Allenby, commander of the force that conquered Palestine, defeating the Turks in 1917.

MY SON WAS DRAFTED

Poem 11

518 line 1. *"The end of the matter: all has been heard."* This is a quotation from Ecclesiastes 12:13.

About the Translators

/

GLENDA ABRAMSON is an emerita fellow of post-Biblical Hebrew at St. Cross College, University of Oxford, and is a scholar of twentieth-century Hebrew literature.

ROBERT ALTER is an emeritus professor of Hebrew and comparative literature at the University of California, Berkeley. He has written on modern Hebrew literature and on the European and American novel and is a translator of the Hebrew Bible.

CHANA BLOCH is an emerita professor of English at Mills College. A scholar of seventeenth-century English literature, she has translated poetry by Dahlia Ravikovitch and Yehuda Amichai and has published five volumes of her own poetry.

ASSIA GUTMANN (1927–1969) was born in Germany and emigrated to Tel Aviv as a child and then to England in 1946. She had been living with the poet Ted Hughes for some time when she chose to end her life.

BARBARA HARSHAV is a prominent and prolific translator, chiefly of modern Hebrew literature but also of Yiddish and French. She is the widow of the literary scholar Benjamin Harshav, with whom she collaborated on many translations.

BENJAMIN HARSHAV (1928–2015) was born in Vilna, fled with his family to central Russia after the Nazi invasion of Lithuania, and settled in Israel in 1948. He taught at Tel Aviv University and, beginning in 1986, at Yale University. He was an eminent scholar of comparative literature, a poet in Yiddish and Hebrew, and a translator of poetry from several languages into both Hebrew and English.

TED HUGHES (1930–1998), one of the outstanding British poets of his generation, became a close friend of Yehuda Amichai and collaborated with him on the translation of a volume of Amichai's verse, *Time*, as well as poems from other books by Amichai.

CHANA KRONFELD is a professor of Hebrew and comparative literature at the University of California, Berkeley. She is the author of a book on Hebrew and Yiddish modernism and of a critical study of Yehuda Amichai and has collaborated with Chana Bloch on the translation of Amichai and of Dahlia Ravikovitch.

STEPHEN MITCHELL is a prolific translator of a wide variety of literary works, modern and ancient, from many languages. In addition to translating many early Yehuda Amichai poems, he has translated from the Hebrew a volume of the selected poetry of Dan Pagis.

RUTH NEVO is an emerita professor of English at the Hebrew University of Jerusalem, where she specialized in seventeenth-century English literature. In addition to

her English version of "The Travels of the Last Benjamin from Tudela," she has translated a volume of poems by the early twentieth-century Hebrew poet H. N. Bialik.

TUDOR PARFITT is emeritus professor of modern Jewish studies at the School of Oriental and African Studies. He has written widely on the Jews of Africa, the Middle East, and Asia.

HAROLD SCHIMMEL was born in the United States and immigrated to Israel in 1962. Initially writing in English, he has published several volumes of Hebrew poetry. He has translated many poems by Yehuda Amichai, with whom he was close, as well as Hebrew poetry by U. Z. Greenberg and Avot Yeshurun.

LEON WIESELTIER, a prominent cultural critic who served for many years as the literary editor of *The New Republic*, is the Isaiah Berlin Senior Fellow in Culture and Policy at the Brookings Institution and a contributing editor and critic at *The Atlantic*. He has written on politics, philosophy, history, and literature. His personal book *Kaddish* has been widely acclaimed.

Index of Titles and First Lines

Note: Poem titles are italicized. First lines that begin with the title are not included.

Permission Acknowledgments